# CURRICULUM DESIGN TECHNIQUES

# CURRICULUM DESIGN TECHNIQUES

Annabelle Nelson
Prescott College

WCB Wm. C. Brown Publishers

**Book Team**

Editor *Chris Rogers*
Developmental Editor *Sue Pulvermacher-Alt*
Production Coordinator *Carla D. Arnold*

**Wm. C. Brown Publishers**

President *G. Franklin Lewis*
Vice President, Editor-in-Chief *George Wm. Bergquist*
Vice President, Director of Production *Beverly Kolz*
Vice President, National Sales Manager *Bob McLaughlin*
Director of Marketing *Thomas E. Doran*
Marketing Communications Manager *Edward Bartell*
Marketing Manager *Kathy Law Laube*
Production Editorial Manager *Colleen A. Yonda*
Production Editorial Manager *Julie A. Kennedy*
Publishing Services Manager *Karen J. Slaght*
Manager of Visuals and Design *Faye M. Schilling*

Cover design by Jeanne Regan



Library of Congress Catalog Card Number: 88–64098

ISBN 0–697–07859–0



Printed in the United States of America by Wm. C. Brown Publishers, 2460 Kerper Boulevard, Dubuque, IA 52001

10 9 8 7 6 5 4 3 2 1

To my Mother *Elizabeth Nelson*
To my Advisor *Barbara Etzel*

# CONTENTS

## CHAPTER 2 LEARNING THEORY 23



## CHAPTER 3 OBJECTIVES AND CRITICAL ELEMENTS 41



## CHAPTER 4 TASK ANALYSIS AND SEQUENCING 47

# PREFACE

The book is aimed at the classroom teacher, special educator, or teacher training consultant. The goal is to transfer specific, practical techniques of curriculum design that will enable the teacher to write the equivalent of a unit from a published curriculum test with one difference, namely that this teacher-made unit will precisely communicate the salient qualities of the concept and actively involve the learner at a level that will insure mastery.

The motivation for writing this book came from my days as a teacher trainer for a compensatory education program for urban schools in cities like Kansas City and Indianapolis. I found that most of my efforts were not aimed at helping teachers improve their teaching, but were instead aimed at problem solving student failure brought about, in part, from inadequate curriculum texts. I was fixing holes in texts by creating individualized curriculum adaptations.

My intent, through this book, is to impart to teachers the techniques that are usually the territory of curriculum designers or cognitive psychologists specializing in learning. Teachers are professionals and, as such, should be in control of the curriculum in their classrooms. Knowledge of curriculum design techniques can help teachers pick and choose what they need from texts and write curricula for the other topics they would like to include.

The first chapter may be odd to some since it spends a great deal of time on the theories of John Dewey and Jean Piaget, while the remainder of the book focuses on curriculum design techniques that originate in behavioral psychology. The explanation of this seeming paradox is the fact that the philosophy of the book is eclectic. The book's philosophy is based on the idea that it is most appropriate to choose the curriculum philosophy that is best suited to the type of material to be taught.

Dewey and Piaget are emphasized because they provide a firm basis for experiential education, which is an essential element for teaching thinking skills and enhancing creativity. However, I believe that there must be some encouragement to use higher levels of thought such as basic skills, concepts, and vocabulary of various subject matters. The behavioral techniques are presented as *tools* to communicate necessary skills to learners. The intent of the book is to encourage experiential activities through philosophy and to empower teachers to be masters of communication through various techniques.

The content of the book has evolved through in-service workshops for teachers on instructional materials design and a series of eight college classes for college education students. References are used sparsely in the book, primarily because much of the material, specific definitions, and techniques have been developed by the author through these classes and workshops. However, original works that are seminal in terms of curriculum design are noted to guide learners to these sources and recognize very significant contributions. Also, a "Further Reading" section at the end of the book refers readers to current work in curriculum design.

Many of the concepts in the book have a unique emphasis when compared to other works. For example, the process of task analysis is presented as a tool to examine a learning task from a student's eyes and world view. The book has a primary focus on elementary education, but examples and concepts are also applicable to secondary teaching.

One of the basic premises of the book is the concept that teaching is not what the teacher does, but how the learner responds to what is presented. Therefore the book is designed to model this concept by actively involving the reader in the content. "Action Items" are interspersed throughout the chapters to make the material applicable to teaching and encourage reader interaction. Other curriculum design techniques modeled by the book are objectives for each chapter, careful sequencing, consistent formats for new information, prompts for recognition of factual information, and open-ended questions to encourage reflection and generalization.

After testing the material with many future teachers, I am confident that this book will help teachers gain confidence and skills to make even difficult-to-teach concepts positive and successful learning experiences for students. The material, though, is not meant to be a panacea or contain all the answers to curriculum design. The future teacher is encouraged to take these techniques and mesh them with other curriculum philosophies and personal teaching style to develop a unique, eclectic curriculum approach.

Annabelle Nelson
September, 1988
Prescott, Arizona

# ACKNOWLEDGMENTS

My mother is a teacher, and she has the natural gift of communicating in a way that other people understand. Growing up with her as my most important teacher made me a teacher. Besides my mother, I would like to acknowledge my advisor at the University of Kansas, Barbara Etzel. She validated my idea that *how* you presented information to people was of vital importance in communicating effectively. In addition, many students helped in the development of this material. These students tolerated my repeated attempts at communicating what I thought I knew about curriculum design. Examples of work by the following people appear throughout the book: Bridget Lombardi, Craig Rubens, Kellie Sloane, Christina Washburn, Joi Krelle, Natalie Hill, and Harry Plumlee. One of my best curriculum design students, Bev Santo, now teaches others what she knows. Finally, I would like to thank Linda Clark, who stayed with me during many revisions of the manuscript, and John Moore and Susan Burton for help with proofing and editing.

# 1
CHAPTER

# CURRICULUM THEORY

## OBJECTIVES

Identify curriculum philosophers contained in this chapter with either the experiential or systematic curriculum approach.

Note two factors which would distinguish the experiential and systematic approaches.

Define Dewey's ideas of psychologizing learning and the learning tendency and give an example of applying these concepts to a teaching situation.

Define Piaget's stages of cognitive development, noting ages and general characteristics of each stage.

List two general approaches that could be applied to teaching based on Piaget's theory.

Define the nature-nurture controversy.

Explain the developmentalist, interactionist and behaviorist views on the determinants of learning.

Speculate on how to balance the use of both the systematic and experiential curriculum approach.

## PROBLEM

Teachers experience curriculum as the textbooks which appear in their room.

## SOLUTION

Empower teachers with specific curriculum design techniques, so that teachers, instead of textbooks, control the curriculum.

The curriculum is the course of study in a given school. It is composed of organizational methods and teaching techniques for communicating content material to learners. Many curriculum texts include methods and strategies for organizing content. This book is different in that it documents the hands-on techniques of curriculm making, offering specific practical ideas that teachers can use to design materials which will work to communicate effectively. The goal is for teachers to have the skills of curriculum designers to troubleshoot problems in published texts and create learning experiences for difficult skills or concepts that teachers wish to include in the curriculum.

Teachers are usually not trained in curriculum methodology. They do not have the skills to create and design curriculum materials that will effectively transfer skills and concepts. Because of this, teachers, for the most part, rely on publishers to create materials. The problem with this is the fact that published curriculum materials, no matter how effective, will not work will all students for all concepts. Teachers need to know what to do when the materials fail.

Relying on published texts for curriculum methodology has other problems. It carries with it the assumption that teaching is "covering information" in a book. However, learning does not consist of the transmission of information from a book to a student. To be effective, a teacher must shift from thinking that learning is presenting textbook information to focusing on how to prompt thoughts and actions by learners. Educators are prone to pay attention only to the information they present from texts rather than to examine learner responses as the primary method for creating curriculum methodology. To be effective, instructional methodology must propose techniques to actively involve the learner in acting on information.

An enthusiastic teacher can be effective because a spark is passed from the teacher to student. That energy charges the student's interest and prompts a reaction to the subject matter. But schools cannot rely solely on enthusiastic personalities to enliven subject matter and generate interest and response. Methodologies exist that take into account the relationship of presentations to student response. These methodologies avoid a one-sided approach to curriculum. They shift the educator's attention to look at students' responses.

Two major methodologies guide the design of curriculum materials. One is experiential instruction, which heightens students' interest by scheduling intrinsically motivating activities. Activities are as real-life as possible, in or outside the classroom, since these are the most powerful in stimulating student interest. When students' instructional activities approximate adult "work," students feel a sense of worth. This prompts learners to do their best, and this "work" is more interesting and diverse than anything presented in a textbook.

The second approach might be called systematic instruction. This is designed to increase the efficiency of teacher-student interaction and successfully communicate a message between teacher and student. Systematic instruction emphasizes the importance of students' responses to curriculum as the determinant of effectiveness. The goal of the systematic instruction approach is to analyze a skill or concept and then to design materials and activities that will lead students to master specific objectives.

The following sections review the evolution and philosophy of both approaches, concluding with recommendations on which approach is called for by various learning contexts. The two approaches are not exclusive. Each has its time and place and complements the other. Experiential Instruction, defined first, when applied to the classroom, helps learners build thinking skills, creativity and problem-solving ability; Systematic Instruction, defined later in the chapter, can be used by teachers to effectively communicate basic skills, vocabulary and concepts which are necessary building blocks for more sophisticated learning.

## EXPERIENTIAL INSTRUCTION: JOHN DEWEY

The experiential approach arises from theories and research on how children learn. It assumes that children have a natural bent for learning. If left alone without a teacher, children will interact with their environment and gain some understanding or knowledge. Learning occurs more spontaneously and effectively when children's natural development is matched by learning activities. The assumption that children have an internal learning force that propels them toward knowledge under appropriate circumstances is akin to the actualizing tendency defined by Abraham Maslow.[1] The actualizing tendency is described as a drive in people which leads them to positive development. Once people contact this tendency, it leads to personal growth and integration.

In an analogous way, educators who subscribe to an experiential education approach believe their task is to create circumstances that allow children's natural learning forces to unfold. By matching instruction with the way a child learns when left alone, teachers enhance motivation. If children experience learning as an automatic extension of themselves, they feel self-fulfillment and can eventually take direction for their learning.

John Dewey was the first American educator in this century to recommend the experiential instruction approach.[2] His work was published as early as 1902 and continued on through the 1930s. One of Dewey's predecessors was Pestalozzi, a Swiss educator, who worked in the eighteenth and nineteenth centuries.[3] Pestalozzi proposed object lessons to awaken children's interest. In a subject like science, Pestalozzi brought specimens of animals into the classroom so children could have some concrete representation of the subject matter. One of Pestalozzi's primary contributions was stressing the importance of making learning relevant to the children's immediate world.

Dewey's work built on Pestalozzi's ideas and made far-reaching recommendations. Dewey's approach was termed "child-centered," since he believed that all instruction must begin within the child's world view. He recognized that children saw the world differently from adults. It followed that instruction would be most effective if it could respond to children's perception instead of forcing children to conform to the way adults perceived the world.

Several cultural forces in the early twentieth century influenced Dewey. One was the work of Charles Darwin. Another was the change in children's lives wrought by the Industrial Revolution.

### Action Item

An application of Dewey's learning tendency to teaching would be to watch the learner carefully and plan learning activities drawing on demonstrated interest. If you notice that a learner is drawn to puzzles and often makes detailed drawings, how might you orient your reading instruction to this student?

## Social Darwinism

The Theory of Evolution revolutionized the biological sciences, and concepts from this theory spread to other disciplines, including education. Educators focused on the fact that the human embryo developed physiologically through stages whose forms closely approximated the evolutionary ladder—fish, amphibian, mammal—and developed a parallel theory for social development. According to social Darwinism, each human in an individual lifetime progressed through the stages in which humans had evolved over the course of history (i.e., no distinction between self and nature, egocentric individualism, social cooperation and so forth). Very young children's social development approximated that of cave dwellers. As children grew, their social development evolved to the Greek period, to the Roman period, then to the Middle Ages. Dewey applied this theory to education and said that children's social evolution would quicken and emerge in a natural course of events. His writings often included the words "embryonic" and "emergent." According to Dewey, education's task was to set a stage for social evolution, and his philosophy seemed more concerned with social than academic development.

For Dewey, and other educators in the early twentieth century, the aim of schools was to produce responsible citizens who could take their places in a democratic society. Like Maslow's actualizing tendency,[4] Dewey's evolutionary force was as strong as that of biological evolution which would propel each child to unfold socially. And as a by-product, the intellect would develop.

## Occupations

Dewey's professional career spanned the industrial revolution. He saw firsthand the influx of rural Americans to jobs in the city, leaving farm life behind. Dewey felt that this brought a profound change in children's lives. No longer did children have integral roles in sustaining the family. Children on farms helped take care of animals and assisted with craft projects to make tools and clothes. Dewey said that previous to the Industrial Revolution, youngsters had "occupations" in the home and the community. By allowing children occupations, adults invested them with trust and responsibility. Children were intrinsically motivated to imitate adults. Creating occupations as the curriculum would give children activities that were scaled down versions of what adults did in life and, consequently, would unleash a natural interest in learning.

These observations about occupations involved in farm life prompted Dewey to recommend that schools include occupations for young children as the main form of instruction. If school approximated life, then it would become dynamic and meaningful for the learner. As a result, occupations in school could be pre-Industrial Revolution home activities, including cooking, crafts, animal care, and wood construction. Moreover, occupations were also generic; hence they stood for all activities that approximated life outside the classroom.

---

**Action Item**

---

Dewey might think that an apprenticeship model for education would do the most in enhancing learner motivation, since students would be involved in "real-life" work. If you are teaching a unit on weather, how might you create a mini-apprenticeship to enhance learner interest?

---

## Psychologizing Learning

Dewey's belief in social Darwinism was the basis for a unique recommendation to psychologize learning for children. Dewey said that children perceived the world very differently from adults. He outlined general developmental stages through which children progressed and said that in the early stages, the children's world view was holistic. Children did not cut time into pieces.

Children also discovered information in a very concrete manner, which meant that they primarily experienced their world through touch and movement. Thus, to psychologize learning, teachers would present activities in a holistic and concrete manner or, in other words, would think as a child or learner when viewing a concept for the first time. This does not mean that Dewey took away content or facts from the curriculum through written word. He was an advocate of mental activity as much as "doing" or physical activity. He used action to provoke mental activity.

To Dewey, social Darwinism created a technique for psychologizing learning. He said the best way to present a concept to children is to think back as to how humans first used or discovered the concept. An example would be Newton's discovery of gravity. Newton threw apples off towers to discover gravity. Therefore Dewey's recommendation to teach the concept of gravity would be to take children to a tower and have them throw off apples. The concept is psychologized since it is presented in a concrete manner. Social Darwinism helps since most concepts were usually first discovered or at least realized through direct concrete interaction with the environment.

If teachers followed Dewey's dictum of pursuing holism in instruction, then individual subjects would not be taught. Occupations presented from a child's world view would be the hub of school activities. If reading and math naturally fit in with the occupation, then they would be included, but not as a "rule of thumb." One activity in Dewey's school was to go to a farm, shear sheep, wash the wool, card the wool, and spin the wool. Either knitting or weaving the wool followed. Another activity was to dig ore and to go through the entire process of converting the ore into a usable product. Such occupations could span a whole year of school time. Teachers today can use Dewey's insights by focusing the curriculum on contemporary occupations from mechanics and meteorologists to computer operator.

### Action Item

In Montessori classrooms there are often map puzzles of the earth and the continents. How might this practice violate the principle of psychologizing learning? (Hint: Does a two-dimensional map of the world fit a child's world view?) How might you introduce maps to a young child in a way that incorporates his or her perspective of the world?

## Discipline and Cooperation

At the time of Dewey's writing, many criticized his work, stating that children could not learn discipline or responsibility in this child-centered approach. If children were always presented with activities that fit their natural development, then they would never be able to function well in the adult world. Of course, Dewey could not take these criticisms seriously since he firmly believed that children's natural development would unfold into just what society needed: creative and responsible adults.

But what about discipline? Dewey had the idea that discipline was not effective if it was imposed externally on a child. Discipline of the inner self was the goal, and this was accomplished by enticing children into an activity that they would enjoy because it fit a natural instinct. The activity, such as work with ceramics, would be designed so that it would require more and more discipline over time. Dewey believed that children's natural instincts were inquiry, conversation or communication, construction, and artistic expression. Instincts could be used by teachers to build discipline by presenting children with an activity which allowed for expression of one of the instincts, like artistic expression. Then by slowly increasing the difficulty of the activity, teachers could lead children to self-discipline.

Dewey also had an answer for teaching children cooperation and responsibility. If occupations were used in schools, part of the activities would require students to function as a community. Adults often band together in government, business, or community ventures. Children could imitate these activities and thereby learn cooperation and civic responsibility. To accomplish this, Dewey recommended student government and activities which required group cooperation as a part of the school curriculum.

### Action Item

A current educational strategy that uses group cooperation to teach discipline and encourage learning is "Cooperative Learning."[5] To accomplish this, teachers create groups of four students with heterogeneous skill levels. Groups are given problems to solve. To practice the idea of "Cooperative Learning," create a problem you might give to a group requiring a solution that would have a relevant impact on the students' lives. (An example would be to give long division problems on how to divide art supplies that the groups would use later for an art project.)

## Dewey Applied to Education Today

During the early part of the twentieth century, Dewey offered a radical notion about educating children. His aim was to enliven education and enrich children's lives, instead of forcing children to conform to adults' notions of correct behavior. Dewey envisioned schools as a dynamic force for children to find the learning force within. Granted, Dewey's ideas are dated, and his developmental stages do not correspond to current research in child development, most notably the research of Piaget. Social Darwinism is not a valid sociological concept, and some of Dewey's ideals were so general that it was hard to put them into practice. There are many educators, even those committed to experiential instruction, who believe that basic instruction in reading and math is necessary.

However, Dewey was the firebrand of the experiential instruction movement. Many of his ideas are unique and quite functional today. The concept of psychologizing learning, of thinking how to teach a concept in light of a child's world view, can prompt very effective instruction. This will invariably involve concrete presentations, a strategy congruent with current research in developmental psychology.

Educators throughout the twentieth century have reaffirmed Dewey's emphasis on occupations or making learning like life. Maria Montessori, whose philosophy influences large numbers of preschools today, made recommendations that were identical to Dewey's.[6] Montessori's curriculum involves children in "practical life" activities. Children imitate adult actions in learning. Montessori preschools are also child-centered in that students choose what activities they will participate in each day.

In a different way, Jerome Bruner recommended bringing real life into the classroom.[7] Bruner was active in the discovery movement in science education spawned by the Russian-U.S. space race after Sputnik in 1957. Bruner said that scientists and practitioners of other subjects should be brought into the classroom to teach children. Bruner's approach influenced much of the science and math curriculum of the 1960s. There are still a few adherents to the discovery approach, but Bruner's influence has waned considerably.

John Holt, whose writings were aimed at reforming education in the 1960s, has in the 1980s taken Dewey's philosophy to a radical extension.[8] Holt's newsletter, "Growing Up Without School," supports parents in keeping their children out of public schools. According to Holt, parents are not to become the children's teachers, but rather need to give children permission to learn as their natural interest and development dictate.

John Dewey's most significant contribution to the experiential education approach was to acknowledge that children have a native learning capacity, and education was best when it responded to this capacity. Dewey recommended occupations, making school like life, and psychologizing instuction to children's world views.

## PIAGET

As John Dewey made a significant contribution to experiential education, so did Jean Piaget.[9] However, Dewey and Piaget had very different perspectives in their studies of children's learning. Dewey's aim was to change society through children's education; he was a social activist. Dewey saw education as an extension of society, and his goals were to make schools a more intergral part of the organism of society and to enhance learning by making schools mirror society.

On the other hand, Piaget, a Swiss developmental psychologist writing in the early twentieth century, was motivated by something very different. He was not concerned about cultural influences on education or how to make education improve society. In fact, Piaget wanted to remove cultural influence from his study of children's cognitive development; he was interested only in the process of learning. Piaget wanted to find out how humans know or find out about the world around them in order to reason in a logical manner. Piaget traced, through careful observation and experimentation, the path that children proceed through in acquiring reasoning skills.

A scientist, Piaget valued logical reasoning as the end product of cognitive development. Through his research, Piaget concluded that children progress through four general stages of cognitive development: sensori-motor, preoperatory, concrete operations, and formal operations. (See Table 1.1 for the ages of children during these stages and the general behavioral characteristics associated with these stages.) Piaget and his followers maintain that the progress through these stages is invariant. In other words, all children will progress through the sequence of these stages in the same order: first sensori-motor, then preoperatory, and so forth. What does change is the amount of time children spend in each stage. A portion of all children will progress much faster through the stages, and others will progress at a slower rate. Researchers have discovered that in certain native cultures, people never develop the capacity for formal operations. This is also true of some individuals in Western cultures. Assisting individuals' progress toward formal operations is critical, since reasoning skills are essential to higher order learning.

**Table 1.1 Piaget Stages**

| | |
|---|---|
| Sensori-motor ↓ | 0–2* years • motor development; sensing environment |
| Preoperations ↓ | 2–7 years • development of symbols through language and role play; no logic |
| Concrete Operations ↓ | 7–12 years • logic with the help of physical actions |
| Formal Operations | 12 on • logical abstract thought in the interior of the mind |

*Ages vary across children but order is invariant

## Operations

Operation is Piaget's central concept in explaining thought processes. *An operation is an internalized action that is reversible.*

The words action, internal, and reversible must be defined to clarify the meaning of an "operation." An action throughout Piaget's work is something that is done to transform the environment. In the *Child and Reality,* Piaget calls this "praxis." Praxis or action is not a set of reflexes to the environment, but rather a coordinated set of movements to accomplish some end. An internalized action is one that occurs within the mind and is separate from the environment. In order for a human to be capable of internalized actions, Piaget traces a path of years of interacting and manipulating the environment. That is, many, many actions are done by a child to "test" the efficacy of an operation before it can be interiorized. Finally, enough sensory impressions and reactions are stored in the mind so that a person can call up internal images or representations of the environment, and then the mind can manipulate the images to predict an outcome. An action cannot be fully interiorized until a child attains the stage of formal operations, usually at about the age of 12. However, some operations could be interiorized during the concrete operation stage at a much earlier time (e.g., addition), since there are always transitions across stages. However, a child would not be in formal operations until the majority of operations could be interiorized.

The reversibility of an operation means that the action is propositional or hypothetic-deductive in nature, such as mathematical operations. For example, subtraction is the reverse process of addition, and division is the reverse process of multiplication. A reversible action can be made or unmade in the internal action of the mind. This allows a human to reason abstractly without the validation of carrying out the action in the environment. For example, a person could surmise what would happen if a certain amount of weight were put on the very edge of a cliff. The person could then remove the weight, rearrange the cliff surface, and replace the weight with a heavier one, all in the interior of the mind.

The hypothetic-deductive or propositional nature of an operation aligns it with the reasoning process used in the scientific method. If a person is capable of an operation, he or she can create a hypothesis or proposition and predict the outcome. The person can also test the hypothesis by creating an experiment in order to validate the hypothesis.

---

**Action Item**

---

When people develop the capacity to do operations in their minds, they are essentially acting like scientists. They can propose hypotheses and figure out logical ways of verifying the hypotheses. Why might a teacher wish to create environments which help children think in operations? Do you have any notions of what you could include in a classroom to encourage this development?

---

## Cognitive Stages

Piaget's developmental stages take a child through the cognitive reorganization steps needed to perform operations that approximate hypothetic-deductive thought. During each stage, the child comes closer to the abstract, logical reasoning skills characteristic of formal operations. It is important to note here that Piaget was not just talking about learning additional skills when children progressed from one stage to another. The major distinction between the stages is the idea that a child goes through a fundamental restructuring of how the environment is perceived and processed.

During the sensori-motor stage, children use their senses to react to and engage the environment as much as they can. For example, an eight month old child continually mouths objects to sense them. During the preoperatory stage, this pursuit of intense sensory experience continues, along with the representation of the environment with symbols. Children start to develop language and create symbolic activities, such as games and role plays of adult life. For the most part, children at this stage are not capable of logic but, rather, make up explanations to fit reality as they perceive it. To a preoperational child, the sun goes into the ocean to take a drink; and two lines of pennies, with the same number but with different spacing, do not have the same quantity because one line looks longer than the other.

The sensory experience of the first two stages is necessary before a child gains enough sensory information to begin to use logic, at about age seven, during the next cognitive stage of concrete operations. In concrete operation, children can conduct a logical action but cannot interiorize this action in their mind. Work with materials in the environment is necessary to deduce outcomes. For example, students must manipulate objects to add at first. After many years of experimenting with logical operations by manipulating objects, children, at about the age of 12, begin to have the capacity to conduct interiorized operations at the formal operation stage. Teachers can assist students through all of these stages by encouraging experimentation with the real world environment.

## Assimilation and Accommodation

According to Piaget, the transitions between stages are always occurring, and there is no static state. Children are continually shifting how they process reality through the mechanisms of accommodation and assimilation. These concepts were adapted from biology by Piaget. From a biological viewpoint, organisms, as they adapt to their environment, take in (assimilate) materials such as food, and make them a part of their structure. Organisms also change (accommodate) their structures to adapt to the environment around them. According to Piaget, a similar process occurs with the cognitive development of humans. Children take in sensory information from their environment and fit it into their self-built cognitive structures to explain how reality works. At the same time, some of the information they perceive contradicts the structures they have created, so that the entire structure will, at times, be changed to fit the new information. This process of assimilation and accommodation is happening continually for children. The transition from one stage to another occurs when there is a major accommodation to sensory input from the environment which overwhelmingly contradicts a previous stage. For example, once a preoperational child learns the concept of quantity, then he or she will no longer be "fooled" by the appearance of one line of three pennies looking longer than another row of three pennies (e.g., O O O, OOO). A child in concrete operations will reject the appearance of these two lines of pennies and surmise that the two lines are equal. The child has accommodated a structure to fit new information.

---

**Action Item**

A child will accommodate, or change, a structure in the mind when he or she receives enough information from the environment that the structure does not work. An example would be a young child who adds "ed" at the end of every verb to make it past tense. When the child says "getted", he or she is corrected by an adult. After a few times the child accommodates the information and shifts the structure to make room for exceptions to the rule. Accommodations underscore the importance of errors in the learning process. How can you, as a teacher, create an environment that treats errors not as a negative phenomenon, but as practice to find out new information?

---

## Conservation

The transition from preoperation to concrete operations is marked by attaining the ability to conserve quantity, weight and volume under transformation. Whether or not a child can conserve volume, for example, can be tested by showing the child two equal lumps of clay in the same shape. The child would be shown the two lumps of clay and would note how the two lumps were the same. Then the adult would change the shape of one lump so that it would be very tall in relation to the other lump. The shape of the clay has been transformed. A child in preoperations, who is not yet logical and who does not conserve, would say that the taller form contained more clay. However, the concrete operations child, who had seen the transformation, would conserve the quantity, since he or she would know that nothing new had been added or nothing had been taken away from the lumps of clay. Thus concrete operational children conserve, while preoperational children do not conserve. The attainment of conservation is somewhat of a mystery since it is an idea never directly taught.

With his research, Piaget verified that children have an interior energy that propels them to develop a series of cognitive structures in an invariant order, as long as there is appropriate interaction and stimulation with the environment.

---

**Action Item**

The ability of a child to conserve marks a shift in a child's development from a magical world, in which the sea drinks the sun, to a logical world, in which the earth moves around its axis blocking the view of the sun. What kind of experiences can you create for children to make this transition to logic? (Remember Piaget's emphasis on experience.) Do you think that watching television would assist this process? How about video games?

---

## Nature vs. Nurture

In psychology and education there is always a debate about whether the individuals' environment or genetic make-up is most important in influencing how they think, feel and behave. This argument is sometimes called the nature-nurture argument. Is it our biological heredity that primarily influences learning, or is learning the result of cultural and environmental influences? Dewey would fall on the nature side of the argument, saying that cognitive development is similar to biological evolution. However, Piaget is called an interactionist and believes that it is neither nature nor nurture that solely promotes learning. According to Piaget, both nature and nurture must interact to create cognitive development. The possibility of development lies dormant in the child until the environment or the child's actions on the environment stimulate cognitive development from the sensori-motor stage to formal operations.

This is an important distinction in discussing educational implications. To Dewey, a teacher can set children loose and learning will take place with very little stimulation from a teacher or the environment.

However, it is more difficult to apply Piaget's work to education. It may be inappropriate to apply Piaget's theories to education because he was not at all interested in pedagogy. Nonetheless, this has not stopped most educators. There are many curricular materials that claim to be based on Piaget. Since Piaget showed us how children learn, it does seem to be a natural extension to apply his theories to curriculum construction.

---

**Action Item**

Which side of the nature/nurture controversy you land on will determine many aspects of your teaching strategy. If you believe that nature is the most important determinant, you may do nothing, since a learner's biological heritage will predict teaching outcomes. Or, you might try to create a positive, emotionally supportive environment to allow a student's natural tendencies to unfold. If you are a nurture person, the pay-offs in the student's environment for desired behaviors would be of critical importance. Take one side or the other of the nature/nurture equation and speculate how you might help students to develop a positive self-esteem.

---

## Environmental Interaction

The recommendation that can be inferred from Piaget's theory is the concept that interaction with the environment is the central most important factor in stimulating cognitive development. Hands-on activities that encourage sensing and experimenting with the environment are critical. Some activities that would pave the path to formal operations would be: stacking up stones and seeing what happens when the stones fall down; trying to dam a creek with dirt; gathering leaves from trees and comparing each leaf, and so forth. Hence, sensory-rich, concrete interaction with the environment that includes experimentation enhances cognitive development.

Some curriculum philosophers have incorporated this interpretation of Piaget's work into their recommendations. For example, Jerome Bruner's recommendations for science curricula in the late 60's were based directly on this aspect of Piaget's work. Bruner called his curricular approach an "inquiry" or "discovery" approach. He encouraged educators and curriculum writers to create materials that led children to discover concepts for themselves by manipulating materials. Bruner also thought that most concepts could be taught to any age child as long as they were presented in a concrete manner. He recruited scientists and mathematicians to write curricula, thinking that they would be more in touch with basic concepts.

One problem with Bruner's inquiry approach was the fact that, in some ways, he lost track of the invariant progression of the use of logic through Piaget's developmental stages. Children are not capable of logical thought until they have reached the stage of concrete operations, which usually comes at age seven. Even though logic is possible at this stage, not until age 12 do children have enough sensory input stored in memory to deduce information in an abstract manner without the aid of concrete objects in the environment. Many of the math and science curricula based on Bruner's ideas used inquiry, but also presented very abstract theoretical information, sometimes with only visual representations in workbooks. For example, set theory was presented to children in math texts as readiness for addition. Practicing mathematicians can see the relationship between set theory and addition, but to children in concrete operations, the relationship is obscure. Bruner's adaptation of Piaget's theories did not relate to children in the preoperatory or concrete operations stage. However, Bruner's emphasis on a discovery approach is sound, as long as it accounts for learners' cognitive developmental stages.

## Concrete Materials

One appropriate extension of Piaget's research to curriculum is the idea that materials must be presented in a very concrete manner which will allow for experimentation. It is a matter of controversy whether or not Piaget's theory would imply that teachers must arrange activities that are concrete and require experimentation to stimulate children's natural progression toward logic, or whether it is enough to let children direct themselves. The most general application of Piaget's theory would imply that extensive interaction with the natural environment, whether or not the interaction is led or created by teachers, would be enough to foster intellectual growth.

## Movement

The manipulation of the environment through physical action or movement is another curriculum recommendation that can be distilled from Piaget's writing. This is overlapping with experimentation and presenting concrete experiences, but it emphasizes that children must move and physically act on their environment to stimulate their development. Praxis, which is necessary for the later acquisition of formal operations, is a series of integrated actions to accomplish a goal during the sensori-motor stage. Children must physically act before they can logically deduce. These ideas on movement would contraindicate having children sit in desks and write words in workbooks, unless they were writing lessons designed to teach handwriting.

### Action Item

The last three sections, Environmental Interaction, Concrete Materials, and Movement, contain the most practical aspects of Piaget's theory for the educator. Think of a specific lesson you may want to teach and brainstorm how you might include experimentation with the natural environment, manipulation of concrete materials, and movement by learners. (An example might be the relationship of the amount of surface area to body temperature. Learners could experiment with animals of different sizes in settings of various temperatures.)

## CURRENT APPLICATIONS OF PIAGET'S TEACHINGS

Piaget outlines stages children progress through on their route to logical abstract thinking capabilities. Piaget's theory clearly points out that children will not progress through these stages automatically unless there is adequate sensory and environmental stimulation. This makes the case for schools providing curricula that give children adequate sensory stimulation, opportunities to experiment and manipulate the natural environment, and physical explorations with concrete objects.

Piaget's theory was designed to understand cognitive development or the changes in the structures of a child's mind used to make sense of perceptual information. The theory does not necessarily deal with the issue of the acquisition of skills, and, as such, would not preclude systematic instruction of these skills, as long as the opportunities existed simultaneously to experiment with the natural environment as a basis for developing more sophisticated cognitive structures (i.e., formal operations).

Some educators use Piaget's theory to say that specific skills should not be taught. The rationale used is the argument that once a stage such as concrete operations is attained, then the skills educators think are important will come naturally. However, there are little data to support this. An equally defensible educational interpretation of Piaget's theory would be the idea that certain curriculum content should be taught, as long as it is appropriate to a given stage and as long as sensory input and experimentation opportunities remain high.

Rudolf Steiner, an Austrian educator who was a contemporary of John Dewey and Maria Montessori, emphasized movement in the learning process, which echoed the implications of Piaget's work.[10] Steiner predated Piaget and did not have the body of research to support his theories, but the emphasis on children's physical movement presents a similarity to Piaget. To Rudolf Steiner, the purpose of education was to awaken in children what he called "supersensible perception" to help children's creativity flourish. (Current educators now would call his terminology "intuitive perception.") To accomplish this, Steiner recommended the inclusion of art and craft activities as a central part of children's educational experience. The curriculum that he outlined included painting, drawing, sewing and knitting, constructing fabric dolls, modeling with clay, carving with wood, working with metal, and participating in sports and drama activities. Steiner maintained that this physical work prompted by art was formative for children's development in order to express their emotional and spiritual feelings. Both Piaget and

Steiner would encourage children to be very active with their hands and bodies; for Piaget, it would be in experimentation and, for Steiner, it would be in construction and creation.

Piaget's work prompts curriculum makers to develop rich, sensory experiences for children and to include experimentation with concrete objects in the environment and movement activities. It would probably not be necessary to have teaching goals for academic skills, but instead, teachers would create the most vibrant experiences possible that prompted the maximum physical response from children. It is important to note that Piaget was not interested in skills acquisition. Dewey said that children would learn to read and do math and acquire basic skills as a matter of course without direct instruction. But Piaget did not address this issue. It would not be contradicting Piaget to say that skills acquisition was separate from basic structural cognitive development. Children need basic cognitive structures to learn certain skills but, at the same time, skills may not develop without any exposure or instruction.

## SYSTEMATIC INSTRUCTION

The roots of both the experiential and systematic instructional approach lie in the progressive movement of the early twentieth century. This period was most closely associated with John Dewey, but included many other educators in America and Europe and was built upon philosophers' and educators' work of the nineteenth century, such as Pestalozzi, Cormenius, Froebel and Herbart. The aim of the progressive movement was to make education respond to people's lives and social conditions. A common thread through most of these philosophers' writings was to use education as a tool to reshape society and improve the living conditions of the lower class. This included preparing citizens to take their places in a democratic society.

Progressive education was a reaction against the formalism in education that was based in the colleges and Latin grammar schools of the nineteenth century. In the formalist's philosophy, education's purpose was to pass on classical knowledge, create discipline, and teach sustained effort of the mind and logical thinking. Usually, however, only the wealthy could afford this education. Progressive education, on the other hand, emphasized integrating subject matter and making it relevant to children's lives. There were two trends in the progressive movement: the first was the child-centered approach; the second was the measurement movement. In the early 1900s, these two trends were not disparate; they were on one hand the philosophy, and on the other hand the tools necessary to counteract formalism.

The measurement trend was applied to improving education in two distinct ways. First, measurement was used to determine what would be most beneficial for students to learn. This was done by analyzing how adults used information. For example, newspapers and cookbooks would be analyzed to see what words to teach in reading. Second, measurement was also used to determine if students had actually profited from instruction. Batteries of tests were constructed for many skills and concepts to check students' acquisition and retention of information.

The measurement movement was most strongly represented by the National Education Association's Committee on the Economy of Time. This committee began meeting in 1911 and met for eight subsequent years. The committee's work was to use the scientific method to determine socially worthwhile curriculum goals which would be relevant to students' lives as adults. The committee used measurement to construct tests and to inventory current curriculum topics as they related to contemporary life.

These were the roots of the current systematic instructional approach. It is important to note that during the early twentieth century, the idea of measurement did not conflict with Dewey's child-centered curriculum. Measurement was a tool to improve education and to help realize the progressive movement's goal. The measurement movement was the practical side of the experiential philosophy.

## Objective Writing

In the first third of the twentieth century, Harold Rugg[11] and Franklin Bobbitt[12] were associated with the measurement movement. They refined the analysis of adult activities to produce objectives for teaching. Objective setting, as a teaching tool and a curriculum development tool, was then picked up later in the 1960's and 1970's by behaviorist B. F. Skinner[13] and educator Robert Mager.[14] A behaviorist, unlike a developmentalist or an interactionist, discounts the need for teaching to a student's developmental stages. To a behaviorist, what is learned is a function of the environmental consequence of certain behaviors, *not* the result of a student's inner development. The emphasis is on the environment around the student. Behaviorists do take into account biological factors which affect behavior and broad social and intellectual stages of development, but, in general, the environment is emphasized as the primary determinant of behavior. Therefore a behaviorist takes the nurture side of the "nature-nurture" controversy.

The behaviorist contribution to curriculum writing in the 1960's and 1970's was the refinement of objective writing proposed earlier by the measurement movement. One aspect of objective writing, according to Mager, is writing an objective with enough specificity so that it is clear when the learner has reached the objective. If Mager's recommendation for objective writing is followed, the testing of learning follows naturally from writing an objective, since the specific objective can become the basis for testing. Objective writing was Mager's primary contribution to the evolution of the measurement movement in education.

Skinner's impact was more comprehensive. Skinner developed programmed learning. In this system, an objective was broken down into steps that were ordered from simple to complex to prompt a learner to respond accurately. Skinner's programmed learning also included ways for learners to check their responses immediately for accuracy. One aspect of programmed learning was the fact that it invariably used paper and pencil tasks as the medium of instruction, since this created the simplest manner of sequencing work and giving immediate feedback. This fact made it unacceptable to advocates of the experiential instruction approach since students were limited in how they could experiment with their environment.

A later development in systematic instruction by Sigfried Engelmann and Douglas Carnine was the procedure of conducting a "conceptual analysis" of an objective to determine steps that instructional materials should follow.[15] Using conceptual analysis, Engelmann and Carnine develop "routines" to teach concepts. A routine is a series of questions and answers by students and teachers to arrive at a successful demonstration of a concept. A routine also includes examples to show common attributes of a concept and how it can be applied to new situations. Chapter 6 contains examples of Engelmann and Carnine's work. Their work is a sophisticated evolution of objective writing.

### Systematic and Experiential Instructions

Both systematic instruction and the experiential approach are student-centered. However, this is manifested in different ways, depending on the approach. In the experiential approach, the focus is on students' social and cognitive development and how to present activities that are a natural extension of those developmental stages. With the systematic method, the strategy is to create objectives and then test students in order to place a student at an objective that has not yet been learned. In this manner, learning can be easily assimilated by students. The experiential approach designs activities that will fit a student; the systematic approach adapts content to fit a student. The latter can complement the experiential philosophy by giving specific methods for effectively teaching skills or concepts which are determined necessary for a student, either by the student or society. Currently, however, educators see the student-centered and the measurement approaches at odds. Throughout the twentieth century, the two approaches have cycled through stages of popularity because of the failure of one to meet all of learners' needs. The experiential approach emphasizes creativity and encourages learners to choose their own curriculum, but does not teach basic skills. The systematic approach teaches basic skills, but does not encourage creativity and learner choice.

## DEVELOPMENTALISTS, INTERACTIONISTS, AND BEHAVIORISTS

There are three major positions in psychology on what influences learning. These are developmental, interactional, and behavioral approaches. Developmentalists believe that nature or genetic endowment is the biggest determinant in learning. Interactionists believe that it is a combination of nature and nurture or environmental conditions outside of a person that influence learning. And a behaviorist believes that environmental conditions are the single most important variable in what people learn.

In relation to curricular content, the developmentalist position (Dewey and Holt) would say that the content must be totally responsive to students' instincts and natural inclinations. Nature is emphasized as the determinant. This makes curriculum design simultaneously easy and difficult. It is easy since no curriculum need be made. Children or students choose what they want to study. But it is very difficult because once students make their choices, teachers must design, create, or collect materials and activities that relate to what the student has chosen. A student-centered curriculum can mean long working nights for teachers attempting to respond to curricular needs. Even in the student-centered curriculum, teachers do choose the curriculum content on some level because teachers select the array of choices. This array, in effect, limits student choice to what the teacher thinks is important. It is possible at times for the student to initiate the choice of learning outside of what a teacher may provide. The probability that this would happen increases with the age of the student. But the point is that even in a student-centered approach, some selection of content does happen.

Not all developmentalists are advocates of a total free choice situation for students to choose the content of what they will learn. John Holt is an advocate of this. But other developmentalists like Rudolf Steiner and Maria Montessori advocate that specific skills be taught and that the instruction must be matched to children's behavioral and cognitive stages. Steiner and Montessori say that children cannot make an informed choice at a young age, since children have no idea of what will help them as adults. It is the teacher's duty to make judgments about what to include in the curriculum.

Piaget is an interactionist because he observes that development of internal cognitive structures does not happen without sufficient environmental stimulation. Therefore, development is dependent on an internal drive *and* action on the environment. Piaget combines both nature and nurture in his view of learning.

Behaviorists, on the other hand, stress nature as the predominant force in learning. The environmental reaction a student's behavior evokes will teach concepts and skills. Behaviors emerge as they are modeled and reinforced in the student's environment. If reading is modeled in a child's environment and then approximations toward reading (e.g., looking at books) are reinforced (e.g., the parent smiles and touches the child), then the child will eventually learn to read. A behaviorist ignores stages and readiness and the student's inner learning tendency. Instead, the behaviorist sets a learning objective, assesses the student's behavior in relation to that objective, and then goes about arranging the environment to accomplish the objective.

Behaviorists are criticized as being too skill oriented and not addressing creativity and thinking skills. Developmentalists and interactionists are criticized for not attending to basic skills and content. Possibly each approach reflects a piece of reality and can be applied in appropriate circumstances to enhance learning.

Table 1.2 summarizes the curriculum theorists noted in this chapter. A developmentalist or interactionist perspective fits the experiential approach to curriculum design, while a behaviorist perspective fits the systematic approach to curriculum design.

## INTEGRATION: EXPERIENTIAL AND SYSTEMATIC

Dewey's philosophy and Piaget's research would lead us as educators to create a curriculum and its appropriate materials to approximate life as much as possible. The curriculum would respond to students' cognitive development and world view, would expose children to extensive experimentation with the environment, and would prompt students to movement and physical reaction to their environment. Probably both Dewey and Piaget would say that the content of the curriculum does not matter, since the school of life and the natural environment would prompt children to learn what they needed to know.

**Table 1.2 Comparison of Curriculum Theorists**

| Developmentalist or Interactionist or Behaviorist | (D) (I) (B) | Teacher's Role | Teach Basic Skills | How People Learn |
|---|---|---|---|---|
| Dewey | D | guide | no | by doing, imitating adult occupations |
| Piaget | I | n/a | n/a | by experimenting and interacting with natural environment |
| Holt | D | allow children to choose | no | by being allowed to choose what they learn and how they learn |
| Montessori | D | guide | have available | by being given choices of self-correcting activities appropriate to their stages |
| Steiner | D | model, create art activities, through building a relationship | yes, at right age | by active involvement, awakening of supersensible perception through art, movement, music, crafts |
| Bruner | I | create discovery activities | yes | by having scientists create curriculum in student's view; by discovery |
| Rugg | D & B | n/a | yes, after analyzing use by adults | by being given relevant learning activities |
| Skinner | B | program learning | yes | by being given tasks appropriate to skill level and being given immediate feedback |
| Mager | B | set goals and objectives | n/a | by communicating clear objectives and goals |
| Englemann | B | analyze task, construct routines | yes | by being given systematically analyzed activities that precisely communicate a concept |

The systematic instructional philosophy, on the other hand, would say that it is appropriate to set goals for children's learning and create sequences of activities to lead children to accomplish these goals. Systematic instruction advocates cite research to indicate that when left to their own devices, students do not acquire the learning that society might call survival skills, such as basic reading and math skills.

Even though most see these approaches as contradictory, symbiosis is possible. Each approach has a unique contribution for curriculum planning. Furthermore, the two approaches can lead educators to determine topics of study to include in a curriculum as well as methods for teaching the topics and the creation of instructional materials. Merging the two creates a vehicle for dealing with the two concerns of curriculum making—content and methodology.

The experiential approach and its supportive data give educators confidence that students can be trusted and that learner response to the environment is the best teacher. For the most part, students can be allowed to choose their own course of study. For young children, field trips and open inquiry opportunities with the environment, along with activities that approximate what adults do in their daily life, can awaken children's learning capacities and faculties and thus expose students to how humans first discovered certain concepts and principles. For older children and college students, working as apprentices or interns would be indicated. Systematic instruction would teach younger children basic academic skills and teach older students research skills, independent study strategies, and how to find information.

Basic skills and vocabulary are necessary for more creative and sophisticated learning. In this way the two curriculum approaches can be tied together. Systematic instruction can set the stage for the experiential approach to take over. Teaching skills before encouraging creativity parallels the stages psychologists report in the process of creativity. First there is a collection of information stage where individuals store basic information. Then there is an incubation stage where no work is done. After a period of time, there is a flash of insight in which the stored information is recombined in novel ways. Finally there is a documentation stage in which the insight is tested. This model of creativity supports the proposal of combining both curriculum methodologies—one for basic skills and one for creativity.

The curriculum makers' job is first to insure that students have vibrant, experiential, experiment-filled choices for activities. The next task is to devote energy to systematizing instruction in basic skills: reading comprehension, writing skills, mathematics, research skills, and independent study strategies. The remainder of this book delves into the specifics of systematic instruction and outlines the techniques to be used to create a curriculum which will insure that each learner possesses these basic skills. This, in turn, will release teaching planning time and instructional time for more emphasis on the experiential approach.

---

## QUICK REVIEW

Can you match the term with the definition?

| | |
|---|---|
| **Occupation** | Presenting information from student's world view |
| **Social Darwinism** | A stage about 0–2, child testing senses |
| **Psychologizing Learning** | A stage 12–on, abstract logic |
| **Operation** | A stage 7–12, logic with concrete help |
| **Sensori-motor** | An activity that approximates real life |

| | |
|---|---|
| **Preoperations** | The theory that each human's social development approximates humankind |
| **Concrete Operations** | A theory that children must contact the environment to develop |
| **Formal Operations** | An internalized, reversible logical action |
| **Developmentalist** | Theory that children will grow into what they need to, naturally |
| **Interactionist** | A stage 2–7, symbols, use perception, not logic to make conclusions |

## EXTENSION QUESTIONS

1. Give an example of what Dewey would include in a curriculum that would be an occupation.

2. How would you use social Darwinism to teach courtesy?

3. What would Dewey's strongest recommendation for curriculum making be?

4. What would an interpretation of Piaget suggest for curriculum making?

# 2
CHAPTER

# LEARNING THEORY

## OBJECTIVES

Define stimulus control, stimulus discrimination, stimulus generalization, cueing, sequencing, modeling and prompting.

Explain how the concept of stimulus control prompts a teacher to examine learner responses.

Give examples of a teaching situation when the use of cueing would be appropriate.

List three general teaching applications of stimulus control concepts.

## Problem

Teachers don't communicate.

Some children don't learn.

A preschool teacher sits down with a small group of young children. She lays out approximately 10 shapes: some are triangles, some are circles and some are rectangles. She talks about triangles and how triangles have three points. She asks the children to pick up the triangles and to feel them. The teacher is satisfied that she is doing an effective job of conveying the concept of triangles to her students. She then mixes up the 10 shapes and asks Nathaniel to choose a triangle. To her surprise Nathaniel chooses a red circle. She then realizes that all of the triangles she had presented were red. Instead of paying attention to the three points of the triangle, Nathaniel was paying attention to the color red.

This scenario happens frequently in teaching environments, not only in preschool, but also at the elementary, secondary, and college level. Teachers give confusing or ambiguous communication by not carefully thinking through the ramifications of the stimuli they present.

This chapter defines terms used in an area of psychology which is called learning theory. When these terms are understood, the acquired knowledge prompts educators to think with precision about the way they communicate. To assist in the acquisition of this knowledge, terms and examples of the terms are presented. The chapter ends with conclusions and generalizations to apply information from learning theory to systematic curriculum design.

**Stimulus:** Any discernible event occurring in the environment at a given point in time.

The fact that a stimulus is a discernible event at a given point in time means that an individual can perceive the event as an entity in time and space. A stimulus can be anything that occurs within or without us and prompts a human to say, "Yes, that's happening." For example, a person smiling at another person is a stimulus; walking outside and feeling a cool wind is a stimulus. In an educational setting, a stimulus can be a phrase said by the teacher to give direction, a word written on the board, a problem on a sheeet of paper, or even a thought that a student has that prompts another event. The main thing to remember in understanding the word stimulus is that it must be discernible.

---

**Action Item**

---

When a teacher asks a question, what other stimuli besides the content of the question could be prompting student response? (Some other stimuli that are operating could be noises outside, words on the blackboard, the facial expression of the teacher and so forth.)

---

**Stimulus Control:** When a given discernible event prompts a response or reaction by a person.

Stimulus control[1] means that a stimulus actually *controls* a behavior, i.e., when a stimulus enters a person's environment, a certain behavior occurs as a response. Most teaching is actually an attempt to achieve stimulus control. Preschool teachers show children an object that is red and say, "What color is this?" Stimulus control is achieved if a child says, "Red." The color red prompts the verbal response, "Red." In solving a differential equation, the teacher's intent is the hope that the student will be prompted to carry out the correct logical deductions to solve the equation correctly. Stimulus control is achieved if the equation prompts the solution.

The concept of stimulus control can be used both for transferring basic skills and for prompting higher order cognitive operations. For example, teachers may want students to infer an answer to a comprehension question on a story, where pieces of information are given which students must put together independently for an answer. The stimuli are the story, the teacher's questions after the story, and the stored memories in the learners' minds that relate to information in the story. All of these stimuli prompt answers by the students that are not necessarily "right" answers but make sense in the context of the information given by the story. If learners cannot respond to an inferential question, or if there is no stimulus control, then it is the teacher's task to examine the stimuli, the story, the questions, and previous information gained by the student, so that the stimuli can be adjusted to prompt an appropriate answer.

An easily remembered example of stimulus control is a stop light. The stimulus is the color of the light; this color invariably prompts a response of either stopping, slowing down, or moving.

If a teacher understands the definition of stimulus control, then it will become clear that the process of teaching is about establishing a relationship between a certain stimulus and learner responses. This makes it impossible to maintain a one-sided view of teaching in which all that is important is what a teacher says and does, and it is merely the students' job to respond. *The notion of stimulus control clearly makes the point that what is involved in teaching is shifting, adjusting, and adapting a stimulus so that the students' responses will be optimal to the learning situation. The learners' responses are the key, not the teacher's actions.*

---

### Action Item

---

What stimuli control or prompt the behavior of saying hello to another person? (A smile on another's face or the proximity to the person could be the stimulus. What other stimuli could be operating?)

---

**Discriminative Stimulus ($S^D$):** The specific discernible event that prompts a given behavior.

In the situation where a green light prompts a person to engage a clutch, the green light is the discriminative stimulus. It is the discernible event in the environment that prompts the behavior. In the "teaching-red" example, the discriminative stimulus was the red object. Ideally, if the concept of red has actually been taught, then any object that is red, or partially red, would be the discriminative stimulus. For the most effective communication in teaching, teachers must pinpoint the exact discriminative stimulus to prompt a response. Sometimes this is denoted by the symbol $S^+$, meaning correct stimulus.

### Action Item

An example of a discriminative stimulus for the response of solving a calculus equation is the written problem on paper. Think of a stimulus that you would like to become a discriminative one in your future classroom. (How about the words, "Be quiet."?)

**S-Delta:** Discernible events in the environment which do not prompt a given behavior.

When the discriminative stimulus is a green stop light, the S-Deltas are the yellow light, the red light, the light pole, the billboard behind the light pole, the neighboring cars, a passenger's voice in a car, and so forth. In establishing stimulus control, it is important to consider what the S-Deltas are as well as what the discriminative stimulus is. A discriminative stimulus exists not only in a world of its own, but also in comparison with other stimuli. A student needs to know what a stimulus is and what it is not. Otherwise, a student will make incorrect generalizations of the stimulus. In the triangle teaching situation, the discriminative stimulus was the triangle, and one S-Delta was the color red. If the teacher had thought this through and presented as many comparisons as possible between the discriminative stimulus and various S-Deltas such as red, circle, big, little and so forth, there would not have been confusion in what the teacher was trying to get across to Nathaniel.

Sometimes S-Delta is denoted by the symbol $S^-$, meaning incorrect stimulus.

### Action Item

The primary educational application of an S-Delta is the fact that it is helpful for teachers to show learners when concepts do not apply. For example, a proportion problem will not work if there are not analogous relationships between the numbers on both sides of the equal sign. It is helpful to demonstrate incorrect ways of setting up a proportion problem—as well as correct ways. Think of a concept you may want to teach and brainstorm on how to show learners incorrect applications of the concept.

**Stimulus Discrimination:** Responding to one stimulus differently from another stimulus.

An example of stimulus discrimination and discrimination training can be seen in the teaching of addition problems that require regrouping. (Regrouping is the same process as carrying.)

$$\begin{array}{r} 15 \\ +13 \\ \hline \end{array} \qquad \begin{array}{r} 15 \\ +18 \\ \hline \end{array}$$

A student must learn to discriminate when regrouping is necessary and when it is not necessary. Students demonstrate stimulus discrimination when they regroup a ten into the top of the ten's place on the left and not on the right; this is done by placing a small one on top of the left column of the problem.

It is important for a student to discriminate when and when not to apply a concept or skill. When a skill or concept is first learned, the tendency is to overgeneralize that skill. It is as if the student has a new toy and is saying, "Does it work here? Does it work here?" By presenting instances of when the new concept can be applied and when it cannot be applied, a teacher helps students attain stimulus discrimination. It has happened that once a student learned to regroup, he or she has put ones over tens columns on every addition problem that is seen, regardless of the need to regroup. In this case, students are not clear on the discriminative stimulus and the S-Deltas.

What is the discriminative stimulus to regroup? This is the concept of having an answer of more than ten in the ones column. A teacher can say, "Add the ones column. Is the sum more than ten? Do you regroup?" This type of communication is keying a student in on the exact stimulus that will prompt the correct solution. A sum that is less than ten is an S-Delta.

Another example that demonstrates the importance of teaching stimulus discrimination is found in teaching the difference between the concepts of longitude and latitude. Latitude should be a discriminative stimulus for visualizing the lines that extend horizontally around the globe and longitude should be a discriminative stimulus for visualizing lines that extend vertically around the globe. If discrimination is not established, errors result.

A few words may be in order at this point about errors and the learning process. A part of applying stimulus control procedures to designing curriculum materials is to enhance effective communication and to decrease the errors that learners make in responding to various stimuli. There is some controversy on the role of errors in learning. In Piaget's theory of cognitive development, errors are very important in helping the process of accommodation, or altering an incorrect cognitive structure. Without errors, a person would not accommodate. However, it is important to note that Piaget is talking about major shifts in cognitive development, not specific skill or concept acquisition.

Stimulus control procedures are designed to teach specific skills and concepts. Learners can still have many open-ended activities which allow errors. But in teaching basic skills and concepts, it is important to avoid confusion. When people make errors in learning a new concept or skill, sometimes error patterns are created that are hard to break. Most people have had the experience of learning someone's name incorrectly and then having great difficulty in relearning the correct name. Stimulus control procedures can prevent such error patterns from forming.

---

**Action Item**

---

A simple example of the necessity of teaching stimulus discrimination is to help first and second graders distinguish between addition and subtraction problems. The problems look just the same except for the sign. Think of other skills or concepts which will need extra attention to help learners discriminate.

---

**Stimulus Generalization:** Responding to one stimulus in the same way as another stimulus.

In stimulus *generalization,* a person applies a skill or concept outside the situation in which it was learned. The same response is applied to a variety of discriminative stimuli. In stimulus *discrimination,* a person limits the number of discriminative stimuli that are responded to.

The more similar two stimuli are, the more apt a person will be to generalize a response from the stimulus that has already been taught to a second unknown stimulus. This is called the *law of stimulus generalization.* For example, when young children start to learn to use the past tenses of words, they first learn the "ed" ending, such as, "He typed the page." After learning the "ed" ending, children try it on all other verbs—goed, comed, sended, and so forth. Children generalize the use of the "ed" ending to all verbs since these are similar words to the child; they are applying the law of stimulus generalization. This law can help teachers choose stimuli to either promote discrimination or generalization. Similar stimuli are chosen to promote generalization, and dissimilar stimuli are chosen to promote discrimination.

---

**Action Item**

---

The main application for stimulus generalization in teaching is to prompt learners to internalize a concept from a specific example and apply it in a new situation. An example of a situation where you might want to prompt stimulus generalization would be helping a learner who has memorized a formula for computing a volume of a rectangular solid to apply the formula correctly in a word problem. What techniques could you use to promote generalization?

---

**Stimulus Gradient:** A range of stimuli along one dimension in a sequence in which each step is a gradual change along that dimension.

A prime example of a stimulus gradient is color. The gradient is created by arranging the hues of color, such as orange changing to red, in conjunction with the increase in wave frequency of the color. The stimulus gradient explains that the more similar stimuli are, the more likely a student will generalize a response. Therefore, the closer in wave length orange is to red, the more likely it will be that a student will call the color red.

The following graph shows the relationship between similar stimuli and frequency of responses.

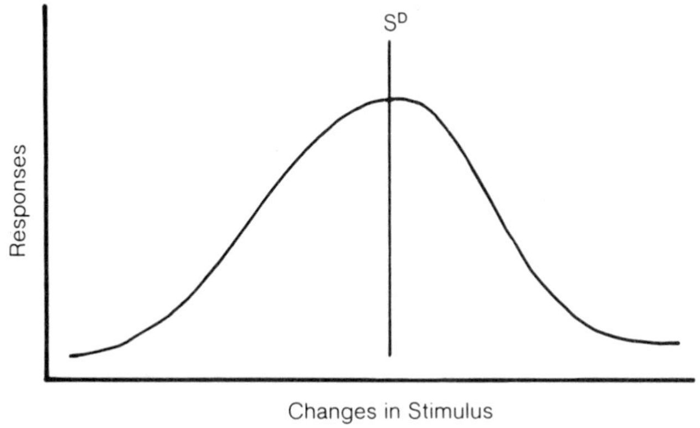


The discriminative stimulus that a student has been taught to respond to is in the middle. The closer the two stimuli are together on the stimulus gradient, the more apt a learner will be to respond to them as if they are the same stimuli. Therefore a learner will respond to one stimulus as if it were another one as long as they are close together on the gradient.

What are the applications to education? If a teacher wants to prompt stimulus *discrimination,* then two stimuli should be selected that are as far apart as possible on the stimulus gradient. Often young children have difficulty discriminating between the letters *b* and *d.* The similarity in form makes stimulus discrimination difficult. In order to help a student discriminate between these, a teacher could change the form of one of these letters so that it appears less similar (e.g., *l* ɔ and *d*).

Another tactic would be to teach the letter *b* with other letters that are very different, such as an *x* or *w.* Then the teacher could present the letter *d* separately with letters that are very different, and finally bring the two together.

If a teacher wants to promote stimulus *generalization,* then stimuli that are similar would be chosen. Consider the example of a child who is very aggressive toward other children. The teacher cannot find a solution. The child is transferred into a special classroom and placed in a very structured environment with specific consequences for following rules. The child's behavior improves and he is to be transferred back into the regular classroom. How can teachers help the child generalize what has been learned in the special class back to the regular class? BY MAKING THE STIMULUS CONDITIONS AS SIMILAR AS POSSIBLE. The child had a study carrel in the special class and was on a point system, earning points for correct behavior which could be traded in for free time. The carrel and the point system could be used in the regular class as well.

The concepts of discrimination, generalization and stimulus gradient alert teachers that learners will tend to overgeneralize concepts or skills inappropriately and may need help in discriminating the limits of application. Conversely, students may also need help in generalizing skills and concepts to new situations. Hence, the rule of stimulus generalization and the concept of a stimulus gradient provide techniques in achieving stimulus discrimination or generalization as the case may warrant.

---

**Action Item**

---

The primary teaching idea that can be derived from the stimulus gradient is to teach generalization by presenting concepts in a manner which emphasizes their similarity. On the other hand, to teach discrimination you present concepts that emphasize their differences. Imagine that you are teaching the difference between velocity and speed. How could you make these concepts as different as possible to achieve discrimination? Imagine, also, that you are teaching identification of the root word after a prefix has been added. The students already know how to identify a root word with a suffix added. How could you make finding a root word with a prefix as similar as possible to doing the same task with a suffix to achieve generalization?

---

**Sequencing:** Arranging stimuli in an order from simple to complex in terms of a student's ability to respond correctly. Step One is easier for a student than Step Two which is easier than Step Three, and so on.

Applying stimulus control concepts to curriculum materials can result in the creation of an instructional sequence which starts with a stimulus that is already discriminative and transforms that stimulus across steps into a brand new stimulus while maintaining correct responding. This is accomplished through cueing and sequencing. An example of sequencing to teach addition would be in the following list of skills. The teacher would create practice for each skill in the sequence listed below. Practice would continue with one skill until it was mastered, and then the teacher would proceed with the next skill.

## Example 1 Sequence to Teach Addition (Preschool)

| | |
|---|---|
| **Step One** | Rote Counting (Counting numbers in sequence without reference to objects.) |
| **Step Two** | Counting Objects |
| **Step Three** | Labeling Numbers (Saying the name of a number's symbol.) |
| **Step Four** | Number-Numeral Correspondence (Linking objects counted to symbol.) |
| **Step Five** | Equal Sign |
| **Step Six** | Plus Sign |
| **Step Seven** | Addition Problem (numbers 0–2) with Objects to Manipulate |
| **Step Eight** | Addition Problem (numbers 0–2) without Objects, but with number line |
| **Step Nine** | Addition Problems using 0–2 |
| **Step Ten** | Addition Problems using 0–5 |
| **Step Eleven** | Addition Problems using 0–7 |
| **Step Twelve** | Addition Problems using 0–10 |

These simple to complex steps assist students in correct responding. The strategy is to break the concept into pieces and present a piece at a time so that a student can readily absorb new information. One piece is added onto the next piece to build the concept and to further enhance accuracy.

### Action Items

When sequencing is used correctly, a teacher provides small pieces of content a learner can assimilate that progressively lead to the acquisition of a concept. How could you sequence instructional activities that go from simple to complex to teach learners how to find a main idea in a story? Can you think of a situation in which you would *not* want to sequence instruction? (Hint: Creativity requires divergent thinking or tolerating a lot of different ideas at one time which are not necessarily logically related.[2] In what situations would you sequence instruction and in which would you not want to?)

**Cueing:** Using a technique to increase the likelihood that a student will respond correctly.

There are several ways to cue correct responses. These are superimposition, stimulus shaping, stimulus fading, modeling and prompting.

**Superimposition:** Putting an $S^D$ (discriminative stimulus) on top of a new stimulus to prompt generalization of this response to the new stimulus.

In superimposition, the idea is to find a stimulus already acting as an $S^D$ that prompts a response similar to the response that is to be taught. The goal is to transfer a response from one $S^D$ to another stimulus that is unknown to the student.

An example could occur when a teacher is helping preschoolers to label the numerals 1, 2, 3, 4, and 5. (Labeling is not the same as counting. It is looking at the form of the number and saying its name.) This teacher could cue the labels in some way. Frequently teachers, particularly preschool teachers, will cue responses by superimposing a picture of something a child likes or is familiar with, like a flower, a bee, a bird, and so forth, on the object. The problem with this cueing strategy is that the picture has no relationship to the response that is desired. A picture of a bird is an $S^D$ for either the word bird or the name of that bird, a robin, for example; it is not an $S^D$ for a number label.

To make the practice of superimposition most efficient in prompting a response to a new stimulus, it is necessary to choose an $S^D$ that prompts a response that is at least similar to the one desired in the teaching situation.

To accomplish this, the teacher could use a picture that starts with the same sound as the number in the example of teaching number labels. The response to the picture would then be relevant to the word of the label. Example 2 shows superimposition of pictures on numerals. The words shown by the pictures are zipper, wiggle, tiger, thumb, and fish, and each begins with the same sound as the number. Therefore the sound will cue the number's name.

**Example 2 Superimposition: Names of Numbers (Preschool)**

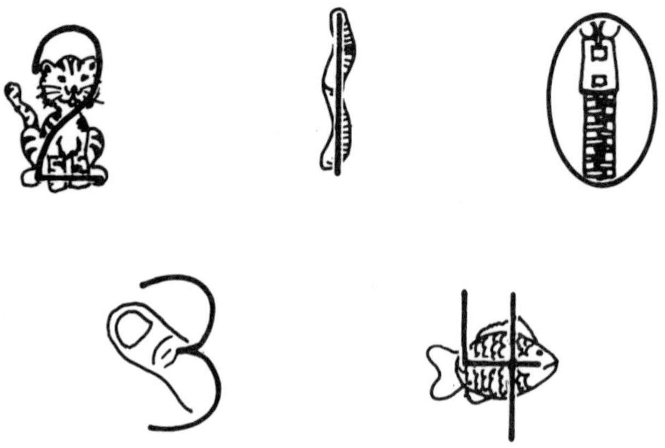

Textbooks or instructional programs that use superimposition usually superimpose color on a stimulus to prompt a correct response. For example, there is a reading series that has a different color for each letter to denote a different sound. Another example is a handwriting series that colors each line with a different color to help a student distinguish between the top, middle and bottom line. The shortcoming of these cues is the fact that they are unrelated to the response that is to be generated. Since the cues do not direct a student's attention to the relevant features of the $S^P$, the student has nothing to rely on when the cues are gone.

**Stimulus Fading:** Gradually adding or removing parts of a stimulus.

In stimulus fading, visual cues are added on the stimulus to prompt a correct response, and then these cues are gradually removed until the student is responding without the aid of the cues. It is not the same process as superimposition, since a picture is not always added. However, stimulus fading can also be used to remove a superimposed picture gradually across steps. For example, the pictures on the numbers in example 2 could be slowly removed by fading the intensity of the drawings across several steps.

Handwriting books usually use a form of stimulus fading to teach children to make letters. Usually the letter to be made is presented and the student traces that letter; then in two or three trials the letter is dotted and the student makes the letter connecting the dots. A more systematic sequence of fading in teaching number writing is depicted in example 1.

Notice that after a certain point, the process of fading changes. In the first ten steps, fading occurs by removing parts of the form of the number. This is designed so that a student will focus attention on the point where the number begins. But after step ten, the fading then removes the intensity of the lines instead of taking away pieces of the form. This is designed so that the entire form of the number is represented visually to the child. Otherwise, the student will try to connect the starting part of the letter and the piece of the letter that is remaining (  ) and, hence, lose track of the complete form.

**Stimulus Shaping:** Gradually changing the form of a stimulus.

In stimulus shaping, one begins an instructional sequence with a familiar stimulus and then gradually the form of that stimulus changes into the form of a new unfamiliar stimulus. This is different from superimposition and fading because in both of these cueing procedures, there is some aspect of the final stimulus that is always presented from the very beginning. In shaping, the stimulus transforms into anther one.

Kathyrn Schilmoeller used stimulus shaping to teach children to choose a Kanji symbol that stood for a certain picture.[3] (Kanji is the Japanese and Chinese writing system.) Children were to examine a Kanji symbol on the top of a card and then choose one of three pictures on the bottom of the card which matched.

Schilmoeller used stimulus shaping to change the picture of the object transformed into the Kanji symbol. At first, the picture is at the top of the card and a child simply finds the picture that matches it below. For example, at the top a sun would be presented and underneath one of the three choices would be an identical sun which the child was to choose. Over time, the sun at the top was changed into the Kanji symbol for sun in gradual steps.

## Example 3 Stimulus Fading: Number Writing (Preschool)

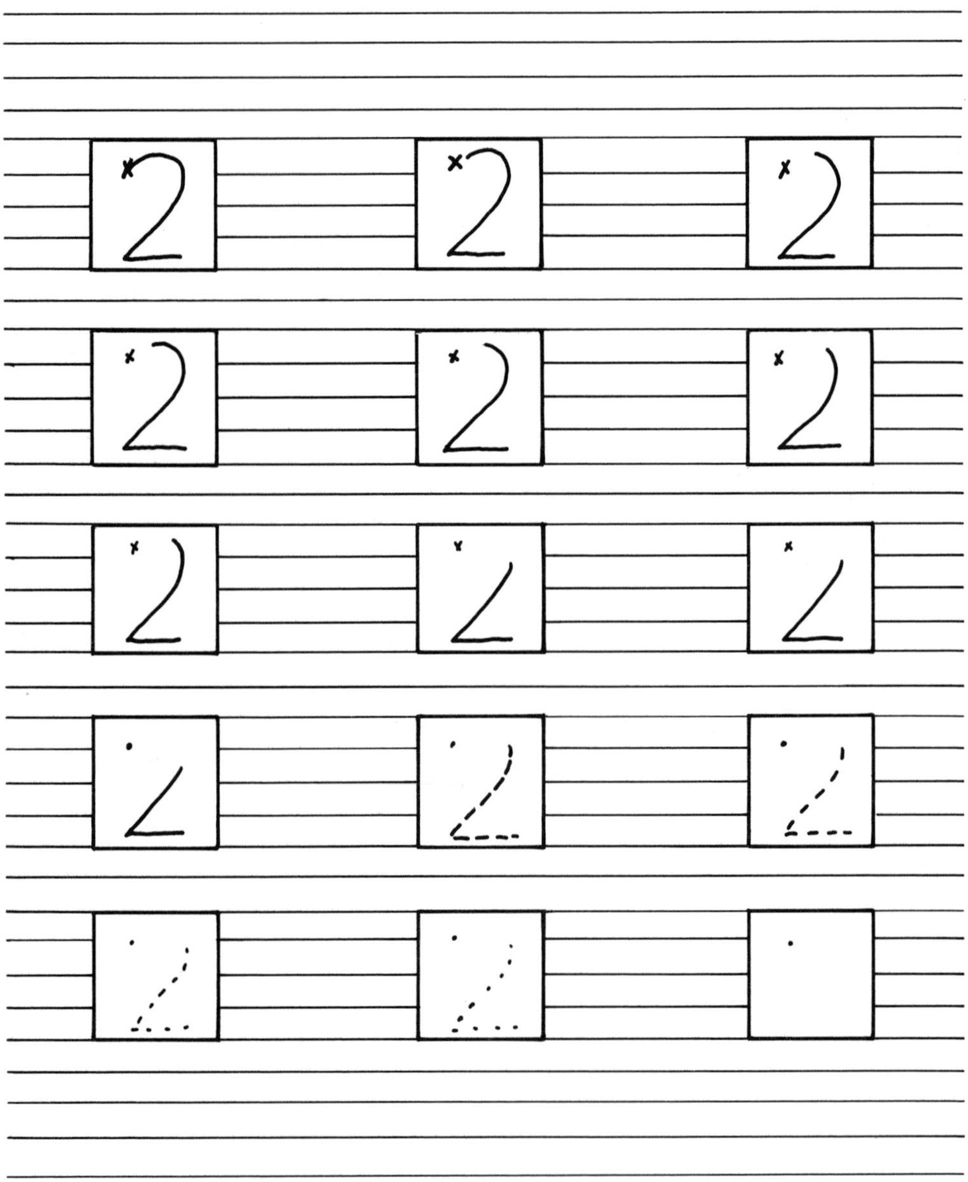

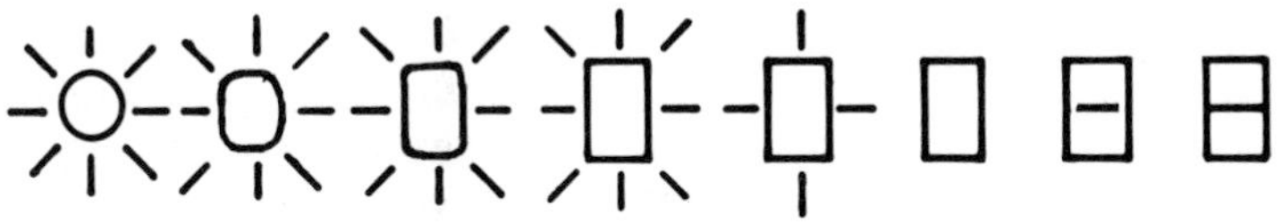

Sun Kanji Symbol for Sun

Shaping can also be used in changing the topography of responses, as well as in changing a stimulus shape. An example of using shaping to change responses is a case in which a catatonic schizophrenic was taught to speak. A psychologist noticed that the man often looked at gum in the psychologist's pocket. The psychologist went up to the patient and showed him the gum. When the man made a small grunt, he gave him a piece of gum. This continued for a while; then the psychologist would model a sound and give the patient the gum only when the patient made that sound. Then the psychologist required the patient to put two sounds together and, finally, to make a word. The response of the patient was shaped since the topography of the response was gradually changed over time.

---

**Action Item**

---

Cueing techniques, such as superimposition and stimulus shaping, are best used to help with the memory of vocabulary words and formulas. The idea is to add a visual or verbal prompt to help memory. Think of a vocabulary word that either you have had difficulty remembering or that your students have had difficulty with. Add a visual or verbal cue or change the shape of some part of the word to aid memory.

---

**Modeling:** Someone shows the response that is expected.

**Prompting:** Someone tells a student the response, or some portion of the response, right before or during a learner's response.

Prompting and modeling are cues that a teacher can use to help students respond correctly. In this case the cues are the teacher's words and actions. Oftentimes, modeling occurs first and is followed by prompting to cue correct responses. Modeling is used initially to demonstrate how to respond to a brand new or very difficult task: then prompting follows the model to help a student complete the task independently.

Both modeling and prompting could be used in an instructional sequence to teach children to count objects. When a new number is introduced, the teacher models the response. ("Count these objects. Watch me. One (point), two (point). Now you do it.") Then, in three steps, the teacher prompts the response by first saying the response loudly with the student, first in a normal voice, and then in a whisper. When a new number is introduced, the modeling and prompting sequence of loud, normal, and whisper is repeated. The sequence systematically progresses from simple (one object) to complex (ten objects), and the use of the cueing techniques, modeling and prompting.

## Action Item

Modeling is showing how to solve a problem or answer a question. Prompting is telling how to solve a problem or assisting a student in gradually becoming independent in performing what is required. Most teachers do a good job of modeling, but do very little prompting. How could you prompt a learner in solving a long division problem to bring a number down in the appropriate place, after multiplying a number by the divisor?

## Example 4 Learning Theory: Teaching the French Word "Marcher"—To Walk

**Discriminative Stimulus ($S^D$)**
The word paired with its meaning in English or paired with a mental image of walking.

**S-Delta**
All other French words.

**Superimposition**

Walking while saying marcher (the movement is superimposed on the word).

**Stimulus Shaping**

**Fading**

1. Gradually removing the intensity of the letters of the word "walk" superimposed on "marcher".
2. Gradually changing the shape of the exaggerated "h" in marcher.

**Modeling and Prompting**
To model, a teacher says, "This word is marcher. What is it? Marcher means to walk."

To prompt, a teacher says, "What does marcher mean? Wa ______" (Teacher walks.) "What French word means walking? Ma ________"

**Stimulus Gradient:**
French words which sound like marcher would be close to marcher on the gradient. Since they sound like marcher, a student might mistake the words for marcher.

**Stimulus Discrimination:**
Selecting marcher from other French words which sound like marcher.

**Stimulus Generalization:**
Using marcher in its correct form to agree with a noun (e.g., nous marchons).

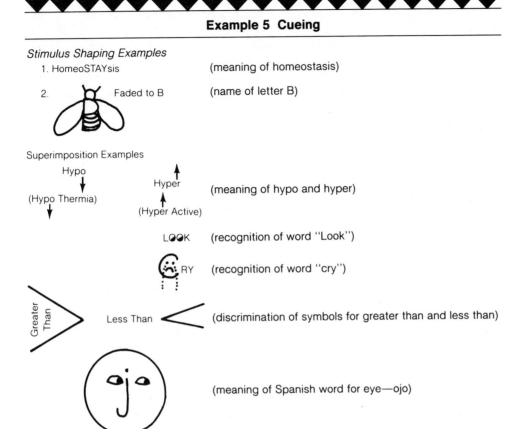

**Example 5 Cueing**

*Stimulus Shaping Examples*

1. HomeoSTAYsis — (meaning of homeostasis)
2.  Faded to B — (name of letter B)

Superimposition Examples

Hypo ↓ (Hypo Thermia) ↓ — Hyper ↑ (Hyper Active) ↑ — (meaning of hypo and hyper)

LOOK — (recognition of word "Look")

 RY — (recognition of word "cry")

Greater Than 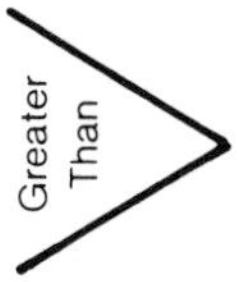 Less Than  — (discrimination of symbols for greater than and less than)

 — (meaning of Spanish word for eye—ojo)

## SUMMARY: STIMULUS CONTROL PROCEDURES ADAPTED FOR EDUCATION

If teachers think in terms of stimulus control concepts, they gain powerful tools to communicate concepts and skills efficiently. Moreover, a number of shifts in teachers' perceptions of the learning process can result.

First, teachers become precise in thinking about what aspect of stimulus complex is most critical. This analysis pinpoints the key aspect of a concept or skill, unlocking solutions for students. This type of analysis also specifies which aspects of the stimulus should be disregarded to alleviate confusions. Furthermore, the discriminative stimulus and the S-Delta's can be pointed out to students.

The concepts of stimulus discrimination, stimulus generalization, and stimulus gradient help teachers communicate to students the refinement of newly learned concepts and skills. Teaching students stimulus generalization prompts the transfer of learning from one application to another and promotes the synthesis of new learning with previously acquired information. In essence, stimulus generalization helps students internalize learning so that it can be used and transformed in new situations. This is complemented by stimulus discrimination since discrimination gives students the cues on the limits of applying concepts in new situations.

Another powerful shift that stimulus control concepts can prompt in teachers is the careful examination of students' responses to stimuli or teaching experiences to see if stimulus control is actually operating. The basic intent of stimulus control is to improve the teacher-student communication process so that the teacher is saying, "This is the critical element to pay attention to, these elements do not make much difference, this is the situation where you can generalize these elements, and this is the situation where you cannot." The teacher's job is to determine if communication occurred. A message was sent, but was it received? The teacher knows if it was received by seeing if the student does indeed respond to the critical element. If this happens, a relationship has formed between the stimulus and response and there exists stimulus control. However, if the student's response does not show this, then the teacher knows communication did not happen and the message must be readjusted accordingly.

Stimulus control, cueing techniques, and sequencing (superimposition, fading, shaping, modeling, and prompting) work together to decrease errors and prompt correct responses. This removes the student's frustration and anxiety reactions to difficult concepts, and also combats error patterns which can interfere with later learning. The strategy is to start an instructional sequence with a concept that is already familiar to students and then transform that concept into a new, more difficult one, while maintaining students' interest and motivation. Motivation will always stay high when students experience success. That is one of the greatest benefits stimulus control can contribute to curriculum design, i.e., to systematize the sequencing of the presentation of difficult concepts so that students succeed in learning. The cycle of communication becomes complete; the message is sent and received.

The cueing techniques are fun and creative and can attract students' attention, particularly that of young students, because these techniques are tangible and immediate. Cues are probably the most useful in learning rote memory tasks and discriminating between easily confused concepts. Sequencing, on the other hand, can be used in every aspect of teaching by transferring students' learning from a familiar concept to a more difficult one.

---

## QUICK REVIEW

Can you match the term with the definition?

| | |
|---|---|
| **Discriminative Stimulus-$S^D$** | A range of stimuli along a gradual progression of change |
| **S-Delta** | The stimulus that does not prompt a behavior |
| **Stimulus Control** | The stimulus that prompts a behavior |

| | |
|---|---|
| **Stimulus Gradient** | The more similar a stimulus is to an SD, the more probable a similar response will occur |
| **Stimulus Generalization** | A discernible event in the environment which prompts a given response |
| **Stimulus Discrimination** | Responding differently to two different stimuli |
| **Law of Stimulus Generalization** | Responding the same to two different stimuli |
| **Stimulus Shaping** | Saying part of a response with a student |
| **Superimposition** | Putting a familiar stimulus on top of an unfamiliar one |
| **Stimulus Fading** | Changing the topography of a stimulus |
| **Sequencing** | Saying or showing the expected response |
| **Prompting** | Creating a series of steps which move from simple to complex |
| **Modeling** | Removing parts of a stimulus gradually |

## EXTENSION QUESTIONS

1. How are John Dewey and Jean Piaget alike in their ideas of child development?

2. Are stimulus control procedures opposed to Dewey and Piaget's ideas? Why or why not?

3. How might a teacher use reinforcement and extinction to teach a concept? Do you think this is a good idea? Why or why not?

4. Why might it be important to isolate the discriminative stimulus in a learning task? Be specific. Give an example.

# 3
CHAPTER

# OBJECTIVES AND CRITICAL ELEMENTS

## OBJECTIVES

Define the purpose of writing an objective.

Express two qualities of a good objective.

Explain one method for writing an objective.

List one frequent problem that teachers have in writing an objective.

Define the purpose of a critical element in helping a learner master an objective.

## PROBLEM

Teachers are unclear about what aspects of concepts to emphasize for effective communication.

An objective is defined as the intended outcome of teaching. In teaching, it is of the utmost importance to have a learning outcome and to perceive clearly what is to be taught. If a teacher has a very clear image or vision of what students will be like at the end of teaching, then it will be easier to actualize the vision. Sports psychologists and coaches often ask athletes to image themselves performing perfectly. Research beginning in the 1940s shows that imaging a performance improves athletic performance as much as actual physical practice.[1] Psychologists use the same technique to help individuals overcome fears, inhibitions, poor self-images, and phobias. Imaging goals or changes in behaviors and attitudes can positively influence an outcome.

If a teacher has a clear image of the end learning outcome, then other things fall into place as well. If what is to be learned can be perceived well, then it can be clearly communicated. The steps that are needed to take students from where they are before instruction to the desired end goal are then definable. A clear image also eliminates confusion over what to communicate. Most students have experienced a teacher who creates interesting activities but, at the same time, does not have a central objective in mind.

Specifying the end outcome of instruction allows teachers to know when they have achieved their teaching aim. If teachers' objectives are very general and ambiguous, then the teaching process is always in a state of flux. There is no point of departure to say, "Yes, indeed, this learning happened."

Objectives need to be distinguished from goals, since both terms, objectives and goals, are used frequently in the field of curriculum design. For purposes here, a goal is defined as a general, overarching aim of teaching. An objective, on the other hand, is the specific outcome of a teaching sequence or unit.

An example of a goal for a social science class may be; "Students will sense the dependence of the United States on other countries' resources." Several objectives may be written to attain this goal. The job of the objective is to specify an outcome related to this goal which will precisely direct the teaching process. An objective translates a goal to teaching procedures. Therefore, an example of an objective for the above goal would be: "When asked the question orally, which country supplies the U.S. with fresh produce and raw materials needed for industrial production, students will verbally respond with the names of five countries."

Objectives are best when they describe the setting conditions of performance, specify some level of criteria, and use observable verbs. Precise verbs are a key to good objective writing. Objectives which use generalized verbs (i.e., gain an understanding of or, be familiar with) are essentially useless in guiding instruction.

*Objectives are important because they—*

1. Give an image of the learner at the end of teaching.
2. Give a basis for creating teaching steps to reach the intended outcome.
3. Clear away extraneous information and prompt straightforward communication about what is to be learned.
4. Provide a reference point to know when teaching is complete.

There are a number of pitfalls in using objectives. One is the fact that some teachers are not able to make the shift from thinking about their own behavior to thinking about what they want a learner to do in a teaching sequence. When asked to write an objective, some teachers will say what they will do, as opposed to what they hope their students will do. For example, one teacher wanted to create a teaching sequence for children to make picture dictionaries and then use them to remember the sounds of the letters. When she went about writing objectives, she wrote objectives for herself, such as, "I will give the students pictures beginning with the letters *a* and *b* and ask them to sort them onto the *a* and *b* pages in the dictionary." This is an objective since it gives the teacher an image of what the end goal of her activities in a lesson will be. However, it is not an objective for the learners' behavior. It does not say what students will be able to do at the end of the teaching exercise. To prevent this pitfall, teachers can actually image students' performances.

Another pitfall of objective writing is that it can make the teaching process too controlled and linear. Teachers can be so locked into their desired objective that they do not encourage horizontal explorations of concepts that arise spontaneously in a teaching sequence. This can be easily solved by thinking of objectives as a guide. The teaching steps that emerge from the objectives are a framework for teaching. But the objectives or steps do not exclude emerging needs if something intriguing rears its head. Thus, horizontal extensions of concepts and skills are to be valued.

One important consideration in writing an objective is to include discrimination and generalization aspects of the skills or concepts within the objective. This insures that teaching is not a rote activity, prompting students to memorize information and respond correctly in only limited applications of a concept. *A higher order of learning takes place when it is internalized and can be generalized to new situations.*

## OBJECTIVE EXAMPLES

The following objectives were created by teachers in a curriculum design class.

Examine the attributes of these objectives. Analyze each objective below in respect to these questions.

1. Does the objective portray a clear picture of the learning to take place?
2. Does the objective give specific enough information to decide when teaching is complete?
3. Does the objective include generalization of the concept?

### Example 1 Objectives: Reading Food Label (Secondary Consumer Affairs)

a. List the six items required by law to be on a food label.
b. Identify the predominant or main ingredient in a given food product.
c. Interpret the nutritional information found on a label.
d. Identify the various forms of sugar, both obvious and "hidden" in a food product.
e. Identify the chemical additives found in a given food product.
f. Choose the best food based on the above factors.

## Action Item

An objective needs to be specific enough so that you can visualize the learner meeting the objective. Write an objective for comparing and contrasting the theories of evolution and Creationism.

## CRITICAL ELEMENTS

The next step in curriculum development, after writing an objective, is to specify the critical element of the learning task. This process is also termed concept development, or analyzing a concept to specify what to emphasize in the teaching process. This is the discriminative stimulus, i.e., the stimulus that will prompt a correct response. What is the most important thing to which a student should pay attention? This is the heart, the core, of unlocking a concept so that it becomes a student's own. Isolating the critical element of a task is a necessary first step in curriculum design. It may be that in some concepts there are a series of critical elements, attended to in a sequential fashion to solve a task. For example, in solving an algebra equation with one unknown, the first critical element would be the equal sign, the next would be the location of the unknown, the next would be recognizing the need to clear the side of the equation with the unknown, the next would be to remember that one must do the same operation to both sides of the equation and so forth. In this case, it would be important to teach one until it is understood and then to go on to the next one.

Since most teachers have already mastered the concepts they are attempting to communicate, it is often difficult to think back to the first time they encountered a concept. The discriminative stimulus aspect of the concept is lost because use and understanding of the concept has become automatic. It is essential that a teacher examine the critical element.

To determine the critical element, the most useful procedure is to examine the task from a logical standpoint and say, "What is the one most important element of this?" Another question a teacher can ask is, "When I respond, what is the aspect of the question, problem or task that I pay the most attention to in order to respond correctly?" Sometimes this must be approached on a trial and error basis. If a teacher designates a critical element and then creates a teaching sequence based on that concept, he or she may find that students do not learn the concept or cannot respond correctly. Then the best tactic is to return to the drawing board and choose another critical element. Learners' responses can point the direction to determining a more functional critical element that will guide learners to the appropriate response. In most cases, however, the first critical element defined by teachers will work.

The study used to exemplify cueing in chapter 2 clearly demonstrates the importance of pinpointing the critical element. In the Schilmoeller study in which children were taught to match pictures with Kanji symbols representing that picture, Schilmoeller gradually changed the form from the picture into the symbol. This was done to direct a student's attention to the shape of the Kanji symbol and its relationship to the picture. The critical element was the shape of the form. Also, in the number labeling sequence described in chapter 2, the critical element was designated to be the beginning sound of the number's name.

A critical element is not the central theme of a lesson. It is the specific aspect of the presenting question, problem or task that when attended to, will be the key to unlock the solution or answer. In other words, it is the most important item to catch the learner's attention.

**Example 2 Critical Elements**

| Stimulus | Critical Elements |
|---|---|
| The sound of the letter "a" | The shape of the mouth (open, smiling) |
| 2 + ___ = 5 | The equal sign |
| When it is safe to cross a street for a blind person | The feel of the curb, the sound of cars from both directions |
| The difference in Freud's and Rogers' theories of development | Choice |

**Action Item**

A critical element is the essential aspect of a task that is most important for the learner to pay attention to. For example, in compass work with maps, it is critical for the student to visualize where magnetic north is on the globe to know whether to add or subtract degrees of declination from true north. What critical element would you emphasize if you are teaching learners to write a topic sentence for a paragraph?

## SUMMARY

The first two steps of curriculum writing, objective writing and isolating the critical element, are essential to the later efficacy of the materials. An objective that is specific and written in terms of the learner's thoughts and behaviors at the end of the teaching process gives the teacher a clear perception of the end goal of teaching. This allows the teacher to organize instruction to match the goal. Curriculum materials can fail simply because there is no clear perception of what is to be communicated.

Isolating a critical element gives a learner power in assimilating a concept or skill. That which is most important or the key to discrimination can be emphasized in the curriculum materials. Laying a solid foundation through these two curriculum making techniques promotes successful learning.

## QUICK REVIEW

Can you match the terms?

| | |
|---|---|
| **Objective** | The key to solving, performing the objective. What is the most important thing for the learner to pay attention to? |
| **Critical Element** | A clear picture of the learning to take place |

## EXTENSION QUESTIONS

1. Of what value is imaging the learner performing the objective in writing an objective?

2. What are some of the questions you can ask to determine the critical element of an objective?

3. How can emphasizing the critical element in an objective teach learner independence?

4. How can you determine whether or not an objective is written in terms of what the learner can do at the end of an instructional sequence instead of what the teacher will do?

# 4 CHAPTER

# TASK ANALYSIS AND SEQUENCING

## OBJECTIVES

Define the purpose of a task analysis

Note one frequent error in writing a task analyses.

Explain a method for conducting a task analysis.

Recognize a correct task analysis.

Define the difference between a task analysis and sequencing.

Express the cardinal rule of creating a sequence.

## PROBLEMS

Teachers assume certain knowledge by learners which results in the omission of information which is necessary for learning.

The next step in curriculum design is a process called task analysis. The task analysis is produced by examining the behavior and thoughts of a student competently performing the objective. A task analysis also isolates the prerequisite skills a learner must have or understand before he or she can even begin learning the new concept in question. A task analysis can be accomplished in a number of ways. One way is to visualize a student perfectly performing the objective. Once the image is set, then the task analyzer sequentially writes down the steps that the student progresses through to perform the task. The teacher also logically thinks through what the prerequisite skills are before a student can even start the first step of a task. Some tasks, particularly manual tasks or athletic tasks, can very easily be analyzed in a sequential basis using this visualization technique. Another task analysis method is to actually watch someone complete the task and then write down the necessary steps.

For tasks that are more conceptual in nature, watching or visualizing someone completing the task is not enough, since many of the steps involved are occurring in the mind and not all of the steps needed are occurring in a linear order. The brain often processes information in a simultaneous manner. In cases of highly conceptual matter, the method is to logically analyze all of the different concepts necessary in order to successfully perform the task and then to list the possible thought process a learner may be working through while performing the objective. In order to determine the prerequisite skills, the concept that seems to be the easiest is analyzed to see what skills are necessary before it can be performed or understood.

Thus, there are two basic methods of task analysis: (1) Visualizing performance of the objective and writing down the steps in sequence; (2) Listing the component concepts of a task, regardless of sequence.

**Task Analysis:** Listing the steps a learner would go through (mentally or in action) to competently perform the objective.

A task analysis is completed so that:

1. A teacher will not assume that students understand certain component skills or concepts that are essential in completing the task, but are automatic to the teacher.
2. Students will not be asked to complete tasks for which they do not know the prerequisites.
3. Teachers can use a task analysis as a basis for creating an instructional sequence that streamlines communication and prompts successful acquisition of a concept.

An example from a kindergarten curriculum math material shows how a problem can arise by not conducting a task analysis. The task involved is for children to look at a number of objects and then put an *x* in a box in front of the numeral (visual representation of the number) that stands for that number. If one were to do a task analysis, the following steps would emerge:

**Example 1 Sequence: Counting Objects (Preschool)**

Look at the objects.

Count the objects starting at the left.

Say a number aloud or in the mind as each number is pointed to, starting with 1, and proceeding in sequence.

Remember the last number that was counted.

Examine the choices of numerals.

Remembering the number of objects counted, find the numeral that represents that number.

Put an *x* in the box of that number.

Does this seem like an arduous mental exercise to teach something as simple and straightforward as finding a numeral to match a certain number of objects? This is clearly an elementary task to an adult or even to a seven year old.

Just for a minute, though, think as a five year old would think when shown this task. The first thing is figuring out which aspect of the stimulus complex on the page to direct attention. The child has to discern what parts of the stimulus complex go together to make up the problem to solve. It is easy for an adult to say that obviously these objects go with that number, but a kindergartener must learn what a problem means visually and spatially.

It is not rare to see kindergarteners moving through the pages of math books, putting "x's" in every box on a page, not realizing that only one out of two choices must be marked for each problem. Some curriculum texts do not appear to use a task analysis, since component skills of a task are omitted. For example, most kindergarten math books omit teaching the skill of naming numerals. Children are asked to count the objects and find the correct numeral without knowing that numeral's name. They know how many objects there are, but they do not know that a 4 stands for the number 4. Some kindergarten teachers experience a great deal of frustration when using these books because they think the problem is the children cannot count. But the problem is relatively simple—identifying the names of numerals.

The idea of conducting a task analysis to streamline curriculum development is not a new notion. In 1911 the National Education Association established a Committee on the Economy of Time. This committee met over eight years and issued a number of reports. One of their objectives was the determination of socially worthwhile knowledge by the tabulation of actual human activities. Harold Rugg was one of the key people involved in this.[1] The committee did analyses on a large scale to determine what concepts should be taught in schools. For example, to determine what math skills and concepts should be taught, a task analysis was done of the math skills needed to act competently in the adult world. An analysis of math skills in a cookbook, in computing factory payrolls, and in understanding advertisements produced a list of arithmetic operations to be included in schools.

Learning research makes it possible today to use task analyses in a more sophisticated and specific manner. Specific concepts can be analyzed to develop effective instructional sequences.

The following task analysis example demonstrates how a concept can be examined in a very specific way as a preface to creating curriculum materials. This task analysis examines a problem on proportion from an eighth grade math book.

### Example 2 Correct Task Analysis (Junior High Mathematics)

**Objective**

When given a word problem stating a relationship of one number to a second number, the student can determine a proportion to solve for an unknown that has the same relationship to a third number.

(Ex. Donna earned $5.76 for 4 hours of baby-sitting. At that rate, what would she earn for 3 hours?)

**Critical Element**

Recognize the relationship of two numbers and how that relationship can be used to determine how one number changes when the other number is changed.

**Task Analysis**

1. Realize it is proportion problem. (Attend to critical element.)
2. Write quantities in proportion equation
   a is to b as x is to c
   Check to see that like units are in the denominator and in the numerator.
3. Solve equation:
   Multiply cross products
   Multiply both sides of inverse of number next to "x".
   Solve by division.
   Express answer in appropriate units.

**Prerequisites**

division; multiplication; reducing fractions; fractions; solving for unknown in equation.

Some people have great difficulty in writing task analyses. Instead of analyzing a competent performance of the objective, these individuals list the steps they would use in teaching the objectives. The problem with this approach is the fact that the thought process is directed toward how to teach and not toward analyzing the components of a task to insure that nothing is omitted in communicating the elements of the task. It takes some practice to get in the swing of examining what is happening in the learner's mind as he or she is performing a task. The following two examples may give more clarity to the process. It is important to practice the process until the teacher can perceive from the mind of the learner how to recreate the process of solution. Seeing from the learner's eyes is the key to effective curriculum design.

### Example 3 Correct Task Analysis (Elementary Language Arts)

**Objective**

Given two sets of words, child will be able to match the words from each column that end alike.

**Critical Element**

1. Child recognizes the ending sound unit of words.
2. Child is able to match similar ending sounds in different words.

**Task Analysis**

| *Column #1* | *Column #2* |
|---|---|
| band | bump |
| near | stand |
| jump | hear |

1. Child recognizes two separate columns of 3 words each.
2. Child reads 1st word of Column #1.
3. Child recognizes ending sound of that word.
4. Child reads 1st word of Column #2, and notices ending sound.
5. Child remembers 1st ending sound and determines if it is same as 2nd word read in Column #2.
   a. Child may need to repeat words and say ending sound after each word to facilitate clarity.
6. Child repeats steps 2–5 with 2nd word and 3rd word of Column #2.
7. Child reads 2nd word in Column #1, and then repeats steps 3–6.
8. Child reads 3rd word in Column #1, and then repeats steps 3–6.

**Prerequisites**

1. Child can read the words and pronounce aloud.
2. Child can recognize similar sounds.

### Example 4 Correct Task Analysis (Elementary Science)

**Objective**

When asked by the teacher in a written question, children will list three means of seed dispersal.

**Critical Element**

Children recognize that seeds travel in different ways, depending on their shape and form.

**Task Analysis**

1. Child remembers what a seed is.
2. Child visualizes different seeds he worked with.
3. Child identifies the word "dispersal" to mean the way the seed travels.
4. Child visualizes a seed he has worked with that is plumed or winged.
5. Child connects above shape with flying through the air.
6. Child knows that the wind helps the seed to fly through the air.
7. Child records "wind" as first method of seed dispersal.
8. Child visualizes a seed he has worked with that has stickers on it.
9. Child visualizes that seed carried on an animal, perhaps his dog.
10. Child connects stickers on seed as an agent to attach to animal's fur or hair.
11. Child records "animal surface" as a means of seed dispersal.
12. Child remembers *cue* that "animals" have to do with two of the means of dispersal.
13. Child visualizes a seed that is fleshy.
14. Child visualizes an animal eating that seed.
15. Child visualizes a scat with seeds in it.
16. Child identifies "animal scat" as a means of seed dispersal.

**Prerequisites**

1. Experience with gathering seeds and noting various shapes.
2. Knowledge of vocabulary word—dispersal.

### Example 5 Correct Task Analysis (Secondary Environmental Education)

**Objectives**

1. Students will be able to describe where alpine environments are found and give a general description of the biotic (cushion and mat plants, krummholtz or tree islands, Bergmann's rule applying to many animals) and abiotic (wind, short summers, long, snowy, cold winters, low oxygen pressure) components.
2. Students will be able to describe three plant and three animal adaptations to the alpine tundra biome.

**Critical Element**
(for objective 2) Students must be aware of the abiotic components of the alpine tundra to enable them to think of the adaptations.

**Prerequisites**
Student must have a background knowledge in alpine ecology and understand the term adaptation.

**Task Analysis**

1. Student is asked to describe three plant and three animal adaptations to the alpine tundra.
2. Student images the alpine tundra, a cold wind is blowing, there is a dusting of snow on the ground and storm clouds are building overhead.
3. Student images a pika with its short legs and ears and says, "Animals have shorter appendages to keep them from losing too much body heat."
4. Student images a marmot in a burrow and says, "Some animals hibernate during the winter to avoid having to spend energy storing food."
5. Student images a mountain goat that is very young, hopping around on a sheer cliff face and says, "The mountain goat matures very quickly and is able to live on cliffs to avoid predators."
6. Student images the wind blowing over a small tree and says, "Some trees have stunted growth, krummholtz, to protect them from the cold and wind."
7. Student images a snow bank slowly melting off a meadow and says, "Plants have a short growing season so they have to mature quickly."
8. Student images a limber pine swaying in the wind and says, "Limber pines have bendable branches to keep the wind from breaking them."

## Example 6 Incorrect Task Analysis (Elementary Social Studies)

**Objectives**
To learn concern and appreciation of other people through sharing, helping and working with one another.

**Critical Element**
The presence or thought of another person.

**Task Analysis**

1. How to use gestures of affection (e.g., hugs).
2. How to recognize when others are showing concern.
3. How to greet and leave other people politely.
4. How to understand a good deed.
5. Think of 5 words, 5 pictures, 5 objects which show caring or sharing.

The task analysis above has a number of problems. First, the objective is very general. It is not clear what this curriculum designer means by sharing or helping. Secondly, the task analysis is written from the point of view of what will be done with the learners to teach sharing instead of an analysis of what a learner would know or do to demonstrate sharing. An exercise for the reader would be to correct this objective and task analysis. (Hint: The objective and an analysis could be aimed at a good deed.)

---

**Action Item**

The most common error in writing a task analysis is for a teacher to write down the steps that he or she will use in teaching the concept in question. One technique to get yourself out of thinking in this way is to speculate on what could be going on in the learner's head as he or she approaches a task or problem. Imagine that you want to teach the appreciation of poetry; speculate on the first step of a task analysis for this concept. (Hint One: You may want to write an objective first, since it is difficult to do a task analysis from a goal. Hint Two: A learner may see a book of poems and think. "I liked the sound of that Emerson poem.")

---

## SEQUENCING

The next step in curriculum making is transforming a task analysis to a sequence. *Creating an instructional sequence is the basic art of curriculum making.* The purpose of a sequence is to create an instructional progression to lead a learner to competency and accuracy in responding to a concept.

Sequencing can be done at all levels, from instructional sequences for a specific concept to a sequence of concepts to present in a subject area across several years. The principles of task analysis and sequencing are very powerful and can be used to design a lesson, design a unit, analyze published curriculum materials or create an entire school's curricula.

Curriculum materials often publish a scope and sequence to accompany books. This is usually a chart which gives the titles of concepts within a subject area and gives the order of presentation. The scope is the breadth of topics and the sequence is the order in which they are presented. This is a very general application of the procedure of sequencing. However, as the remainder of this chapter explains, sequencing can be refined to a sophisticated art.

Jerome Bruner talked about sequencing in his book, *Toward a Theory of Instruction.*[2] He claimed that most concepts could be presented successfully if they were presented in the correct sequence. Bruner proposed a spiral curriculum to accomplish this. Bruner said that a spiral of one concept could be created across every instructional level, from kindergarten to college level. For example, if the concept were set theory, kindergarteners would have simple tasks to create sets of similar members. In first grade a slightly more sophisticated presentation of skills would occur. Eventually in high school or college, abstract logical operations on sets would be taught.

Besides the spiral curriculum, Bruner recommended that experts in a given subject area be curriculum designers, since they were the ones who understood the subject matter and could construct the best spiral. There are a number of practical problems with Bruner's curriculum design approach, even though it is conceptually sound. The first is the idea that a mathematician would have great difficulty in empathizing with a child's perception of math skills. Using Dewey's terms, a mathematician would have difficulty psychologizing a concept or making it a part of a child's world view.

Another problem with the spiral idea of curriculum is the criticism that when a concept is introduced on a spiral, not enough practice is given at each point in the spiral to master the concept.

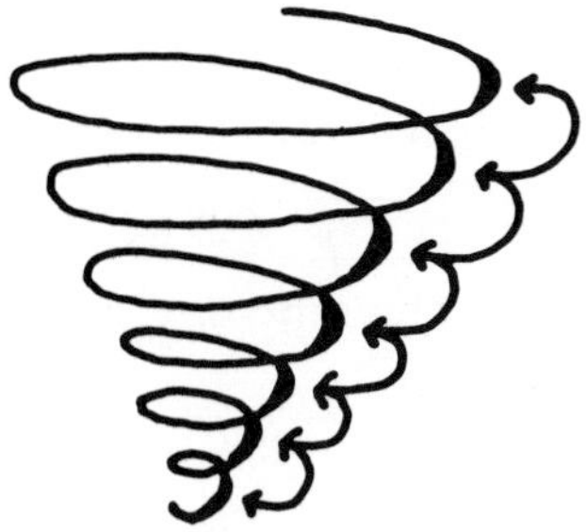

The spiral curriculum concept

The task is not sequenced in a careful enough manner at each point in the spiral. So much attention is focused on creating the spiral across years of curriculum materials, that very little attention focuses on each point in the spiral to communicate effectively. Students get a taste of the concepts as they proceed through the spiral, but do not master the concepts.

Even though Bruner's ideas do not work out practically, the practice of sequencing concepts for instruction can be used to realize the benefits of Bruner's ideas—that any student can be taught anything if it is presented correctly. Starting instruction with a familiar concept and gradually changing that concept over steps until it is a new and more complex concept can effectively teach most concepts.

**Sequencing:** Creating a series of instructional steps that move from simple to complex to teach each skill or concept generated by a task analysis. The first step of a sequence is a skill or concept that the learner has already mastered. Cues are used in a sequence to assist memory.

The cardinal rule in creating a sequence is to *TEACH ONE THING AT A TIME.* It is essential that each step in a sequence teach one skill or concept only. Otherwise, it is possible for students to respond in a confused manner. To use the vocabulary from chapter 2, the purpose of each step in the sequence must be to establish one discriminative stimulus and to help a student see the difference between a discriminative stimulus and the S-Deltas.

One criticism of sequencing is the observation that all students do not need sequencing. Some students catch on quickly. Yet it is possible to design a sequence to accommodate all rates of learning. The technique is to place tests or probes after each step or every few steps of a sequence. (A probe is a mini-test of performance of the end task that the sequence is designed to teach.) The probe serves several functions. First, if after a few steps in the sequence a student is putting the complex task together, then the student's performance on the probe will tell whether or not the rest of the sequence is necessary or whether the student can perform the task without the remaining steps. The second function of a probe is to communicate to a student that a day will come when he or she will be expected to perform the complex task without the help of the steps in the sequence or any cues.

The following sequence is used in an elementary mathematics text to teach division.

**Example 7 Sequence to Teach Division (Elementary Mathematics)**

1. Divide, horizontal format. Written question. The response is cued by pictures that are grouped by the divisor.

   $$15 \div 3$$

2. Divide, horizontal format. Written question. Cues or pictures circled by the number that is the divisor.
   Six eggs divided between two chickens.
3. Divide, horizontal format. No written question. Cues are pictures circled.

   $$10 \div 5$$

4. Divide, horizontal format. Cues are pictures circled. Student must write equation.

   Write equation _____ ÷ _____ = _____

5. Divide, horizontal format. No cues.

   $$21 \div 7 =$$

This sequence does not move from simple to complex. It takes a few jagged turns. The cues used vary and not systematically removed, and step 2 is easier than step 1. Hence, there is a progression, but it is confused.

The following two sequences were created by teachers in a curriculum design class. The sequences list the skill or concept that would be presented at each step of instruction. Notice that one skill is presented at a time. These are in outline form. The next chapter explains how to use specific techniques to flesh out an outline of a sequence to instructional procedures.

### Example 8 Sequence Outline Contractions (Second Grade)

1. Definition of a Contraction.
2. Purpose of Apostrophe.
3. How to Make Apostrophe.
4. Read a Contraction.
5. Know a Contraction is a Two-word Form.
6. Concert Two Words into a Contraction.
7. Contractions of *not.*
8. Contractions of *will.*
9. Contractions of *is.*
10. Contractions of *are.*
11. Contractions of *would.*
12. Contractions with many letters left out.

### Example 9 Sequence to Outline Reading Food Labels (High School Consumer Affairs Class)

1. Define a label.
2. Tell the six points that are on a label.
3. Realize the descending order relationship of ingredients on a label.
4. Define the Minimum Daily Requirements (MDR).
5. Find 6 points on an actual label.
6. Circle the main ingredient on a label.
7. Find the Minimum Daily Requirements on a label.
8. Define the forms of hidden sugar.
9. Choose products with the least hidden sugar.
10. Recognize chemical additives.
11. List the chemical additives.
12. Visit a grocery store and select nutritionally healthy packaged food.

Many textbooks for intermediate elementary and high school content areas rely on review questions. Often, though, the review questions do not match the sequence of information in the chapter they are designed to review.

Lack of correct sequencing is a problem in elementary curriculum books. The listing below of concepts from a fifth grade reader traces several sequences. The sections indicate a chapter. Examine the number of concepts in each chapter and decide whether or not the sequence moves from simple to complex for each concept.

**Example 10 Sequences with Many Objectives (Fifth Grade Reader)***

**Selection 17**

*=suffix sequence

o=probable ending sequence

___=antonym sequence

Baseword of suffix*

Meaning of word with suffix "er"*

Meaning of word with suffix "or"*

Draw conclusion

Identify "interview" form of writing

Identify form of pronoun

Use card catalog to complete a sentence

**Selection 18**

Identify words that make up a contraction

Identify words that make up hyphenated or compound words

Identify an inference drawn from plot/setting/characters

Identify attitudes, emotions or traits of characters

Select from a pair of homophones

**Selection 19**

Identify baseword of a given prefixed word

Identify the meaning of a word beginning with prefix "im"

Identify the baseword of a given suffixed word*

Predict a probable ending o

Identify use of comparison or contrast in a selection

Identify author's purpose

Identify form as a fairy tale

Identify meaning of homograph

**Selection 20**

Identify characteristics of a poem

Identify the form of a written selection as poetry

Identify and describe the effect created by imagery

Identify and explain the meaning of similes

Identify the use of personification

Identify and explain the meaning of metaphors

Identify characteristics of a poem

**Selection 21**

Identify baseword of a given suffix*

Identify the meaning of a word ending with the suffix "age"

Identify the meaning of a word ending with the suffix "on"

Identify the sequence of events in a written selection

Identify the elements of plot/setting/characters that can be verified by fact

Identify the form of a written selection as fiction

Identify the sources to find information

Identify the antonym ___

**Selection 22**

Identify the basewood of a given suffixed word*

Identify the meaning of a word ending with suffix "ness"

Compare or contrast the attitudes, emotions or traits of characters

Predict a probable ending o

Divide a given word into syllables of end-of-line hyphenation

Identify both a synonym and an antonym ___

Identify the meaning of an unfamiliar word

Identify an analogous relationship between two pairs of words

Selection 17 deals with suffixes(*), and this is returned to in selections 19, 21, and 22. Predicting a probable ending (o) to a story is covered in selection 19 and 22. Antonyms ( __ ) are reviewed in selections 21 and 22. Other than this, there are no repetitions of concepts. Out of 43 concepts, only three are directly related. It may be that by taking a bigger sample of the book there would be more overlap. Even so, the number of concepts introduced and the lack of sequencing will create confusion. The curriculum writers violated the basic rule of sequencing—teaching one thing at a time.

The advice to this curriculum author would be to scale down and teach one thing at a time to insure that systematic review builds on essential skills.

**Action Item**

A sequence converts a task analysis into the steps to teach the concept involved. Write an objective, complete a task analysis and then detail the steps from simple to complex of a sequence that you will use to aid a learner to master this objective. It is best to start a sequence with an emphasis on the critical element.

At this point, you may be thinking that this is quite a bit of time to spend in thinking about what you will teach. However, you are retraining your mind to think more precisely in how you communicate concepts. This takes some time and practice. Once you learn to think this way, the process will become easier, and you can design curriculum materials rather quickly.

## SUMMARY: TASK ANALYSIS AND SEQUENCING

A task analysis examines an objective to produce a description of the process a learner pursues in completing an objective in a competent manner. A task analysis is written from the learner's perspective and is a systematic way of accomplishing John Dewey's principle of psychologizing learning. Teachers must see from the students' eyes to accomplish effective curriculum design. Many make the error of writing what they would do to teach an objective, instead of listing the steps a learner would progress through in performing the task after it is acquired, not in *learning* it.

Once a task analysis is completed, the next curriculum design procedure is creating a sequence of the steps one would use to teach the concept. Sequences prompt success if they start with a concept that a learner already knows and then transform this concept into the objective of the sequence. The cardinal rule of sequencing is to teach one thing at a time. Many curriculum materials ignore principles of sequencing and present information in a potentially confusing manner by starting with more difficult information and then proceeding to easier material. The procedure of sequencing can be a powerful tool in enhancing learning. Students enjoy learning more and acquire it more efficiently when experiencing success.

## QUICK REVIEW

Can you match the terms?

| | |
|---|---|
| **Task Analysis** | A series of steps moving from simple to complex |
| **Sequencing** | Listing the steps a learner would go through (mentally or in action) to perform a task |

## EXTENSION QUESTIONS

1. What is the basic rule of sequencing?

2. How does one perform a task analysis?

3. Why is a sequence ineffective in teaching if many concepts are introduced at one time with no systematic follow-up?

4. How does one know if a sequence does not move from simple to complex?

5

CHAPTER

# CURRICULUM DESIGN TECHNIQUES

## OBJECTIVES

Define each technique listed in the chapter and give a practical example of how to apply the technique to a specific concept or skill.

Explain how to create a unit by using objective writing, task analysis, sequencing and three of the curriculum design techniques from this chapter.

For a given objective, choose at least four curriculum design techniques which could be used to communicate the concept or skill to the learner.

Note for later reference the guidelines for choosing a published curriculum text.

## PROBLEM

Teachers see curriculum making as collecting activities.

## SOLUTION

Teach teachers to analyze and plan, based on desired student responses.

Mr. Rick, a fourth grade teacher, is introducing the concept of longitude and latitude. In years past this lession has always been a failure. Students are more confused about the concept after it is reviewed. Mr. Rick has a new idea of using more activities to show longitude and latitude on a map. He plans to show the concepts on a globe and to draw charts on the chalkboard. Unfortunately, it doesn't work. There is still confusion. Luckily, there is help for Mr. Rick.

The following chapter includes definition, rationale and examples of a number of curricular micro-techniques which help a teacher develop a successful strategy.[1] Materials can be planned to help students maximize success. Once the procedures from the previous chapters are completed, teachers can use these techniques to insure learner success.

**Strategy:** A rule that will alert a learner to the critical element.

A strategy gives students something to rely on when a teacher is not there to give assistance. Teaching a strategy also prompts a student to internalize a skill or concept instead of relying on the external prompting of a teacher or book or relying on rote memory. If a student internalizes a strategy, then the knowledge for success is carried within. An example is seen in teaching a first grader addition. If the teacher has taught a given strategy such as, "See the problem 2 + 5. Start counting at 2 and then make a mark over 5 as you continue to count five more places," then when confronted with a new addition problem, the learner has the wherewithal to attack the problem and attempt a solution, instead of guessing or trying to remember the exact answer.

Evidence that teaching strategies assist learning is supplied from research comparing the sight and phonetic approach to teaching reading. In the sight approach, a learner is shown a word, and the teacher says, "This word is ______ . Now you say it." Books that use the sight approach repeat a new vocabulary word a number of times to prompt learners to remember the word.

The phonetic approach, on the other hand, teaches the sounds of letters, and prompts students to blend the sounds into words, once the letter sounds are mastered. The idea is to give students tools to decode unknown words. Not only are individual sounds taught, but also sounds of several letters together, as in prefixes (in), and suffixes (ing).

Research reported by Jean Chall in *Learning to Read: The Great Debate,* indicates that after one year of instruction, learners taught by the sight approach have a larger vocabulary than those taught by the phonetic method.[2] After three years of instruction, however, the students who have learned by the phonetic method have improved over the sight students by a significant amount in terms of recognition of words and comprehension of passages read. The implication is the idea that it may take longer to teach students a strategy, but once that strategy is taught, students can apply the strategy independently to learn new information.

Teaching strategies, therefore, allow learners to take more self-direction for learning and also allow them to be independent of external instruction after a certain point. Strategies can also result in effective communication to students, since the rule should be designed to emphasize the critical element.

**Example 1 Strategy: Solving a Word Problem (High School Math)**

| Step | Key Question | Action |
|---|---|---|
| 1. Read the question | Do I understand what the problem says? | If not, reread. If so, proceed to step 2. |
| 2. Identify the unknown | Is there an interrogatory or command cueing the unknown? | Give the unknown a symbol and write what it is. |
| 3. List known information | What does the problem tell me? What else do I need to know? | Write down what is known |
| 4. Image the problem | Can I see this problem in my mind? | Draw a sketch or graph or representation. |
| 5. Write the guideline | Is this a ratio and proportion problem, a perimeter problem, a triangle problem, or what? | Write the guideline i.e., "This is an even number series problem." |
| 6. Write the formula | Does my guideline have a mathematical form or formula? | Write the formula i.e., $X + (X + 2) + (X + 4) = 200$ |
| 7. Solve | What algebraic or mathematical technique will solve my equation? | Work the problem. |
| 8. Check the answer | Do I know that my answer is correct? | Show a check of the problem. |

Strategies are best used to give students guidelines to solve problems in mathematics or in science. They are important since they can help students become self-directed and independent workers. They are most efficient when they emphasize the discriminative stimulus or critical element of the task.

**Action Item**

An example of a strategy to teach learners to answer multiple-choice quizzes would be as follows:

(1) Read the question carefully.
(2) Read each answer before making a choice.

Think of a strategy you would use to teach learners when to double the consonant before adding the suffix "ing".

**Behavior Rehearsal:** Practice by a student of the desired response. The practice is prompted by a teacher. Behavior rehearsal is usually a routine of questions by the teacher and answers by the student which results in the complete response. A behavior rehearsal can be designed to teach the rule of a strategy. Often teacher modeling and prompting are used and faded out.

There are several rationales for using behavior rehearsal. First, behavior rehearsal gives a nonpunitive, safe situation for students to practice a concept or skill. This is important particularly for a concept which has been introduced previously in a confused manner with student errors. B. F. Skinner discovered early in his research on learning that punishment creates negative emotional responses to a learning situation. Anxiety can impair learning. Behavior rehearsal can overcome a learner's anxiety in a situation that has previously been one of failure. If done correctly, there is very little chance that a student can make an error in a behavior rehearsal routine. In behavior rehearsal, the student is taught to say aloud the answer to the questions in the routine.

Behavior rehearsal works by maximizing sensory input to the learner about what is to be learned. If a student is talking aloud, looking at material, and at the same time moving, then the sense of sight, hearing, and kinesthesia are used. Talking aloud is a strategy that most people use naturally if they need to focus their attention or if they are confused. This increases the auditory sensory input since people hear themselves talking. Movement, as Dewey, Piaget, and Steiner (chapter 1) have pointed out, is a way of actively involving a learner, and internalizing information. Therefore, behavior rehearsal is most powerful when it prompts students to talk aloud and to move in response to a stimulus.

Behavior rehearsal also helps because it graphically breaks down a task into pieces by presenting routines to the learner in a step-by-step manner. Only as much as a student can assimilate is presented in each step. This helps insure retention.

Prompting and modeling are usually integral to behavior rehearsal. Behavior rehearsal routines are created as a series of questions and answers. The teacher asks the first question and then models the answer. The teacher then prompts the student to imitate the model by saying the first word or first few words of the response. For a time the teacher "overtalks" the student as he or she responds, meaning that the teacher says the response with the student but says it a little louder and a little faster than the student. The teacher actually leads the student. After the student is responding correctly, the teacher first fades out the use of the model, then fades out the use of the prompt or the overtalking.

Since behavior rehearsal takes time to develop, it is most beneficial for very difficult situations or for easily confused concepts (e.g., longitude and latitude) or for skills which are essential for later learning (e.g., basic math skills, or dictionary use).

Behavior rehearsal is best used to teach rules or to teach concepts or skills that are very difficult for a given learner. An adaptation of behavior rehearsal that is more practical is using a rhyme or a song to emphasize the critical element of a task.

This is an example of a behavior rehearsal routine to teach second graders the relationship of directions. To teach the sequence, the teacher models the entire routine with the movements. The teacher then models each individual step of the routine, prompting imitation by saying the step with the students as they repeat the model. The teacher continues this procedure until the students can do the entire sequence on their own. Prompting can be added as necessary (e.g., "What do you do first? What do you do next?").

**Example 2 Behavior Rehearsal: The Relationship of Directions (Second Grade Social Studies)**

1. I stand facing North.
2. If I am facing North, then South is behind me, East is to the right, and West is to the left.
3. I point behind me and say, "That is South."
4. I point to the right and say, "This is East."
5. I point to the left and say, "This is West."

**Action Item**

The technique of behavior rehearsal relies on models and prompts. A step in a sequence is modeled and then students are prompted to imitate the model. This process continues until the student can independently complete the steps in a sequence. Create a series of steps to help a learner talk through booting a piece of computer software. Rehearse the steps with someone else, trying to use prompts to assist the learner in rehearsing the sequence until the steps can be performed independently.

**Mental Rehearsal of Imagery:** The student visualizes within the mind a concept, event, or skill. This makes the concept more concrete and aids in memory.

When the mind images something, the senses react as if the event imaged was perceived outside the mind.[3] In effect, the mind interprets an image as if it occurred in reality since the image elicits the same emotional and perceptual reaction. This makes imagery a very useful tool in helping a learner actualize a goal or visualize a concept in a three dimensional manner. In chapter 3, the use of imagery in sports was noted, but it is also possible to apply imagery in learning cognitive tasks.

There are several things to remember in using mental rehearsal or imagery. (Mental rehearsal was a form developed by researchers using interiorized practice to improve sports. Imagery practice or guided imagery is a more contemporary term.) First, students will differ in their ability to evoke an image in their minds. However, all humans can think in images and the ability to use images can improve with practice.[4] This implies that if students express difficulty with imaging, the best teacher response is to encourage further effort, and perhaps lead them through imaging exercises that have more detail and involve more sensory images than in the first attempt.

The second thing to remember about imagery is that certain circumstances prompt more vivid images than others.[5] The more vivid an image, the more effective it will be in prompting an internal response to assist learning and memory. Imagery capabilities are most receptive when an individual is in a relaxed state and the teacher leads that individual in the imagery exercise. The exercise would include a vivid description of what is to be imaged, involving as many senses as possible. Teachers should lead students in relaxation exercises and then prepare a script that includes visual, auditory, olfactory and kinesthetic senses to lead students through the image.

Unlike behavior rehearsal, mental rehearsal does not require a great degree of planning. Implementation can be relatively simple. This makes imagery a useful and easy tool for teachers. It can be used frequently and for a variety of skills and concepts.

Imagery can be used to lead a student visualizing a successful performance, such as writing a word correctly during a spelling test. It can also be used to help students see sophisticated concepts in a concrete way, as in closing the eyes and imaging how the muscle tension of an artery inhibits blood flow.

Imagery is well suited to the science curriculum since principles from nature can be graphically sensed by students through visualizations like the example below:

### Example 3 Imagery: Surface Area Relationship to Temperature (High School Biology)

Begin by taking the students through an imagery session. In the first part they are walking alone on an unforested and exposed mountain. Their clothes are warm enough for day, but they get lost and they must spend the night on the mountain. Temperature drops below freezing. I ask them to imagine how their hands, feet, face and body core feel. They find a partially enclosed crevice and stay in there until dawn. What do they do there? I ask them to think about what they do with their arms, legs, and bodies. Afterward we talk about how they felt and what they did. We especially concentrate on the shapes they put their bodies in.

In the second part of the imagery session they are in a warm place. On this day, there is no breeze at all. Although there is plenty of shade, it is hot even there. It is unusually dry, as there has been no rain for several weeks. Again I ask them how they feel and what they do, especially with their bodies.

Again we discuss what they did. Then we compare the body shapes and positions in the cold with those in the hot. We draw some cold and hot shapes on the chalkboard and compare the amounts of surface area exposed by each. We discuss why we felt better with more or less of our surface areas exposed and how that relates to heat loss and heat retention.

Imagery can also be used in social studies to make other cultures more alive to a student as in the following example:

**Example 4 Imagery: The Relationship of the Native American Dwelling to Environmental Influences (Elementary Social Studies)**

1. Child's image expands to a winter scene with an open fire within the lodge.
   a. Child thinks of a cone placed upside-down, filling quickly with water.
   b. Child relates this to a correctly positioned lodge filling up quickly with warmth.
   c. Fewer clothes need to be worn; less wood collected. Thus a comfortable family resides inside, even with harsh winter conditions "outside."
2. Child's image changes to a summer scene with a hot sun outside; the lodge's skin is rolled up at the bottom, the smoke flaps wide open.
   a. Child recalls that a cooling breeze is created by the natural convection of air (as it moves out the top of the lodge and is sucked in at the lower edges).
   b. The result is a shaded, cool, comfortable home when it may be hot and still outside the lodge.

Imagery is also very helpful in introducing creative writing exercises by awakening creative thought patterns. A significant amount of information also supports the use of imagery to accelerate the memory of basic facts and vocabulary words. Teachers can lead students to imagine a visual symbol with a fact or to see themselves writing the facts with a magic pen in the mind's eye.

**Action Item**

Imagery helps not only to make concepts concrete, but also to affect the body's physiology by slowing down the heart and breath rate.[6] Therefore, using imagery in your classroom will help relax and calm students. Imagery is also involved in creativity[7] and is very helpful in stimulating creativity in writing or art activities.[8] The main key in using imagery is to lead students to visualize a specific scene and use as many senses as possible (i.e., seeing, hearing, touching, moving, smelling and tasting). Write up what you would say to learners to prompt them to image a fantasy scene to use before a creative writing lesson.

**Cueing:** Adding or emphasizing information to a stimulus complex, either through the teacher's words or through the visual presentation of the stimulus. This is done to alert the learner to the critical element of a task.

A cue can assist students in remembering information, can decrease the errors that a learner might make in acquiring information or applying a concept, and can insure that the most critical aspect of a stimulus complex is emphasized. A cue can result from using the techniques noted in chapter 2—superimposition, stimulus shaping, fading, or modeling and prompting by the teacher.

For the most part, published curriculum materials use the model of a correct answer to prompt correct responses. For example, the answer to the first problem on a page is given. One shortcoming of modeling is the fact that a model of the answer to the first problem on a page will not necessarily cue later solutions, since the critical element is not emphasized by the cue. In other words, the student cannot generalize to other problems since the process in coming up with the answer is not cued.

The Laubach Literacy program demonstrates an effective way to use cues to emphasize the critical element of a learning task. The literacy program is designed to teach adults how to read and is used worldwide. The cueing strategy is adapted to each language and country. An object that begins with the same *sound* that the alphabet letter represents is superimposed on the letter. Stimulus shaping is used because the object is in the same form as the letter. These kinds of visual cues aid memory since they are meaningful to the learning goal (i.e., the sound and shape of the letter).

Cueing could be used a great deal in curriculum material, particularly to enhance memory of rote skills. Cues are particularly helpful for memorization of terminology and discriminating between two easily confused concepts. Cues can be both a visual picture of a cue superimposed on the word to be learned and a verbal word cue which will trigger a memory. For example, conifer trees are sometimes easily confused. However, there are very distinctive aspects of each tree that can be pinpointed as cues for students to recall correct names. The shore pine's cone has a little "tail" between the intersection of each layer of seed. Teaching the pairing of the word, tail, and the image, tail, creates a cue to prompt a memory. The essential thing is for cues to highlight the critical element and to focus the student on that aspect of a task.

Movement is also a very functional cue. Many foreign language programs now begin with verbs, and have students make the appropriate movement to correspond to the verb. This accelerates the memory of these words.

**Literal Comprehension:** Repeating the exact facts or information presented. To be used at the beginning of a sequence.

**Generalized Comprehension:** Taking the information presented and applying it in a new way. To be used at the end of a sequence.

Instructional sequences are best when they include steps to teach literal comprehension at the beginning and generalized comprehension at the end. This assists in creating a sequence that moves from simple to complex, since repeating information is easier than applying it in a new way. Also, it is necessary to understand something before it can be internalized.

Internalization means that the information is the student's own and the student can call it up at will. An example of this occurs in a chemistry class when the lesson is the definition of enthalpy and entropy. The teacher has designed tasks such as a multiple-choice test so the student can demonstrate his or her literal comprehension of these terms. Then to prompt generalized comprehension, the teacher would give questions which require applying the definitions in two different situations which have not been discussed in class (e.g., the motion of molecules near the earth's surface vs. the motion of molecules in a space shuttle).

Curriculum planners can use literal and generalized comprehension to prompt higher levels of learning. The first step is to insure that students know the meaning of terms, and the next step is applying that meaning to increasingly difficult situations. The key to understanding generalized comprehension is the idea that there may not be a clear cut answer (e.g., there may be many correct responses).

---

**Action Item**

---

Literal comprehension is necessary before generalization is possible. Some of your learners will enjoy thinking in abstract concepts and will need little help in generalizing information. Others will find it a continual challenge. Imagine that the concept you want learners to generalize is the idea that the physical environment affects the manner in which people build homes. The literal comprehension facts include the knowledge that Hopis live in pueblos and that the Sioux live in tipis. How might you help a learner generalize the proposed concept to how Swiss people build their homes?

---

**Recognition Response:** A recognition response requires that a learner choose a correct response out of a number of choices. To be used at the beginning of a sequence.

**Recall Response:** A recall response requires a student to respond by bringing forth information that is stored in memory. To be used at the end of a sequence.

A cue for the reader to remember the difference is to pair the word, recognition, with a multiple-choice test, and the word, recall, with an essay exam. In creating an instructional sequence to accomplish a learning objective, it is best to include formats of responses that involve recognition, at first, because these are simpler for the student. After students are successful at recognition responses, then recall formats can be introduced. This is a simple way to insure that a sequence moves from the simple to the complex.

Using recognition before recall is also sound teaching. This is so because a question requiring a recognition response is presenting information in a concrete manner. A recall response, on the other hand, is more abstract because it requires a student to call forth information without a prompt and retrieve stored information. The information must have been previously internalized, since it is more than a reiteration response.

Recognition can be used to check on literal comprehension; recall can be used to check on long-term memory of literal comprehension and, also, to check on generalized comprehension. Recall questions can more accurately assess generalized comprehension since the questions are open-ended.

The following sequence from an elementary reading text is designed to teach the use of context to determine meaning from a reading selection. The sequence begins with an open-ended task in which students make up words and ends with a multiple-choice question. These curriculum authors reversed the "recognition before recall" rule. The result is a sequence that has more difficult responses at the beginning than at the ending.

### Example 5 Incorrect Use of Recall Before Recognition (Elementary Reading Context Clues for Meaning)

**Step One**

Point to nonsense word gorking (Gorking, and gorking, as a dragon will, he clambered down the slickery, slockery sides). Create other words that could be substituted for gorking and slickery, slockery.

Student is to invent own words, write them in sentences, exchange sentences. (This is a recall or an open-ended question.)

**Step Two**

Student is to pick correct synonym of underlined word of three choices given.

So I had to make *trial* runs with different foods.

experimental courts lawyers

(This is a recognition question and should be first in the sequence, since it is easier.)

---

A correct example of recognition before recall is sometimes used in chapter end sections by having true/false questions (recognition) followed by open-ended questions (recall). A more sophisticated application of recognition before recall would be to use recognition questions immediately after a chapter. Then after the second chapter, use recall to review information from the preceding chapter. This fosters more long-term memory and a higher level of understanding.

### Action Item

Recognition questions are best used to check on acquisition of factual material, and recall questions are best for helping learners generalize information. Recall questions are also effective in building retention of material if teachers will ask these questions periodically after a concept has been presented.

A recognition question . . .
In which stage did Piaget state that children acquired logic?
(a) sensori-motor (b) concrete operations (c) formal operations

A recall question . . .
What distinguished the concrete operation stage from the formal operation stage?

Think of a concept you would like to teach and write a recall and recognition question. When in a teaching sequence would you use these questions?

**Uniform Instruction:** Keeping the same format throughout a teaching sequence. A format is defined as the way the student is to respond.

Many times students respond incorrectly, not because they do not know a concept, but because they do not understand the way a teacher is asking the question. Therefore, in order not to add confusing information into a learning situation, it is best to use a consistent style in requesting responses from a learner or in presenting information. Sometimes a teacher will vary the terms used in explaining a concept. For example, in a college psychology class a teacher may use the words Freudian and psychoanalytic interchangeably; confusion may result unless it is made clear to the learner that the terms mean the same thing. Another example of this comes from teaching second graders subtraction. It is best if the teacher decides which term to use—"subtract" or "take–away." It could be that the teacher decides to start out with the word "take–away since it is more concrete and then to change to "subtract." If so, a transition should be planned to pair the two words and then fade one out.

Uniform instruction also applies to the visual presentation of questions or problems. A kindergarten math book presents a good example. To make sure that students can make the transition from one format to another, it is a simple precaution for teachers to model and to prompt correct responding to a new format. Stimulus shaping can also be used to transform one format into another.

Another aspect of uniform instruction is to design curriculum materials so that there is always one format which is used consistently in introducing a new concept. Then a second format is used to practice its use, and a third format is used to test its use. In this way the learner is alerted that "This is a new concept. Pay attention."

---

**Action Item**

---

Take a math problem, long division, for example, and write down how you would explain the steps for solution to a learner. What vocabulary would you want to keep consistent over repeated explanations?

---

**Adequate Practice:** Presenting enough instances of applying a concept or skill to insure mastery or understanding.

Some people have the idea that teaching is standing up and presenting information once or twice. This seems to be the assumption many curriculum designers have, since few published texts provide enough practice to promote mastery. In addition, published curricula often compound the lack of adequacy by changing formats quickly. It seems as if curriculum writers try to throw in as many formats as possible, hoping that one will take. This is an ineffective attempt at meeting individual differences. Not only does the material lack adequate practice, but it also presents the practice in inconsistent formats.

One of the most common errors in published curriculum texts is the lack of adequate practice. Teachers can compensate for this by asking students to create similar problems, by creating board games with the material, or by asking peers to verbally ask a partner the questions that have already been asked in writing. To promote generalization of learning, teachers can insure that the format is consistent.

---

**Action Item**

---

Flash cards and games using skills are two standard procedures for adding practice in skills. Imagine that you are a fourth grade teacher and that you have done your best to prompt your learners to memorize multiplication facts, but some learners still do not retain these facts. Think of a creative way to add in more practice.

---

**Tests or Probes:** Checks to see if learners can perform the learning objective.

Teachers must have feedback on whether or not learning takes place and whether or not learners receive the message that was intended. This can happen in a variety of ways. For example, a teacher can ask a student informal questions. If asked, many teachers will say that they know what skills and concepts their students know. However, if there is not a systematic way of checking on each student's performance in relationship to the learning objective, then teachers are relying more on guesswork than planning. A key in designing an instructional sequence is to put in systematic checks on student progress.

One method to accomplish this is to put tests in at every few steps of a sequence. If this is done, the tests are called probes. As a surgeon probes organs during an operation to see what surgery is necessary, a teacher probes learners' skills to see what additional instruction is necessary. A probe gives information on how much of the objective the student has mastered at each step of the sequence. This can be useful in two ways. First, since students have individual learning rates and capacities, it is possible that a student can make "leaps" in learning a concept and put steps together all at one time. If this happens, the student does not need to go through all the steps in the sequence. Probe performance can tell a teacher that a given student needs no more instruction because the learning objective has been met.

If probes are not used, it is at least necessary to have a test at the end of an instructional sequence. Otherwise, it is anyone's guess whether or not learning occurred. The teacher must look to the student to judge the effectiveness of teaching.

Tests and probes can diagnose the success or failure of a sequence. Using a probe at every step of the sequence is useful since it can pinpoint an ineffective step. Students' performance on tests can mirror the quality of instructional materials.

Furthermore, the format of tests is an area of attention for teachers. To assess whether or not an instructional sequence has communicated the learning objective, it is best to use a very similar format for testing as used for teaching. Remember the stimulus gradient and the law of stimulus generalization. The closer the format of the test is to the format used in teaching the skill, the better the likelihood of a correct response. If a teacher wants to see if the student not only knows the learning objective but also can generalize this information to new applications, then formats which were not used in the teaching sequence can be used. It is important for teachers to be clear whether they are testing acquisition or generalization, and then to design formats accordingly.

### Example 6 Various Evaluation Methods

**Recognition Probe: Surface Area (Secondary Science)**

When an animal is exposing maximum surface area, it will be

1. Gaining heat
2. Losing heat

It might do this when it is

1. Hot
2. Cold

When an animal is curled up in a ball, it is exposing

1. Maximum surface area
2. Minimum surface area

**Combination Recognition and Recall Probe: Adverbs (Elementary Language Arts)**

Children are to underline the adverbs, draw an arrow to the verb they describe, and tell what question they answer.

The tiny baby slept *soundly.* (How)

There are no silly monkeys playing *here!* (Where)

The cold wind blows *briskly.* (How)

The summer sun shines *bright* and *early.* (How, when)

My big dog has floppy ears that swing *here* and *there.* (Where)

Only happy smiles leave *there!* (Where)

*Occasionally* laughing, the clown ran *around.* (When, where)

**Combination Recognition and Recall Tests: Word Problems (Secondary Mathematics)**

Five questions asking students to circle the words that cue the unknown.

Five questions where the students are asked to write a short sentence describing the unknown.

## Example 7 Recall Evaluation Methods

**Recall Tests: Adverbs (Elementary Language Arts)**

Children fill in the blanks with adverbs that describe "how" the action (verb) was done.

The tall boy ran _______________ .

The cold wind blew _______________ .

The elegant queen danced _______________ .

The angry man shouted _______________ .

**Recall Generalized Comprehension Questions: Biology (Science)**

Ask students to find pictures of animals. Locate shapes or structures that tend to increase or decrease surface area.
Discuss possible effects these structures have on temperature regulation in these animals.

**Recall Generalized Comprehension Project: Environmental Education (Secondary)**

Ask students to design a plant and an animal that are adapted to the alpine environment; these can be as wild as the imagination allows but must contain some of the actual adaptations studied.

**Error Patterns:** A consistency in the mistakes a learner makes that reflects an incorrect solution strategy.

Analyzing student performances on tests or probes sometimes reveals a pattern of errors which can give teachers clues to a mistaken notion that a student may have formulated. Usually the student has created a critical element of his or her own that differs from the critical element necessary for correct performance.

For example, look at how one third grade student deals with addition problems requiring regrouping. The strategy that the student developed was to write down the sum of the ones column without regrouping a ten into the tens column. The teacher can correct this strategy by starting with the student's response and model how to write the ten above the tens column instead of as an answer. The teacher can also point out that the student has shifted the tens to the hundreds place and give an example of the serious consequences this could have in a real life situation such as computing a grocery bill.

$$\begin{array}{r} 15 \\ +18 \\ \hline 213 \end{array} \qquad \begin{array}{r} 17 \\ +25 \\ \hline 312 \end{array} \qquad \begin{array}{r} 18 \\ +25 \\ \hline 313 \end{array}$$

When tests are given, teachers can also check across students' answers to see which problems were missed consistently by a large percentage of students. This would indicate to the teacher that either it was not a good test item (i.e., the format or the way the question was phrased was misleading), or that the sequence did not teach the item in question.

Examining student work for error patterns is a very functional tool in revising sequences to make them more effective and can also pinpoint where students' incorrect assumptions must be corrected.

---

**Action Item**

---

Imagine that a 10th grade student made the following errors in reading:

For systematic, he read sysmotic.
For wonderful, he read wondeyful.
For calicification, he read calculation.

What is the error pattern? What is the student's incorrect strategy for decoding a word? How might you help the student correct the strategy?

---

**Cumulative Introduction:** Reviewing a concept in a systematic way after it has been mastered by a student.

Cumulative introduction is a technique to insure that once a concept is introduced and mastered by a student, that student retains the concept. This assists in promoting memory retention. In planning a sequence or a series of sequences which fit together, teachers can create a systematic strategy to review previously learned materials.

One principle from the psychology of learning explains how to promote retention. The principle is, "Spaced practice is better than massed practice." As result of this, a sequence can be more effective if it distributes student practice over time instead of concentrating it in one period. Thus, a student would retain more of what was presented if he or she had practiced ten minutes on Monday, Wednesday, and Friday, instead of 30 minutes on Monday. This principle of choosing spaced practice over massed practice is another rationale for using cumulative introduction, since it has the effect of distributing practice over time. Usually a sequence includes massed practice for a time, and then the concept is reviewed at periodic intervals. This also gives students the opportunity to learn a concept if it was not mastered during the initial presentation.

Another positive feature of cumulative introduction is the advantage that it promotes long-term memory. Most teaching situations deal with short-term memory since material is presented, then tested, and not reviewed again. The ideal is to convert short-term memory to long term, which will give students access to learning over time. Promoting long-term memory helps students learn higher order thinking skills that are necessary to synthesize information. Synthesis occurs when different pieces of information from various sources, some just learned and some learned previously, are put together into a central concept. With cumulative introduction, students can acquire more information in their long-term memories and will therefore have more information to use as a basis for synthesis.

### Action Item

Imagine that you have covered the concept of centrifugal force. It was difficult, but you think you succeeded. You do not want to lose the gains that you made. Speculate on how you could return to the concept periodically to build retention.

**Full Range of Examples:** Presenting opportunities for a student to see as many situations as possible in the application of a concept.

Presenting a full range of examples helps students with stimulus generalization and stimulus discrimination. It shows the range and limitations of an application of a concept. The full range of examples should show instances where a concept works and does not work. In this way, a teacher helps students gain an understanding of the basic attributes of a concept and the limits to its generalization. Students can then more readily generalize and synthesize information.

**Exaggerate Differences:** If two easily confused stimuli are presented together, transform them to make them more dissimilar.

Oftentimes texts will present two easily confused examples simultaneously to enable the learner to compare them. The problem with this procedure is the disadvantage that it promotes generalization instead of discrimination. Recalling the stimulus gradient from chapter 2, the best way to help a learner discriminate two easily confused concepts is to make them different.

The rule of uniform instruction and consistent format does not hold for easily confused concepts. Presenting varying formats which emphasize differences helps students make a discrimination. The following sequence demonstrates how to emphasize the difference between the shapes of the letters *b* and *d.*

1. Transform stimuli with stimulus shaping or superimposition.
2. Teach first discrimination in isolation with cue.
3. Introduce very different S-Deltas (e.g., x, y, w).
4. Teach second discrimination in isolation with cue.
5. Introduce very different S-Deltas for second discrimination.
6. Introduce two discriminations together with cues.
7. Fade cues.

## ADDITIONAL CURRICULUM DESIGN TECHNIQUES

Some of the concepts presented in previous chapters can stand on their own as curriculum design techniques. One of these is psychologizing learning or making a concept a part of a student's world view. The following example for a high school biology class makes an abstract concept "real" to the students by having them construct various surface area examples.

### Example 8 Psychologizing Concept: Concrete Presentation of Surface Area

To help visualize this concept, many 1 cm cubes should be available. Pile them up to make a larger cube. Figure the volume of the larger cube and the sum of the smaller ones. It is the same. Then figure the surface area of the larger cube and the sum of the surface areas of the individual cubes. In sum, the smaller cubes will have a larger surface area.

Another powerful technique is sequencing information in order to teach simple concepts that will later be developed in a more sophisticated manner.

This is an example of sequence for a secondary environmental education class.

### Example 9 Sequencing: Simple to Complex Order of Environmental Education Concepts

1. **Community**

   Plants and animals occupying a common environment and interacting with each other.

2. **Niche**

   The role an organism plays in a community.

   Where it lives, where it seeks food and shelter, who are its friends and enemies, what it gives to and takes from the community.

3. **Habitat**

   The physical features of an organism's environment.

   The organism's food, water, shelter and space in a suitable arrangement.

4. **Carrying Capacity**

   The capability of a certain environment to support life.

   Carrying capacity changes throughout the year and from year to year, dependent upon conditions such as rainfall, competition from domestic animals, etc.

5. **Competition**

   Intraspecific-within species-strong because members of the same species have same survival needs, due to occupying the same niche.

   Variability within species reduces competition.

A third technique from previous chapters is using teacher modeling (telling or showing how to do a task) and prompting (asking questions to encourage imitation of the model). This is particularly useful in teaching vocabulary or strategies. See the following example.

**Example 10 Modeling and Prompting: Problem Solving Sequence in Word Problems (Secondary Mathematics)**

**Problem #3:** Katie has a $10 roll of nickels, a $10 roll of dimes and a $10 roll of quarters. How many coins does she have?

**Step 1.** Teacher reads the problem to the class and then rereads and says, "Do I understand what the problem says? It says a girl has one roll each of three different coins and that each roll is worth $10."

**Step 2.** "What is the unknown here? What do I need to find? Well, these words 'how many' are my clue to the unknown. I need to know the total number of coins contained in those three rolls.

"Now I need to give a symbol to my unknown. I could use C for coins or I could use my old friend X. I think I will use C this time."

**Step 3.** "What information does this problem give me to help me solve it? Well, it says I have $10 of quarters, $10 of dimes and $10 of nickels. What else do I need to solve this problem? What if I were a Martian and didn't know anything about dimes, nickels and quarters? I would need to know how many of each it takes to make one dollar, right? Fortunately, we earthlings already know how many: 4 quarters, 10 dimes and 20 nickels. Sometimes we have to add information to the problem, don't we?"

## THE LONGITUDE-LATITUDE PROBLEM

Recalling the teacher's problem at the beginning of the chapter can now be approached using some of these curriculum micro-techniques. Mr. Rick could then calm the confusion in his students. He could exaggerate the differences between the terms longitude and latitude by superimposing a visual and verbal cue on latitude (e.g., a ladder rung between the two *t*'s). He could also present one of the terms first and could provide adequate practice with a recognition exercise. Students could color in the latitude lines on a world map. In addition, an imagery exercise could be added. Students could visualize the planet and see the lines encircling it. Longitude would then be introduced with similar activities. Finally, recall activities would be used for both concepts. A generalized comprehension exercise would test acquisition of the concept. Students would be asked to find ships' locations when given certain degrees of longitude and latitude.

## MAKING AN INSTRUCTIONAL SEQUENCE: STEPS AND EXAMPLES

The following steps are used to create an instructional sequence. These steps represent a compilation of procedures from previous chapters.

1. Write an Objective.
   Write it so that you can tell when you are done teaching and so that it includes both literal and generalized comprehension.
2. Isolate the critical element.
   Can you cue it?
   Can you psychologize it?
   How do you make it concrete?
3. Conduct a Task Analysis. List prerequisite skills.
4. Create a Sequence that Moves from Simple to Complex. Answer these questions as you design it.

Can a strategy be taught? If so what is the strategy.

Does it make sense to use behavior rehearsal? If so write a script with questions and answers.

Does it make sense to use imagery practice? If so, write what you would say to lead through imagery.

Can you cue the critical element or psychologize it?

Can you add a word or visual picture cue?

Will you model and prompt the correct response?

Can you exaggerate differences?

What format will you use? How will you keep it consistent? How will you change the format to prompt generalization?

How will you use cumulative introduction?

What are the S-Deltas? What is a full range of examples you can present to prompt discrimination and generalization of the concept?

How will you provide for adequate practice?

How will you use recognition before recall?

5. Design a test to match the objective.
6. Plan to do an error analysis.
7. Revise sequence.

## AN EXAMPLE OF USING CURRICULUM DESIGN TECHNIQUES

The following example applies the book's procedures in addressing a high school social science class.

The goal is from a high school social science class and it is to teach how the U.S. is dependent on other countries for daily life activities.

This goal does not need to be subdivided since an objective can be written for the goal. The techniques from the previous chapter are used to write an objective, determine prerequisite skills, isolate a critical element and to conduct a task analysis.

### Objective

The student is to think in a divergent manner to review objects or foods in daily life and name three objects or foods from another country that could be used in a day that are not obviously from another country (e.g., these objects would not have recognizable foreign brand names or be a part of a generic group, such as electronics that is easily associated with another country).

### Prerequisites

Knowledge of foreign countries including geographic location, climatic conditions that allow specific agriculture crops, and specific raw materials and manufactured products associated with the countries. Ability to entertain a number of possibilities at once and use deduction to find a solution. Knowledge of the origins of raw materials needed to manufacture products in the U.S. Knowledge of location of reference materials and how to use these reference materials that tell origin of products.

### Critical Element

Noticing subtle factors that would allow a product to be traced to its place of origin and then asking the question, "Where did this come from?"

### Task Analysis

(This is written in terms of what the student would do or think to perform the objective competently. *These are not the steps to teach the objective.*)

1. Note that the task is to isolate three products from my daily life that do not *obviously* originate in other countries.
2. Mentally review and discard things that are obviously from another country—Japanese cars, Japanese electronics, coffee, chocolate, clothes from Taiwan and Korea, etc.

3. Visualize self going through the day and mentally note or red flag any items that may be of origin from other countries:
   a. Foods which need tropical climates to grow.
   b. Oil-based products.
   c. Products using raw materials not found in U.S.
4. Speculate on origin of noted items. Ask self question, "Where does this come from?" Keep asking question until one comes to raw materials of object. Choose three items that probably come from some place outside of the U.S. Say these items.
5. Use reference materials to check that one is correct.

Once a teacher completes the above analysis, this can be converted into a unit of instruction with accompanying materials that will allow students to accomplish the steps noted in the task analysis. To accomplish this, the teacher brainstorms on all the curriculum design techniques in the previous chapter which could be used here.

**Strategy.** The teacher wants the students to use the following strategy. "This item is obviously from another country; I will discard that one. This one is not so clear. Where did it come from?"

**Behavior Rehearsal.** The teacher can use behavior rehearsal to teach students the above strategy. The teacher will bring different objects in and model saying the above strategy. The teacher will then prompt the students to say the strategy aloud, probably in diads or pairs so that the students will not feel uncomfortable.

**Imagery.** Imagery can be used in two ways. First, by leading students in imaging the products in their home, school and in stores where they shop. Secondly imagery can be used in leading students to visualize the source of raw materials, e.g., diamond mines in South Africa, and the manufacturing process of products. Of course, it would be positive to show movies and pictures of all this to assist in the imagery.

**Model-Prompt.** This can be used for the teacher to model divergent thinking of possibilities and deducing a solution. "What about this product? Could it have come from another country? And this one? Where did it come from? What clues tell me it is a possibility?" The teacher could model this with several products brought into the classroom and then give the students pictures or lists or other examples, some very subtle, to work on in diads.

**Superimposition (Cueing).** Several pictures of a globe could have cues superimposed on them to show tropical regions, oil regions, and raw material origins. Also reference materials in the library could have pictures denoting products affixed on the spine of the book to help students find the right reference materials.

**Recall before Recognition.** Sheets could be made which include matching tasks of drawing lines between raw materials and a country, products and a country or products and their component raw materials. This should be done early in the sequence.

**Adequate Practice.** Recall and recognition activities for linking products to countries, resources to global locations and work in diads on using strategy and in using divergent thinking would provide adequate practice.

**Evaluation.** At the end of the unit, students will be asked to write the three products as specified in the objective. The teacher could also probe with this evaluation throughout the unit in order to monitor acquisition.

**Error Analysis.** Students will also be asked to write how they came up with their answers to allow the teacher to see if there are any problems in the students' strategies.

**Cumulative Introduction.** At the end of the unit, the teacher will make a chart of all the products from sources outside the U.S. which the students have generated. Students will be asked to add at least two new items each week. Points will be given for very subtle ones or new ones. Students with the most points will receive an "Interdependence Expert" citation.

**Generalized Comprehension.** An independent project will be assigned after the unit is complete. The project will consist of the students listing 5 cultural practices with an origin outside the U.S. and supporting the list with citations from reference material. Students will also be asked to write a short "Think Piece" on what interdependence means. Is it good? Is it bad? Does it mean we owe something to a country we are dependent on?

After specifying possible curriculum design techniques, a teacher reviews the list of curriculum design techniques and the activities which were listed. She or he lists them in the sequence in which they will be presented. The list must proceed from simple to complex. Model-prompt, superimposition, behavior rehearsal and recall should all come early in the sequence to insure that the sequence will encourage early success. Evaluation measures and generalized comprehension are best at the end of the sequence.

To create the sequence, the teacher needs to think of the logical order to present the information. One possible order is (1) information on the origins of products, (2) location of global resources, (3) presentation of a strategy, (4) review of daily life products, (5) divergent and deductive thinking, and (6) solving the problem.

After the instructor completes a sequence, there should be a feeling of completion. He or she should be able to say, "Yes, after all these activities are presented, I feel confident that students will be able to do the sequence." There should not be the feeling of rushing. Also, it is critical that much learner activity (talking, doing, constructing) is included in the unit.

## CHOOSING A PUBLISHED CURRICULUM

Once teachers know how to design effective curriculum material, then they also can apply these same principles in choosing effective published curriculum materials. Answering the following questions can serve as a guide to the analysis and selection of texts which will assist teaching.

1. Are there objectives listed?
2. Count the number of skills presented in a five page section. Is it more than 5?
3. Find one skill or concept the first time it is presented. Trace it across twenty pages. How many times is it repeated? Is there adequate practice?
4. Is there cumulative introduction or maintenance review?
5. Look at the formats. Are they consistent?
6. Are there too many distracting stimuli which direct attention away from critical elements?
7. Are there tests? Look at a test. Choose one item. Is the item in a previous section? Is the format the same?
8. In a sequence, is recognition used before recall?
9. In a content curriculum . . .
   Does the sequence of review questions match the sequence in text?
   Are important concepts summarized or noted?

## SUMMARY

The curriculum making techniques in this chapter are the practicalities of making curriculum materials effective and enhancing learning in both a literal and generalized manner. Many think teaching is an art and it definitely is. A teacher's intuition and spirit are essential to communicating with students. However, the "technique" can add to the "art" to synergize the success of learning materials. Teachers who adapt these procedures in creating materials for very difficult concepts or skills report that learners enjoy learning when they can understand the concepts being presented. Teachers are enthusiastic because a concept changes from a source of frustration into a successful experience for both the student and the teacher. Very few published materials use all of these techniques. Therefore one can make a significant improvement in instructional materials by experimenting with their use for difficult to teach concepts. Some or all of them can be applied, allowing a teacher to discover which ones fit most naturally with a given teaching style.

---

## QUICK REVIEW

Can you match the term with the definition?

| | |
|---|---|
| **Strategy** | Adding or emphasizing information |
| **Cumulative Introduction** | Visualization within the mind |
| **Recognition Response** | Providing enough responses to insure mastery |
| **Literal Comprehension** | Ordering concepts from simple to complex |
| **Adequate Practice** | Practice by a student of the desired behavior |
| **Recall Response** | Bringing forth the correct response from memory |

| | |
|---|---|
| **Tests or Probes** | Repeating the exact facts |
| **Psychologizing** | Consistency in mistakes reflecting an incorrect solution strategy |
| **Behavior Rehearsal** | Using the same format for learner response throughout a sequence |
| **Generalized Comprehension** | Reviewing a concept systematically to insure mastery |
| **Error Patterns** | Presenting a rule that will alert a learner to the critical element |
| **Mental Rehearsal or Imagery** | Checking to see if learner can do objective |
| **Uniform Instruction** | Applying information in a new way |
| **Cueing** | Choosing correct response |
| **Full Range of Examples** | Making two easily confused stimuli more dissimilar |
| **Sequencing** | Telling or showing how to respond; asking questions to encourage response |
| **Modeling and Prompting** | Presenting a variety of applications of a concept |
| **Exaggerate Differences** | Presenting a concept as a part of a student's world view |

## EXTENSION QUESTIONS

1. What techniques are particularly important to put at the beginning of a sequence?

2. What function can the technique of imagery serve in a sequence?

3. What important information does an error analysis provide?

4. What is the relationship of strategies and behavior rehearsals to critical elements?

# 6
CHAPTER

# TROUBLESHOOTING PUBLISHED CURRICULUM TEXTS

## OBJECTIVES

Define four problems in published curriculum texts.

Explain how to correct at least two of these problems.

Sometimes teachers are stuck with curriculum material that has---

Too Many Skills Presented

Lack of Adequate Practice

Distracting Stimuli

Information Out of Sequence

This chapter shows how to change or add information to published curriculum materials to make them more effective.

## PROBLEM ONE

Too Many Skills

## SOLUTION ONE

Objective Slicing

**_Sedimentary Rock_**

| | *Name* | *Texture* | *Composition* | *Comments* |
|---|---|---|---|---|
| CLASTICS | Conglomerate | Round pebbles | Any kind of rock or minerals | Pebbles held together with sand, clay, and cement |
| | Breccia | Angular pebbles | Any kind of rock or minerals | |
| | Sandstone | Sand-size grains | Quartz (most common) or feldspar and quartz | Grains may be calcite |
| | Siltstone | Very fine grains | Mostly quartz, some clay | Gritty feel |
| | Shale | Microscopic grains and flakes | Mostly clay, some mica | Occurs in layers, no gritty feel |
| NONCLASTICS | Limestone | Coarse to micro-scopic crystals | Calcite or micro-scopic shells | Chalk—microscopic texture, a precipitate or evaporite |
| | Chert (flint) | Microscopic crystals | Chalcedony | Common as cement in rocks, or as masses, a precipitate |
| | Alabaster | Microscopic to coarse crystals | Gypsum or anhydrite | Evaporite |
| | Rock salt | Cubic crystals | Halite | Evaporite |
| | Peat, lignite, or coal | Coarse to micro-scopic plant fragments | Products of plant decay in absence of oxygen | Fragments of plants to fine-grained carbon compounds |

**FIGURE 6.1** Too many skills presented on one page (From *Focus on Earth Science,* by M. S. Bishop, P. G. Lewis and B. Sutherland. Copyright 1976 by Charles E. Merrill Publishing Co. Reprinted by permission of the publisher. All rights reserved.)

*Figure 6.1*[1] shows new skills for a sixth grade science lesson. Sixteen new words are presented on one page. All but the gifted student would have difficulty absorbing this much information. The best troubleshooting method here is to slice the objectives. Instead of teaching all words, a teacher could chop the list into three vocabulary words a week. By presenting three skills at a time, the sequence would effectively diminish the amount of information to be absorbed at one sitting. A teacher could present the first three skills and give practice in the form of word cards, dictation, and student composed sentences which include the new words. Once students master the first three vocabulary words, the teacher can move on to the next three.

The failure of this curriculum to sequence information so that the amount in a lesson is "chewable and digestible" creates a great deal of extra work by a teacher to remediate curricular inadequacies. Curriculum writers could prevent this problem by presenting fewer skills at a time and then giving adequate practice.

## PROBLEM TWO

Lack of Adequate Practice

## SOLUTION TWO

Add in Relevant Practice

A curricular design shortcoming which usually accompanies "too many skills" is lack of adequate practice. Since many skills come at once, it is next to impossible to provide enough practice for students to master skills and concepts.

To add in relevant practice the teacher must examine the materials to determine what the teaching objective is. Sometimes the teaching objective will be explicitly expressed in the teacher's manual. If this is not the case, a teacher must infer the curriculum writer's intent by analyzing problems. Also important to note is the format used to teach the objective. Once this is determined, additional practice can be created which matches the format and leads to mastery of the objective.

One method for adding in adequate practice is to make a game to review the concepts or skills. Games are not functional in introducing new skills, since the concepts or skills cannot be presented in a systematic enough manner. But for adding in adequate practice, they are ideal since they are fun for most students. A teacher can construct a game board which can be used for all sorts of concepts. A new stack of cards can be created for each new skill, with words to define, math problems to solve or generalization questions to tax the mind. A student draws a card and if he or she can respond correctly, then the dice are thrown and the student can move the number thrown.

*Figure 6.2*[2] shows an example of lack of adequate practice. At least three objectives involving Roman numerals (e.g., recognizing and recalling Roman symbols, writing standard numbers for Roman numerals and writing Roman numerals for standard numbers) are presented on one practice page. It would be more efficient to maximize learning and generalization to provide adequate practice on each objective and then to mix the objectives for additional practice. A great amount of practice on each Roman numeral and what it represents would be necessary at the beginning of this lesson.

## ENRICHMENT

### ROMAN NUMERALS

The Roman numeral system uses symbols to name numbers.

| I | V | X | L |
|---|---|---|---|
| 1 | 5 | 10 | 50 |

| C | D | M |
|---|---|---|
| 100 | 500 | 1,000 |

You show the numbers by adding and subtracting the symbols.

I I I
1 + 1 + 1 = 3

X V I I
10 + 5 + 1 + 1 = 17

When I appears before V or X, subtract 1.
IV
5 − 1 = 4

When X appears before L or C, subtract 10.
XC
100 − 10 = 90

When C appears before D or M, subtract 100.
CD
500 − 100 = 400

| | | | | | | | | |
|---|---|---|---|---|---|---|---|---|
| I<br>1 | II<br>2 | III<br>3 | IV<br>4 | V<br>5 | VI<br>6 | VII<br>7 | VIII<br>8 | IX<br>9 |
| X<br>10 | XX<br>20 | XXX<br>30 | XL<br>40 | L<br>50 | LX<br>60 | LXX<br>70 | LXXX<br>80 | XC<br>90 |
| C<br>100 | CC<br>200 | CCC<br>300 | CD<br>400 | D<br>500 | DC<br>600 | DCC<br>700 | DCCC<br>800 | CM<br>900 |
| M<br>1,000 | | | | | | | | |

**Write the standard number for each.**

1. LXIV
2. CCXXII
3. DCLVI
4. MMI
5. XLVII
6. LXXIX
7. CXCV
8. MDLII

**Write the Roman numeral for each.**

9. 28
10. 319
11. 1,986
12. 731
13. 54
14. 185
15. 427
16. 1,342
17. Write the year Columbus discovered America in Roman numerals.
18. Write the year you were born in Roman numerals.

FIGURE 6.2 Lack of adequate practice (© 1988 Silver, Burdett & Ginn. Used with permission.)

## PROBLEM THREE

Distracting Stimuli

## SOLUTION THREE

Page or Format Slicing

Many published curriculum writers use novelty and quick change in hopes of maintaining student interest. It is the same technique that Sesame Street relies on. The assumption is if the stimulation changes fast enough, then learners will watch what is happening. And if they watch, they will learn. This is not quite a correct assumption. It is true that learners will watch when stimuli change quickly. This is called the Hawthorne effect, and in the study that verified the effect, researchers gradually changed the intensity of light in a factory. With each change, workers increased productivity, even when it became almost to dark to see. The variable that increased productivity was the change and not the quality of light. But as we have learned through stimulus control, stimulation must be designed to help a student *focus* attention on the critical element of a task. Even though learners will pay attention to changing stimuli, they may not learn. Learning happens from selective attention.

*Figure 6.3*[3] shows a case of distracting stimuli. The figures are not integrated with the text in a meaningful way. The visual presentation acts to scatter attention instead of focusing it. Teachers can deal with this by telling students to ignore certain parts of pages, or teachers can ask students to pull out pages with information that does not contribute to the sequence. Teachers can also ask students to cover extraneous information with a separate sheet of paper while working.

## PROBLEM FOUR

Information Out of Sequence

## SOLUTION FOUR

Slice What Doesn't Build on Each Step

If teachers encounter pages of texts which clearly do not follow a sequence, the best strategy is to omit those pages, and if necessary, add in more practice of the previous format. The rationale for this is that out-of-sequence material will do more harm than good because it diverts student attention from critical elements. *Figure 6.4* shows a workbook page from a fifth grade reader with out-of-sequence information. Students have not been presented with the meaning of the word *euphemisms* before this page.

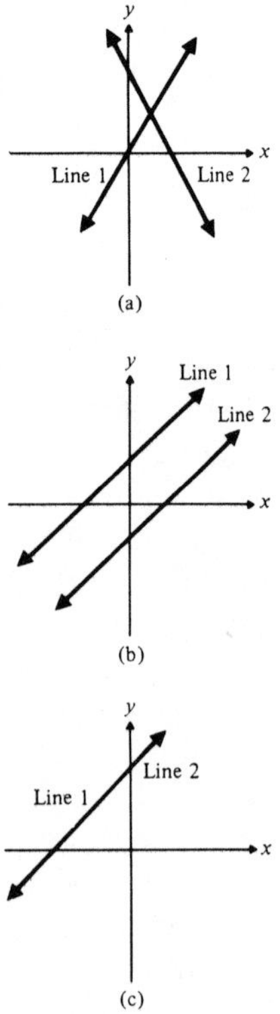

Figure 8.1

To obtain the solution to a system of equations graphically, graph each equation and determine the point or points of intersection.

Example 1 Solve the following system of equations graphically.

$$2x + y = 11$$
$$x + 3y = 18$$

Solution: Find the $x$ and $y$ intercepts of each graph.

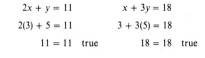

| $2x + y = 11$ | Ordered pair | $x + 3y = 18$ | Ordered pair |
|---|---|---|---|
| Let $x = 0$, then $y = 11$ | (0, 11) | Let $x = 0$, then $y = 6$ | (0, 6) |
| Let $y = 0$, then $x = \frac{11}{2}$ | $\left(\frac{11}{2}, 0\right)$ | Let $y = 0$, then $x = 18$ | (18, 0) |

The two graphs (Fig. 8.2) intersect at the point (3, 5). The point (3, 5) is the solution to the system of equations.

*Check:*

| | |
|---|---|
| $2x + y = 11$ | $x + 3y = 18$ |
| $2(3) + 5 = 11$ | $3 + 3(5) = 18$ |
| $11 = 11$ true | $18 = 18$ true |

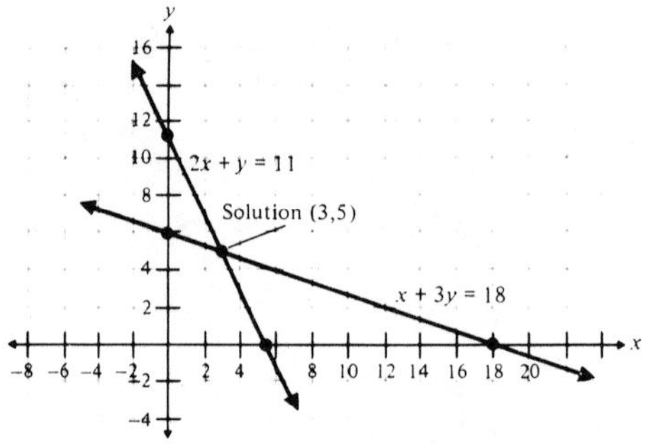

Figure 8.2

The system of equations in Example 1 has a single ordered pair as a solution. This system is an example of a **consistent system of equations.**

Example 2 Solve the following system of equations graphically.

$$2x + y = 3$$
$$4x + 2y = 12$$

Solution:

| $2x + y = 3$ | Ordered pair | $4x + 2y = 12$ | Ordered pair |
|---|---|---|---|
| Let $x = 0$, then $y = 3$ | (0, 3) | Let $x = 0$, then $y = 6$ | (0, 6) |
| Let $y = 0$, then $x = \frac{3}{2}$ | $\left(\frac{3}{2}, 0\right)$ | Let $y = 0$, then $x = 3$ | (3, 0) |

**FIGURE 6.3** Distracting stimuli (From Allen R. Angel, *ELEMENTARY ALGEBRA: A Practical Approach,* © 1985, p. 253. Reprinted by permission of Prentice-Hall, Inc., Englewood Cliffs, N.J.)

**Workbook** Name ______________________________

## Euphemisms

A euphemism is a word or phrase used in place of another word or phrase that may offend some people. An example of a euphemism is the reference to *old people* as *senior citizens.*

**A. Draw a circle around the word or words that best express the meaning of the underlined euphemism in each sentence.**

**1.** The sanitary engineer picked up the refuse.
 a. worker  b. garbage collector  c. delivery person

**2.** John's aunt passed away on Tuesday.
 a. called  b. visited  c. died

**3.** My mother calls herself a homemaker.
 a. housewife  b. woman  c. maid

**4.** Mrs. Stoddard has a domestic engineer to do work around the house.
 a. nurse  b. maid  c. resident

**5.** Most gas stations have restrooms.
 a. bathrooms  b. gas attendants  c. telephone booths

**B. Match the euphemism in Column I with the word it stands for in Column II. Write the letter of your answers on the lines at the left.**

| Column I | Column II |
|---|---|
| ____ **1.** powder room | **a.** clerk |
| ____ **2.** passed away | **b.** maid |
| ____ **3.** domestic engineer | **c.** bathroom |
| ____ **4.** service assistant | **d.** died |
| ____ **5.** sanitary engineer | **e.** garbage collector |

**C. On a separate sheet of paper, write two sentences using the five euphemisms from Column I of Part B.**

FIGURE 6.4 Out of sequence information ("Euphemisms" from *HBJ Reading Program: Landmarks, Workbook*, edited by Margaret Early, et al., copyright © 1987 by Harcourt Brace Jovanovich, Inc., reprinted by permission of the publisher.)

Therefore errors are made because of lack of vocabulary. More careful sequencing would teach the word meaning before its application and generalization. Teachers can spot out-of-sequence material by noticing high frequency of errors. The out-of-sequence material can then be skipped. Otherwise the teacher must add a teacher-made sequence based on principles in chapter 5.

Most curriculum materials after the third grade level are content curriculum. The purpose is not to teach reading or math skills but to cover a subject area like science, history, social studies, or literature. Sometimes these materials are well sequenced and the review questions at the end follow this sequence. This helps students find and pay attention to information considered relevant by the author. However, this is frequently not the case. An adaptation to solve out-of-sequence review questions is to construct a study guide to emphasize relevant information from the text and to direct a student's attention to the material for review questions.

### Action Item

There is one consistent phenomenon that alerts a teacher to problems in a textbook—student errors. After noting the confusion in learners' faces and errors on their papers, the teacher needs to diagnose the problem within the text.

Is it too many skills? If so, the corrective action is to reduce the number of skills. For example, two skills can be presented each day through board work, flash cards or hand-outs. When all of the skills are presented, then the teacher can return to the text.

The problem may be the lack of adequate practice. If this is the case, games, photocopies of the pages or peer tutor work are solutions.

Another problem could be distracting stimuli on the page. Windows cut out of construction paper are a good way to help learners focus on the relevant information on a page.

The final problem may be that the information presented is out of sequence. In this case learners do not have the prerequisite skills to be successful. The choice is to cut the page out, omit it, or save it for a later time.

Interview a teacher of a grade level that you hope to teach or which you are currently teaching. Ask about a page or unit in a textbook that results in a lot of errors. Try to diagnose the problem and prescribe a possible solution.

7

CHAPTER

# A SYNTHESIS OF APPROACHES

## OBJECTIVE

Speculate on a personal curriculum philosophy and how one might integrate various philosophies with one's opinion about how learning happens.

There are three major positions in psychology on what influences learning. As documented in chapter 1, these are the developmentalist, interactionist, and behaviorist approaches. Developmentalists believe that nature or genetic endowment is the biggest determinant in learning. Interactionists believe that it is a combination of nature and nurture or environmental conditions outside of a person that influence learning. And a behaviorist believes that environmental conditions are the single most important variable in what people learn.

What is a teacher to do in light of the developmentalist, interactionist and behaviorist approaches? Usually what happens is that a teacher adheres to one approach or another, and ignores the others. It's as if an educator adopts a religion of learning and then either accepts or rejects information based on that religion. But perhaps there is something applicable in all three approaches. The developmentalists may be right that children do have an inherent curiosity which will promote learning. An interactionist may be correct that stimulation from the environment is essential to catalyze learning and growth. And a behaviorist may be correct that the environment can be arranged to promote learning. But how can this be used to determine the content of the curriculum?

The progressive movement of the early twentieth century evolved to reform education. Before that time, education was only for the wealthy. Pestalozzi, Dewey and others saw education as a means to change society by extending educational opportunities to all people. Progressive ideas (spawned by Dewey) included both a student-centered curriculum (developmentalist) and the use of measurement (behaviorist) to improve education. In effect, progressives combined nature and nurture. The spirit of the progressive movement can be continued today, prompting educators to intertwine the developmentalist, interactionist, and behaviorist perspective to create an effective curriculum.

The basic building blocks of the curriculum could be those skills or concepts that are necessary to learn later skills such as reading, writing, computation, and research skills to find out information in libraries and from other people. After that, teachers could give stduents a wide array of subjects to choose from and could also encourage students to create their own topics of study with teacher assistance. Also, the external environment outside the classroom could be used as a lab to promote as much experimentation as possible.

Such a strategy adopts a behavioristic point of view by arranging the environment to insure that basic skills are taught and also reflects an interactionist perspective by encouraging interaction with the world around the student. Finally, a developmentalist perspective is incorporated, since the bulk of the curriculum is student choice to allow for students' natural learning tendencies to unfold. In sum, the content of the curriculum is student choice, but core skills are taught systematically.

Systematic instruction methodology can be used to insure that basic skills are taught and an experiential approach can be used for other content areas. For example, in elementary schools, two hours a day can be spent in systematic instruction of basic skills, and the remainder of the day can be spent in open-ended, sensory-rich explorations of the learner's surrounding environment.

It is possible to use systematic techniques so effectively that there is no struggle to learn basic skills. Teachers then can be freed to create experimentation with an environment enhancing motivation, as in Dewey's occupations, and thus create a transition for the learner to the real world.

## SUMMARY

Curriculum theories are cyclic in their application to the schools of the United States. A developmentalist and experiential approach was popular at the turn of the twentieth century. In the 1930s when it appeared that learners were not acquiring necessary content, an objective writing movement, or behaviorist and systematic approach, became the predominant philosophy of designing curriculum. In the 1960s a return to the experiential approach accompanied the radical changes in U.S. society created by the Vietnam War. Nongraded open schools were one of the changes during this time. With the release of the *Nation at Risk* report in the 1970s, the pendulum returned to a systematic curriculum philosophy to improve learners' performance on standardized tests.

A wide swing in one direction usually results in a swing in the opposite direction. The challenge for the educator is to develop a sustained curriculum philosophy which incorporates strengths from various approaches to insure that all important elements of learning are addressed.

The purpose of this text is to empower teachers with systematic curriculum design techniques so that they know how to communicate difficult concepts and basic skills to learners. In addition, knowledge of these curriculum design techniques allows teachers to choose and trouble shoot published texts. However, teachers are also encouraged to use experiential techniques whenever possible to bring the world into the classroom and to orchestrate expeditions for learners into the world outside. Both the experiential and systematic approaches are necessary to create well-rounded learners who have both a store of basic skills and the thinking ability to know what to do with the information.

# GLOSSARY

**Adequate practice:**
Providing enough responses to insure mastery

**Behavior rehearsal:**
Practice by a student of desired behavior with prompting from teacher

**Behaviorist:**
A theory that learning occurs as a result of environmental consequences of behavior

**Concrete operations:**
A Piaget cognitive stage, age 7–12, capable of logic with concrete help

**Critical element:**
The key to solving or performing the objective. What is the most important thing for the learner to pay attention to?

**Cueing:**
Adding or emphasizing information to prompt a correct response

**Cumulative introduction:**
Reviewing a concept systematically to insure mastery

**Developmentalist:**
A theory that chidlren will grow into what they need to, naturally

**Discriminative stimulus-$S^D$:**
The stimulus that prompts a behavior

**Error patterns:**
Consistency in mistakes reflecting an incorrect solution strategy

**Exaggerate differences:**
Making two easily confused stimuli more dissimilar to facilitate discrimination of the two stimuli

**Formal operations:**
A Piaget cognitive stage, age 12–on, includes the use of abstract logic

**Full range of examples:**
Presenting a variety of applications of a concept

**Generalized comprehension:**
Applying information in a new way

**Imagery:**
Visualization within the mind to make concepts to be learned more concrete and accessible

**Interactionist:**
A theory that children must contact the environment to develop

**Law of stimulus generalization:**
The more similar a stimulus is to an $S^D$, the more probable a similar response will occur

**Literal comprehension:**
Repeating the exact facts

**Mental rehearsal:**
Visualization within the mind to make concepts to be learned more concrete and accessible

**Modeling:**
Saying or showing the expected response to encourage a correct response

**Objective:**
A clear, specific picture in the teacher's mind of the learning to take place

**Objective slicing:**
Omitting certain parts of a textbook lesson to make the objective understandable to students

**Occupation:**
An instructional activity which approximates real life

**Operation:**
An internalized, reversible logical action in the mind

**Page slicing:**
Omitting certain pages in a textbook to exclude confusing information that is presented out of sequence

**Preoperations:**
A Piaget cognitive stage, ages 2–7, symbols, use of perception in lieu of logic to make conclusions

**Probes:**
Checking to see if learner can do objective

**Prompting:**
Saying part of a response with a student to encourage a correct response

**Psychologizing learning:**
Presenting information from a student's world view

**Recall response:**
Bringing forth the correct response from memory

**Recognition response:**
Choosing a correct response from choices presented

**S-Delta:**
The stimulus that does not prompt a behavior

**Sensori-motor:**
A Piaget cognitive stage, about ages 0–2, a child tests the environment with the senses

**Sequencing:**
Creating a series of steps which move from simple to complex

**Social Darwinism:**
The theory that each human's social development approximates humankind's progress from caveman to civilized human

**Stimulus control:**
A discernible event in the environment that prompts a given response

**Stimulus discrimination:**
Responding differently to two different stimuli

**Stimulus fading:**
Gradually removing parts of a stimulus that have cued a correct response

**Stimulus generalization:**
Responding the same to two different stimuli

**Stimulus gradient:**
A range of stimuli along a gradual progression of change

**Stimulus shaping:**
Changing the topography (the shape) of a stimulus to prompt a correct behavior

**Strategy:**
Presenting a rule that will alert a learner to the critical element

**Superimposition:**
Putting a familiar stimulus on top of an unfamiliar one to cue a correct response

**Task analysis:**
Listing the steps a learner would go through (mentally or in action) to perform a task

**Test:**
Checking to see if learner can do objective

**Uniform instruction:**
Using the same format for learner response throughout a sequence

# FURTHER READING

## CURRENT CURRICULUM DESIGN REFERENCES


Barrow, R. *Giving Teaching Back to Teachers: A Critical Introduction to Curriculum Theory.* Wheatsheaf Books, 1984.

Beane, J. *Curriculum Planning and Development.* Newton, MA: Allyn and Bacon, 1986.

Beane, J. *Sefl-concept, Self-esteem, and the Curriculum.* New York: Teachers College Press, 1986.

Brubaker, D. *Curriculum Planning, The Dynamics of Theory and Practice.* Springfield, IL: C. C. Thomas, 1981.

Connelly, F. M. *Teachers as Curriculum Planners: Narratives of Experience.* New York: Teachers College Press, 1988.

Darling-Hammond, L. "The Over-Regulated Curriculum and the Press for Teacher Professionalism." *NASSP Bulletin* 71(1987): 22–29.

Kemp, J. *The Instructional Design Process.* New York: Harper & Row, 1985.

*Learning and Loving It: Theme Studies in the Classroom.* Ontario, Canada: OISE Press, 1988.

Posner, G. *Course Design: A Guide to Curriculum Development for Teachers.* 3d ed. New York: Longman, 1986.

Pratt, D. "Curriculum Design as Humanistic Technology." *Journal of Curriculum Studies* 2(1987): 149–162.

Tyler, R. "The Five Most Significant Curriculum Events in the Twentieth Century." *Educational Leadership* 44(1986–87): 36–38.

Wadsworth, B. *Piaget's Theory of Cognitive and Affective Development.* 3d ed. New York: Longman, 1984.

Wiles, J. *Curriculum Development: A Guide to Practice.* Columbus, OH: C. E. Merrill, 1985.

# REFERENCES

## CHAPTER 1


1. Maslow, A. H., *Motivation and Personality.* 2d ed. (New York: Harper and Row, 1970).
2. Dewey, J., *The Child and the Curriculum.* (Chicago, Ill.: University of Chicago Press, 1902).
3. Green, J. A. (Ed.), *Pestalozzi's Educational Writings.* (New York: Longmans, Green and Co., 1916).
4. As noted at the beginning of the chapter, Abraham Maslow[1] proposed that humans have an inherent drive or tendency to develop in a positive manner and that the job of people in helping professions is to create conditions which activate this drive. The drive will then guide a person to positive development.
5. Johnson, D. and Johnson, R., *Learning Together and Alone.* (New Jersey: Prentice Hall, 1983).
6. Montessori, M., *The Absorbent Mind.* (New York: Holt, Rinehart and Winston, 1967. Fourth Printing, 1973).
7. Bruner, J. S., *Toward A Theory of Instruction.* (London, England: The Belknap Press, 1966).
8. Gilman, R., "Growing Without Schooling, an Interview with John Holt." *In Context.* Summer, 1984.
9. Piaget, J., *The Child and Reality.* (New York: Grossman Publishers, 1973).
10. Calgren, F., *Education Towards Freedom.* (East Grinstead, England: Lanthorn Press, 1976).
11. Rugg, H. and others, *Curriculum-Making Past and Present.* (New York: Arno Press and The New York Times, 1969).
12. Bobbitt, F., "The New Technique of Curriculum-Making." *The Elementary School Journal.* Anniversary Issue, 1985. pgs. 70–77.
13. Skinner, B. F., *The Technology of Teaching.* (New York: Appleton-Century-Crofts Educational Division, Meredith Corporation, 1968).
14. Mager, R. F., *Goal Analysis.* (Belmont, Calif.: Geron Publishers, 1972).
15. Engelmann, S. and Carnine, D., *Theory of Instruction: Principles and Applications.* (New York: Irvington Publishers, Inc., 1982).

## CHAPTER 2

1. Definitions for the terms in this chapter are found, in part, in Whaley, D. L. and Malott, R. W., *Elementary Principles of Behavior.* (New York: Appleton-Century-Crofts, 1971). These definitions and others have been rewritten and created by the author for work with teachers.
2. Nelson-Burford, A., *How to Focus the Distractible Child* (Saratoga, CA: R & E Publishers, 1985).
3. Schilmoeller, K. J. and B. C. Etzel. "An Experimental Analysis of Criterion-Related and Non-Criterion-Related Cues in 'Errorless' Stimulus Control Procedures." In B. C. Etzel, M. J. LeBlanc and D. M. Baer (Eds.). *New Developments in Behavioral Research: Theory, Method, an Application In Honor of Sidney W. Bijou.* (Hillsdale, New Jersey: Lawrence Erlbaum Associates, 1977).

## CHAPTER 3

1. Twining, W. E., "Mental Practice and Physical Practice in Learning a Motor Skill." *Research Quarterly* 20 (1949): 432–435.

## CHAPTER 4

1. Rugg, H. and others. *Curriculum-Making Past and Present.*
2. Bruner, J. S., *Toward a Theory of Instruction.*

## CHAPTER 5

1. Some techniques in chapter 5 are, in part, based on definitions by Siegfried Englemann and Douglas Carnine in *Theory of Instruction: Principles and Applications.* These definitions and others have been rewritten and created by the author for work with teachers.
2. Chall, J., *Learning to Read: The Great Debate.* (New York: McGraw Hill Book Company, 1967).
3. Klinger, E., *Imagery, Concepts, Results, and Applications.* Volume 2. (New York: Plenum Press, 1981).
4. Ibid.
5. Singer, L., *Imagery and Day Dream Methods in Psychotherapy and Behavior Modification.* (New York: Academic Press, 1974).
6. Qualls, P. and Sheehan, P., "Imagery Encouragement, Absorption Capacity, and Relaxation During Electromyograph Biofeedback." *Journal of Personality and Social Psychology* 41(1981): 370–379.
7. Nelson-Burford, A., *How to Focus the Distractible Child.*
8. Rose, R., "Guided Fantasies in Elementary Classrooms" in *Imagery: Its Many Dimensions and Applications.* (New York: Plenum Press, 1979).

## CHAPTER 6

1. Bishop, M. S., Lewis, P. G. and Sutherland, B., *Focus on Earth Science.* (Columbus, Ohio: Charles E. Merrill Publishing Co., 1976). page 165.
2. Angel, A., *Elementary Algebra: A Practical Approach.* (Englewood Cliffs, New Jersey: Prentice-Hall, Inc., 1985). page 253.
3. Early, M., *HBJ Reading Program: Landmarks.* (Orlando, Fl.: Harcourt Brace Jovanovich Publishers, 1987). page 62.

# INDEX

Page numbers in italics indicate figures; page numbers followed by t indicate tabular material.

# Back Roads of Washington

Seen near BZ Corners, Klickitat County

*Books by Earl Thollander*

BACK ROADS OF NEW ENGLAND
BACK ROADS OF OREGON
BACK ROADS OF WASHINGTON
BACK ROADS OF CALIFORNIA
BACK ROADS OF TEXAS
BACK ROADS OF ARIZONA
BARNS OF CALIFORNIA

*Farm on Lopez Island, San Juan County*

# Back Roads of Washington

by Earl Thollander

Clarkson N. Potter, Inc./Publishers NEW YORK
DISTRIBUTED BY CROWN PUBLISHERS, INC.

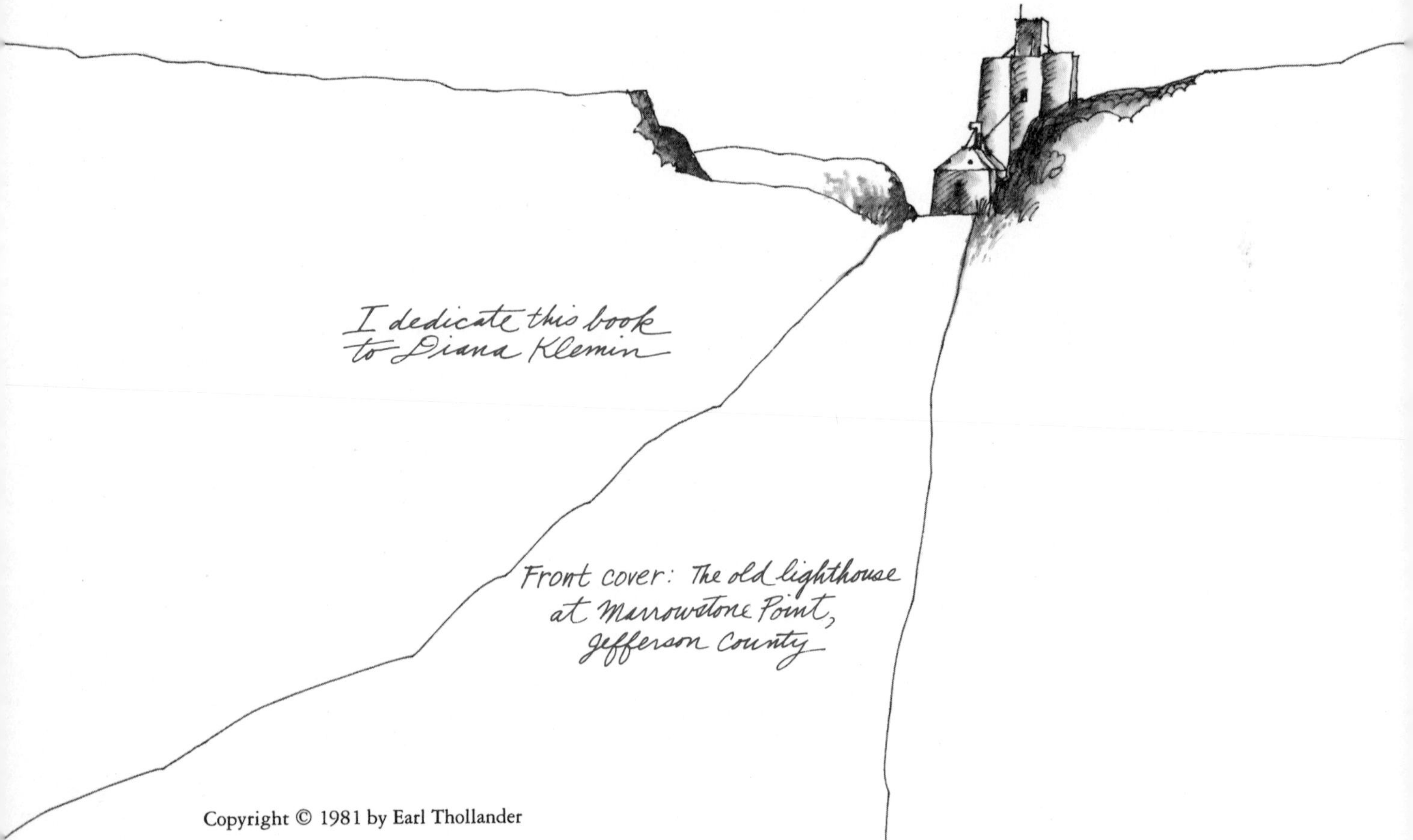

*I dedicate this book to Diana Klemin*

*Front cover: The old lighthouse at Marrowstone Point, Jefferson County*



Inquiries should be addressed to Clarkson N. Potter, Inc., One Park Avenue, New York, New York 10016

Printed in the United States of America

Published simultaneously in Canada by General Publishing Company Limited

Library of Congress Cataloging in Publication Data

Thollander, Earl.
Back roads of Washington.

1. Washington (State)—Description and travel—1951- —Guide-books. 2. Automobiles—Road guides—Washington (State) 3. Washington (State)—History, Local. I. Title.
F889.3.T48 1981 917.970443 81-5128
ISBN: 0-517-542692 (cloth) AACR2
ISBN: 0-517-542706 (paper)

10 9 8 7 6 5 4 3 2 1

First Edition

*Grain elevator at Marlin, Grant County*

# Contents

## Back Roads of Northeastern Washington



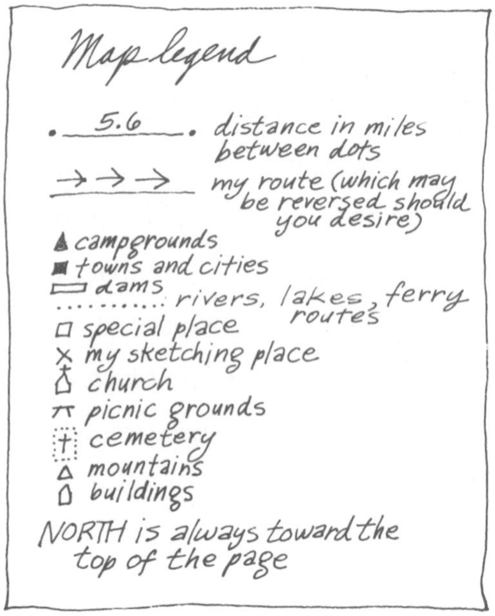

## Back Roads of Southeastern Washington

Yellow Dandelion

Sketching in Oysterville, Pacific County

# Foreword

Bob Meadows knocked on the door of our cottage and came in before we could answer. "Hey," he said, "there's an artist fellow sittin' out there in the field, just a-drawin' away. I'd sure like to see what he'd do if one of them great big b'ars come up and looked over his shoulder."

As it happens, there are no great big b'ars around Oysterville; ours are middle-sized fellows, though fearsome enough at that. But even if a Kodiak brown bear in all its terrible majesty came visiting, I know what Earl Thollander would do: He would make a place for it in his drawing.

He was sitting out there that rainy day because of me. I had written a book, *Oysterville: Roads to Grandpa's Village,* and Earl had agreed to pretty up the pages with sketches of local sights, animate and inanimate—snipe, oyster shells, falling-down fences, and so on. The way he does.

The way he does is a thing to marvel at. For years, Earl Thollander has been exploring the back roads of this nation, sketching as he goes. His means of transportation is a 1972 Chevrolet pickup truck that serves as both studio and bedroom. At intervals he parks off the road, gets out, and begins to draw. You may have seen him sitting on a rail fence, with his pad in his lap, or leaning forward in a canvas folding chair in a field, as on that day in Oysterville. To find the best vantage point, he sometimes climbs into the branches of a tree or onto the roof of a farmhouse.

Each expedition adds a new installment to a unique pictorial chronicle of America. It is an America invisible from superhighways and absent from headlines. In the America recorded by Earl Thollander you will still find covered bridges, steepled country churches, and barns bursting with hay. You can still pause to marvel over a half-opened jonquil or the cemented nest of a mud swallow. It is an America that has never gone away, but that was forgotten for a while. Now that we are seeking it again, Earl Thollander is pointing out the way.

Should the day come, God forbid, when the last covered bridge and steepled church have vanished, Thollander's elegant drawings will remain as testimony—part of the heritage that they record.

You may fairly accuse me of chauvinism when I say that I admire *Back Roads of Washington* even more than its predecessors. I am, after all, Washingtonian by birth and rearing. But I am right. The two-page drawing of Oysterville is sufficient by itself to make this book immortal.

Willard R. Espy

Oysterville, Washington
January 1981

# Preface

Seeing Washington at a leisurely pace,
following where its back roads lead me,
there is time to meet people, to meditate on
history, to take the measure of the land.
I feel close to the earth—its forests, farms,
meadows, wild birds, animals—
and joyful and at peace with man.

Snowbush,
Spokane County

# Author's Note

*Back Roads of Washington* is a nonhighway travel guide through areas of interest and beauty. Each of the book's four parts begins with a sectional map. These will help you locate the back roads on larger maps of Washington State that are available at no charge from many sources, including travel services, chambers of commerce, tourist bureaus, and automobile clubs. Localized maps for all the roads throughout will guide you on specific trips. Unless otherwise indicated, the North Pole is toward the top of the page. Arrows trace my direction of travel, although the routes can easily be reversed. Maps are not to scale because the roads are of varying lengths; however, the mileage notations will provide a sense of their distance. Your odometer will not measure distance exactly the same as mine, but the differences should not be too great. County maps purchased from the Washington State Highway Commission, Highway Administration Building, Olympia, Washington 98504, were essential to me in following the back roads. I also purchased maps at ranger stations when entering forest preserves.

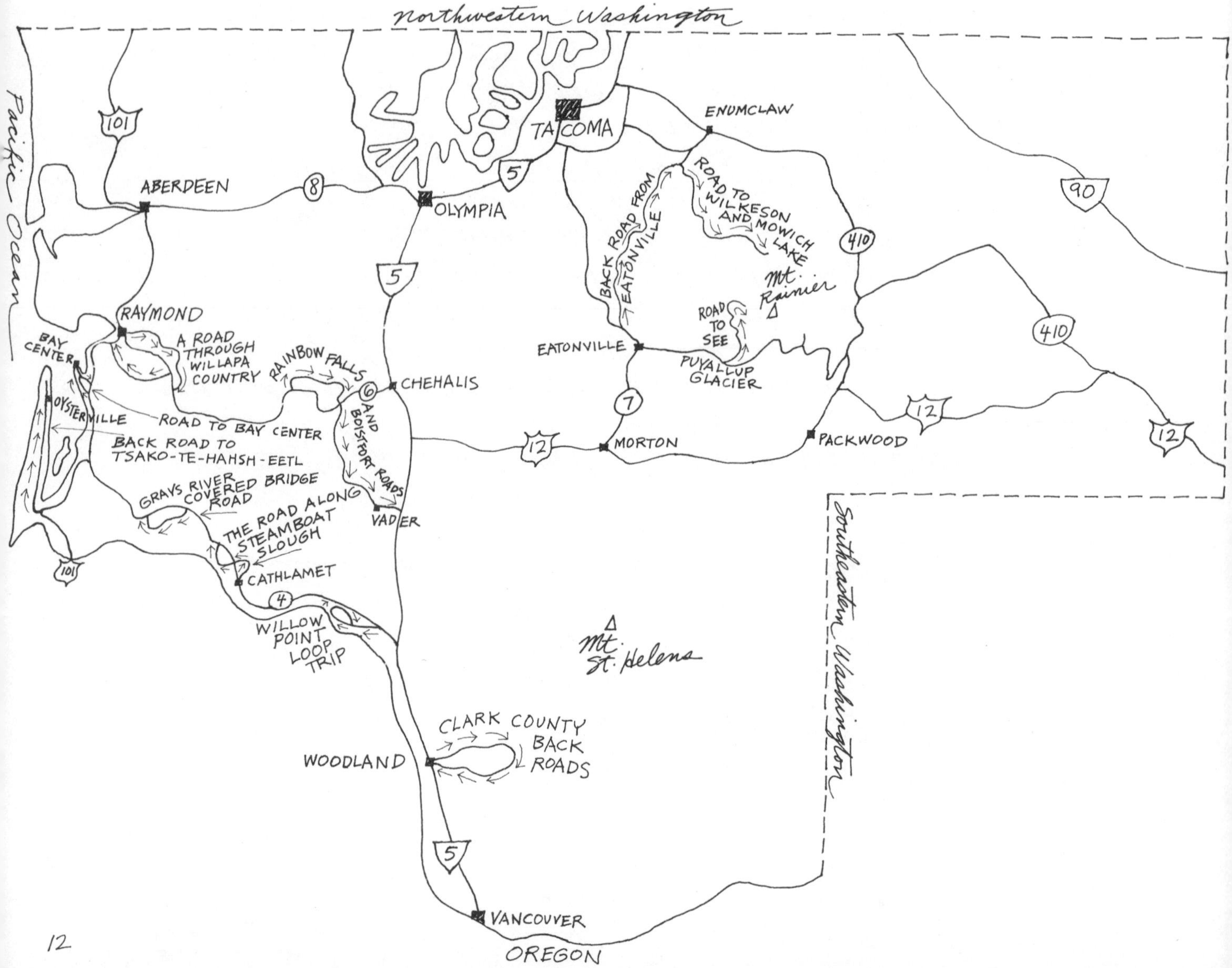

Northwestern Washington
Pacific Ocean
101
TACOMA
ENUMCLAW
ABERDEEN
8
5
OLYMPIA
90
ROAD TO WILKESON AND MOWICH LAKE
BACK ROAD FROM EATONVILLE
410
Mt. Rainier
ROAD TO SEE
RAYMOND
BAY CENTER
A ROAD THROUGH WILLAPA COUNTRY
RAINBOW FALLS
6
CHEHALIS
EATONVILLE
PUYALLUP GLACIER
OYSTERVILLE
ROAD TO BAY CENTER
AND BOISTFORT ROADS
7
12
BACK ROAD TO TSAKO-TE-HAHSH-EETL
MORTON
PACKWOOD
GRAYS RIVER COVERED BRIDGE ROAD
THE ROAD ALONG STEAMBOAT SLOUGH
VADER
CATHLAMET
4
WILLOW POINT LOOP TRIP
Mt. St. Helens
Southeastern Washington
CLARK COUNTY BACK ROADS
WOODLAND
VANCOUVER
OREGON

# Southwestern Washington

I recall the big foreign-bound cargo ships navigating the bends of the Columbia River; a cool, misty evening while camping at Fort Canby State Park; a fresh fish dinner (perhaps the best I've ever had) at South Bend; snow-topped Mount Rainier glistening in the sunshine, and foxglove blossoming six feet tall.

Foxglove, Pierce County

Clark County back roads

The road takes me across the Lewis River and from time to time touches the river as it winds past farms, barns, meadows, and forest land.

The 1876 gristmill at Cedar Creek was sturdily built, and stands to this day for people to enjoy. This custom mill, where local farmers brought their wheat, rye, and buckwheat to be ground, is a fascinating souvenir of Washington's early agricultural history.

Gristmill, 1876, Clark County

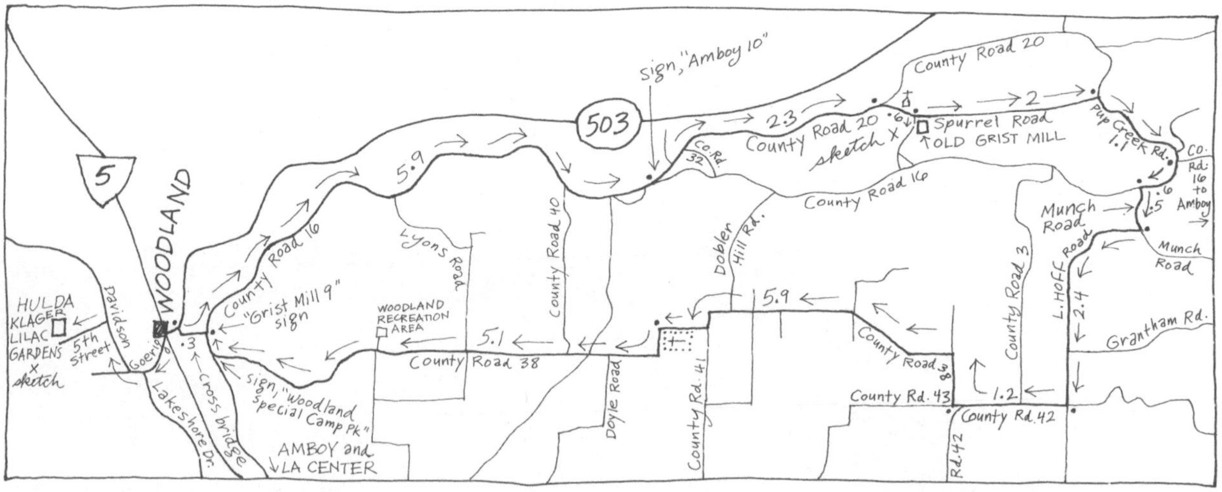


## *The road to Hulda Klager's house*

There are exotic trees and flowers in abundance all around the house of the "Lilac Lady," hybridizer Hulda Klager, in Woodland. The Woodland Federated Garden Club saved the old house and gardens from the bulldozers when she died in 1960 at the age of ninety-six, and the garden club continues to maintain them.

Go anytime, but the best season is spring, when you will see the many Klager varieties of lilacs and experience the charm of Hulda's house and garden at its peak. The doll, in my picture from the Klager home, is nicely handmade of lisle cotton stocking material. Grace Davis's rocker dates from about 1880.

Grace Davis's rocker circa 1880, Hulda Klager House, Woodland, Cowlitz County

*Willow Grove loop trip along the Columbia River*

While riding atop dikes one gets views of pastureland, grazing cows, barns, fishing boats, log floats, and, of course, the Columbia River with its big cargo ship traffic on the opposite shore. The wooded hills of Oregon are a backdrop. The 1,200-mile-long Columbia is one of the largest rivers in the world, draining an area of 257,000 square miles. I will view its greatness many more times in my back road journey through Washington State.

The Columbia River,
Cowlitz County

Old pilings, Columbia River, Wahkiakum County

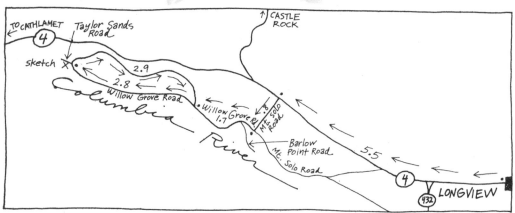

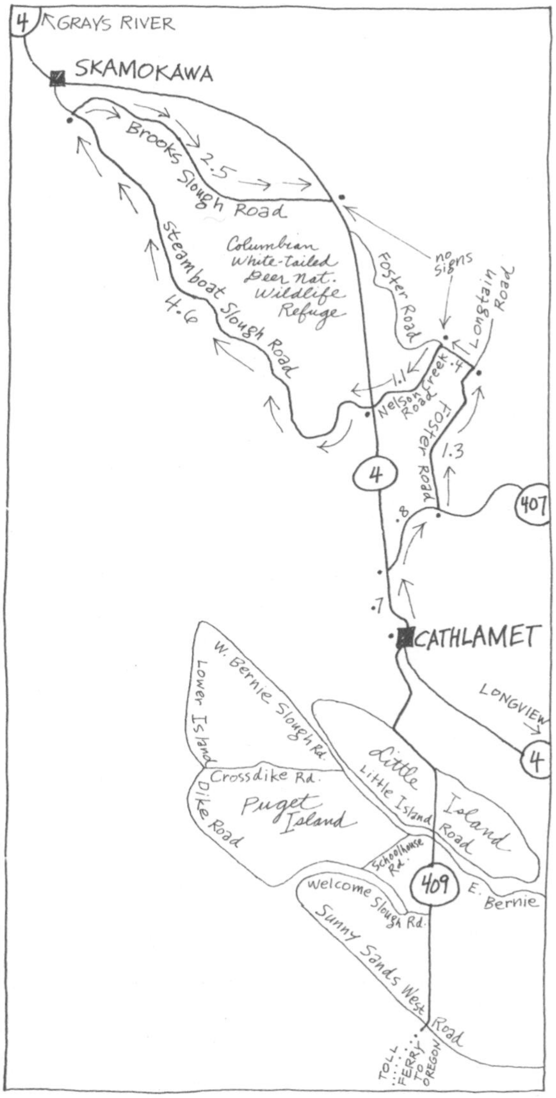


## The road along Steamboat Slough

I travel along dike roads past farms and waterways and am struck by the bouquets of wild grass, flowers, and sometimes young trees that grow from the tops of old pilings. Many are quite decorative, as if specially arranged for the delectation of travelers on back roads.

On Puget Island, south of Cathlamet, are other dike roads. A toll ferry from the island crosses the Columbia River into Oregon.

*Grays River Covered Bridge road*

This trip is through green meadows and forest land with views of Grays River, farms, barns, and cows. The bridge was built in 1905 and is the only covered bridge in Washington still in use by cars. I make my drawing and proceed across it and along a road lined with wild flowers.

Grays River Covered Bridge,
Wahkiakum County

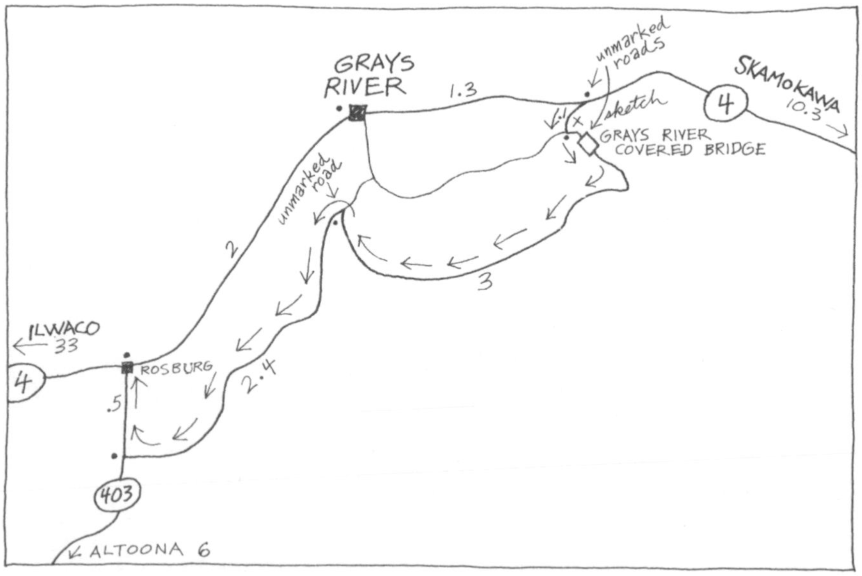

Wild blackberry,
Pacific County

## Back road to Tsako-te-hahsh-eetl

Foliage here is so dense, at times the road seems walled with green. There are some cranberry bogs, a lovely old hillside cemetery nestled in lush green forest and, at Nahcotta, heaps of Willapa Bay oyster shells. Oysterville, called by Indians Tsako-te-hahsh-eetl (*Land of the Red-top Grass and Home of the Woodpecker*), is a charming hamlet where descendants of the co-founder, R. H. Espy, still live. In my drawing you see the 1869 W. W. Little house and the Oysterville Church, its orange and white roof topped by a gleaming gold ball. A venerable organ stands on each side of the interior of the church — no doubt producing music as rich as a stereo hi-fi. An immersion tank below the floor for baptisms, I was told, was used only once, because no drain had been installed.

I observe what I call "hesitation light" in Oysterville. Being near the coast and most often cloudy, the light suddenly brightens or fades, depending upon the intensity of changing cloud layers.

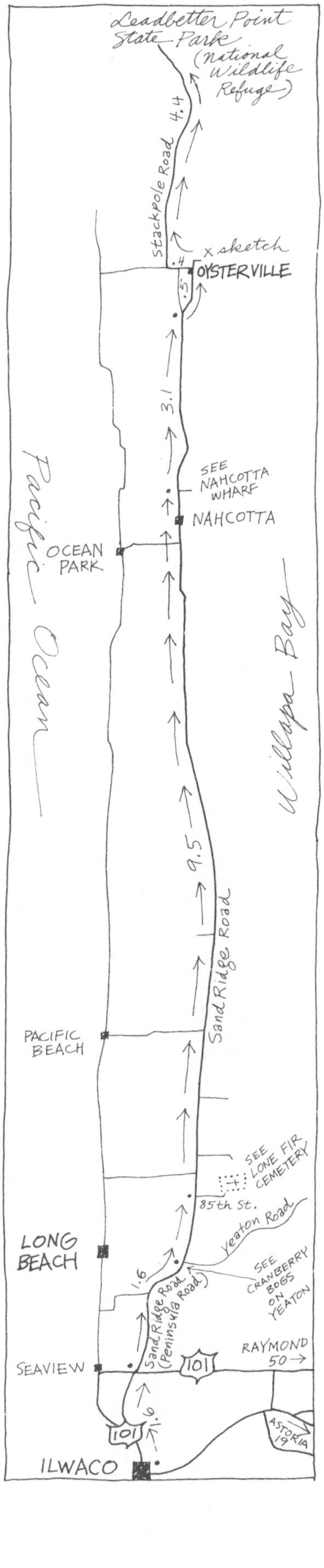

Oysterville,
Pacific County

## The road to Bay Center

Harry Bochau, pronounced Bó-haw, once owned this house in the quiet little fishing and oyster town of Bay Center. I talked to his son, who has since sold it, and learned that the old house had been called "The Château." Harry planted the monkey puzzle tree, a tall Chilean evergreen; I had also seen one at the Hulda Klager lilac gardens. Its intertwined branches and stiff sharp-pointed leaves are a challenge to draw.

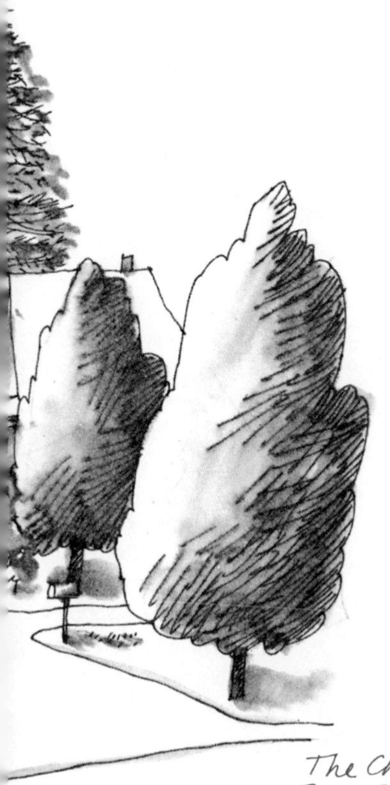

The Château, Bay Center, Pacific County

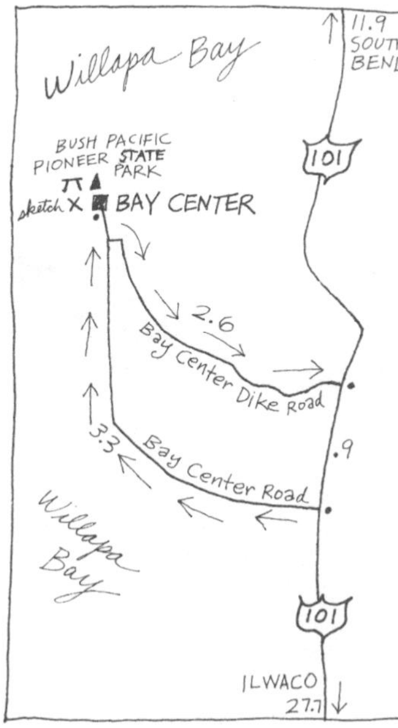

## a road through Willapa country

This is a rolling, verdant landscape of forest and farms — a country for lumbering and dairies. I sketch the Willow River Dairy with its big 1910 barn and the milk parlor on the left, the old 1889 house, and the railroad bridge.

The owner of the farm bicycles out to meet me while I am sketching. She tells me of the many demanding routines that must be maintained on a dairy farm, in addition to the obvious daily necessity of milking the cows. Later I lunch at a hillside cemetery and take in a grand view of Willapa Valley.

Willow River Dairy, 1889, Pacific County

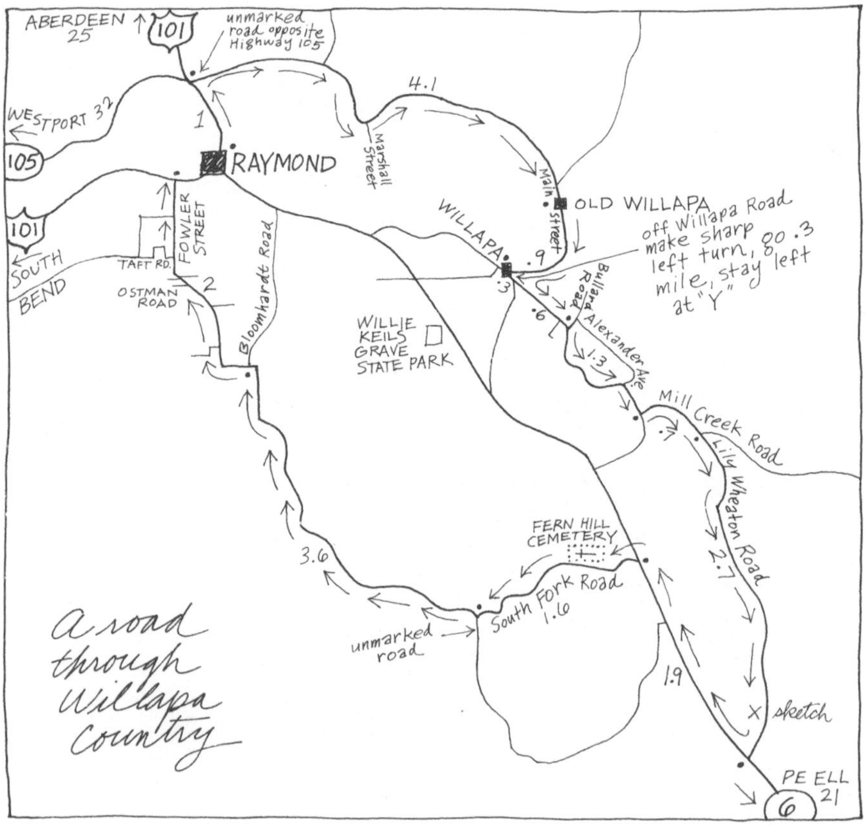


## *Rainbow Falls and Boistfort roads*

Scenes along the road from Rainbow Falls State Park include an old covered railroad bridge (now without train rails), forest, farms, and glimpses of the Chehalis River. Past Boistfort the road runs through glorious farm country—meadows green with crops of corn, hay, and peas.

Wildwood Dairy features a tall, dark blue silo. The young owner left his Dairy Science course at college to run this 170-acre farm.

Chandler Road
3.4
Kobe Road
Elk Creek Rd.
Stevens Rd.
1.4
Toppelt Rd.
1.1
Stevens Road
Leudinghaus Road
.8
3.4
RAINBOW FALLS STATE PARK
OLD RAILROAD BRIDGE
6
PE ELL 5.5
Meskill Road
3
Ceres Hill
6
Ceres Hill Road
3
(ARCHED BRIDGE)
WHITE RD.
.2
CHEHALIS 9
6
BOISTFORT RD.
Curtis Hill Road
Noon Hill Road
King Road
7.4
Hubbard Road
MacDonald Road
BOISTFORT
PE ELL
14.4
X sketch
Wildwood Road
CHEHALIS 24
RYDERWOOD
506

*Canada Thistle, Lewis County*

*Wildwood Dairy, Lewis County*

Puyallup Glacier, Mt. Rainier, Pierce County

*The back road to see Puyallup and Tahoma glaciers*

There are two confused fawns on the road, not knowing which way to go to escape my oncoming vehicle. They finally bolt off through Douglas fir, western hemlock, and red cedar forest, and are soon hidden among vine maple, moss and fern. At the Viewpoint of Puyallup Glacier, its river pounds down the mountain with rock-crushing force, yet on the banks close by, in all tranquility, grow dainty columbine, daisies, penstemon, tiger lily, cow parsnip, lungwort, and other wild flowers.

The Tahoma Glacier, which I sketch on the return trip, plays hide-and-seek with me, great mists and clouds constantly rearranging themselves on the mountain. Outsized horseflies circle, keeping up a constant hum, but they do not bite. Majestic Mount Rainier with its 27 glaciers and 14,410-foot height is stunning and awe-inspiring—what a mountain!

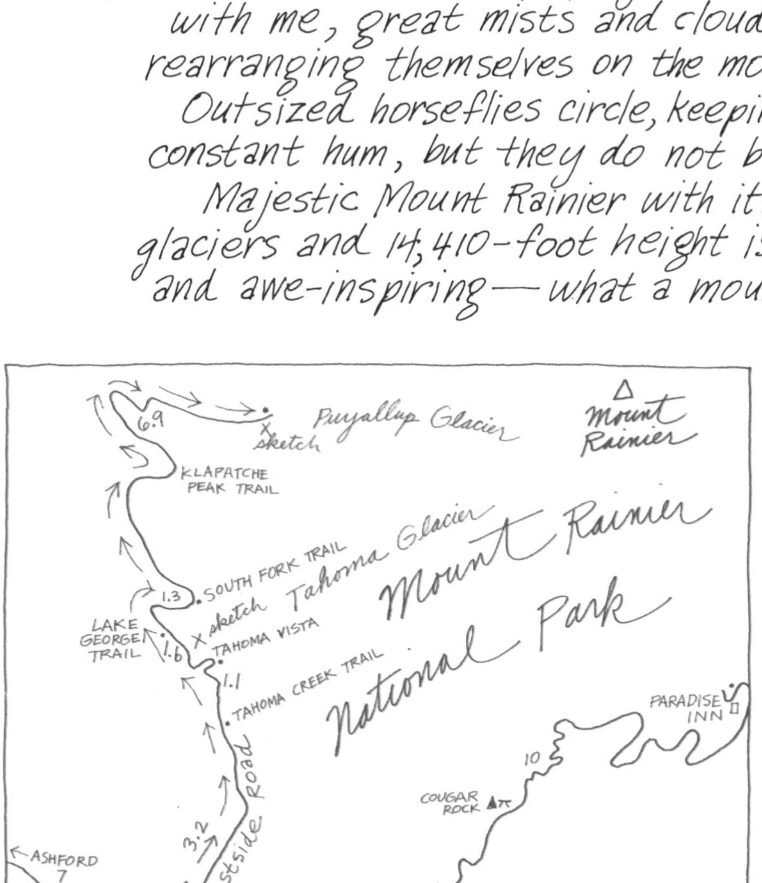

Tahoma Glacier,
Mt. Rainier,
Pierce County

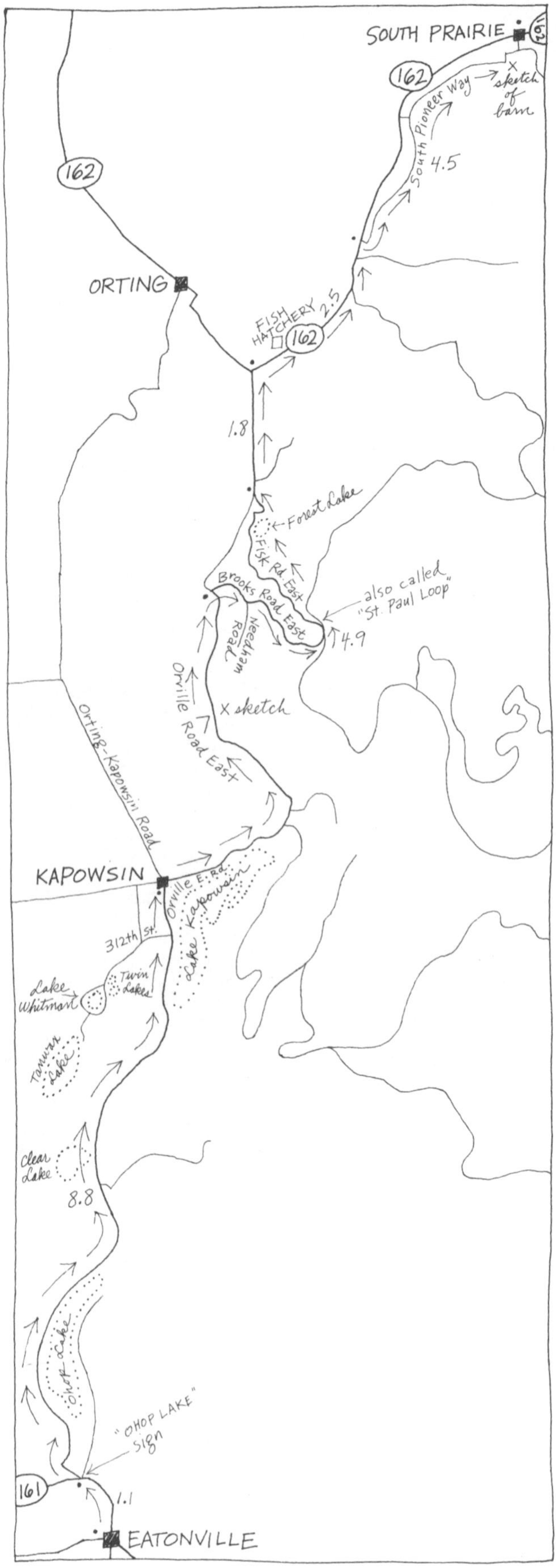


## Back road from Eatonville

The road passes Ohop Lake through the lush meadow and farm landscape of Ohop Valley to Kopowsin Lake and South Prairie town. I stop along the way at the fish hatchery to watch tiny salmon leaping about. One leaps too far! It jumps onto a gravel path and I return it to the water. Near South Prairie I draw the Winters barn. Mrs. Winters tells people who look for the farm, "watch for the ugliest barn!" I equip myself with a can of dog repellent, which Mrs. Winters gives to me in case the big ram should come close and lower his head in my direction. "Don't turn your back on him," she cautions. The formidable ram chews a bit on my folding chair while I sit in the meadow and sketch, but luckily that is all.

*Seen on the road to South Prairie, Pierce County*

Winters Barn,
near South Prairie, Pierce County

## The road to Wilkeson and Mowich Lake

The early settlers of Wilkeson, a town rimmed by conifer forest, were the immigrants who worked in local coal mines. Mining declined in the area around 1912, but in 1883 the nearby Carbonado mines were the second largest in Washington. The nicely restored Orthodox church, topped with a pale blue onion dome, is the oldest of its kind in Washington. It is located on Long Street. If you drive north to Short Street, then east to Cothery Street, you will see a castle.

Holy Trinity Orthodox Church, 1900, Wilkeson, Pierce County

It was constructed by a Wilkeson carpenter who dreamed of building and living in his own castle. The owner isn't home when I visit, but I talk to his neighbor through a screen door as he watches television. "I don't mind a castle going up next door," he comments in good cheer.

I then drive to glacially formed Mowich Lake, which is surrounded by high-ridged peaks and trails that invite investigation.

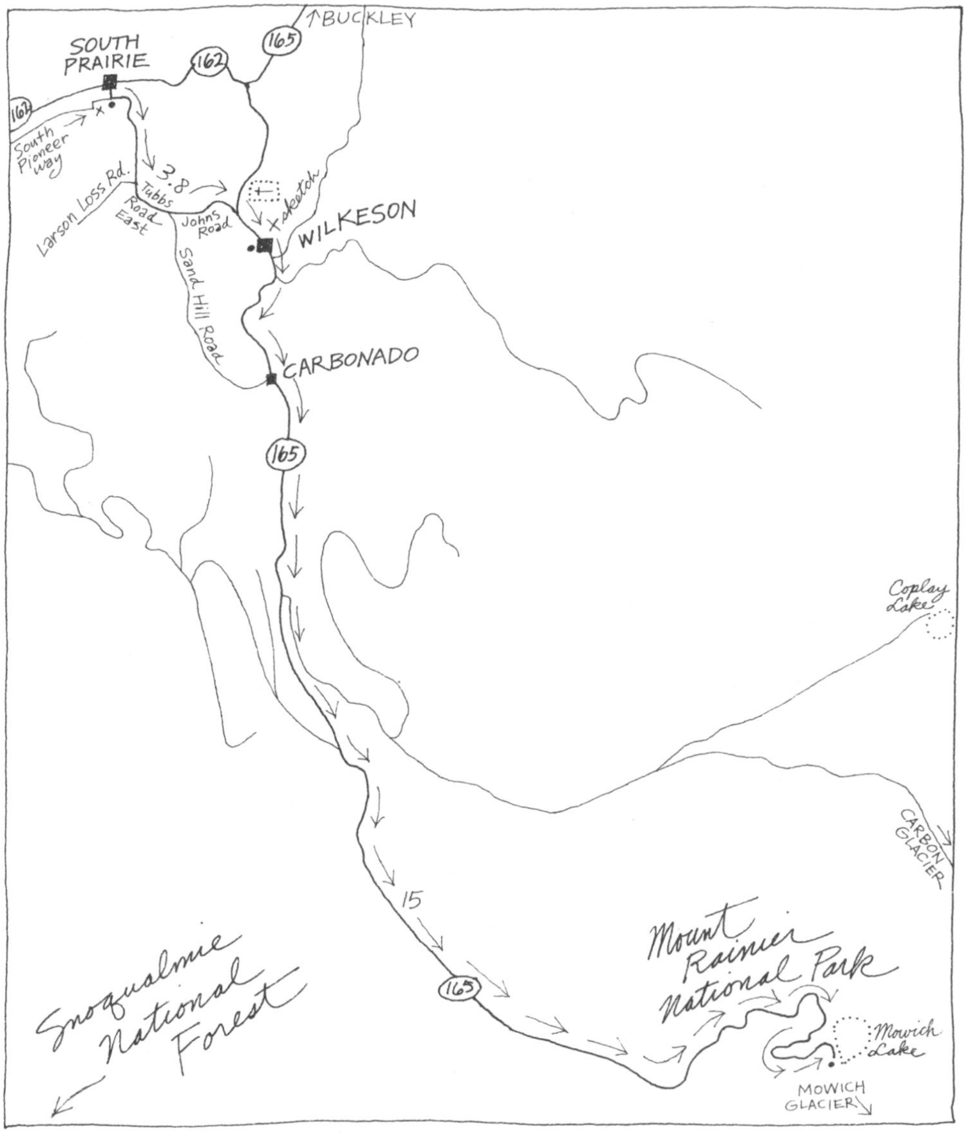

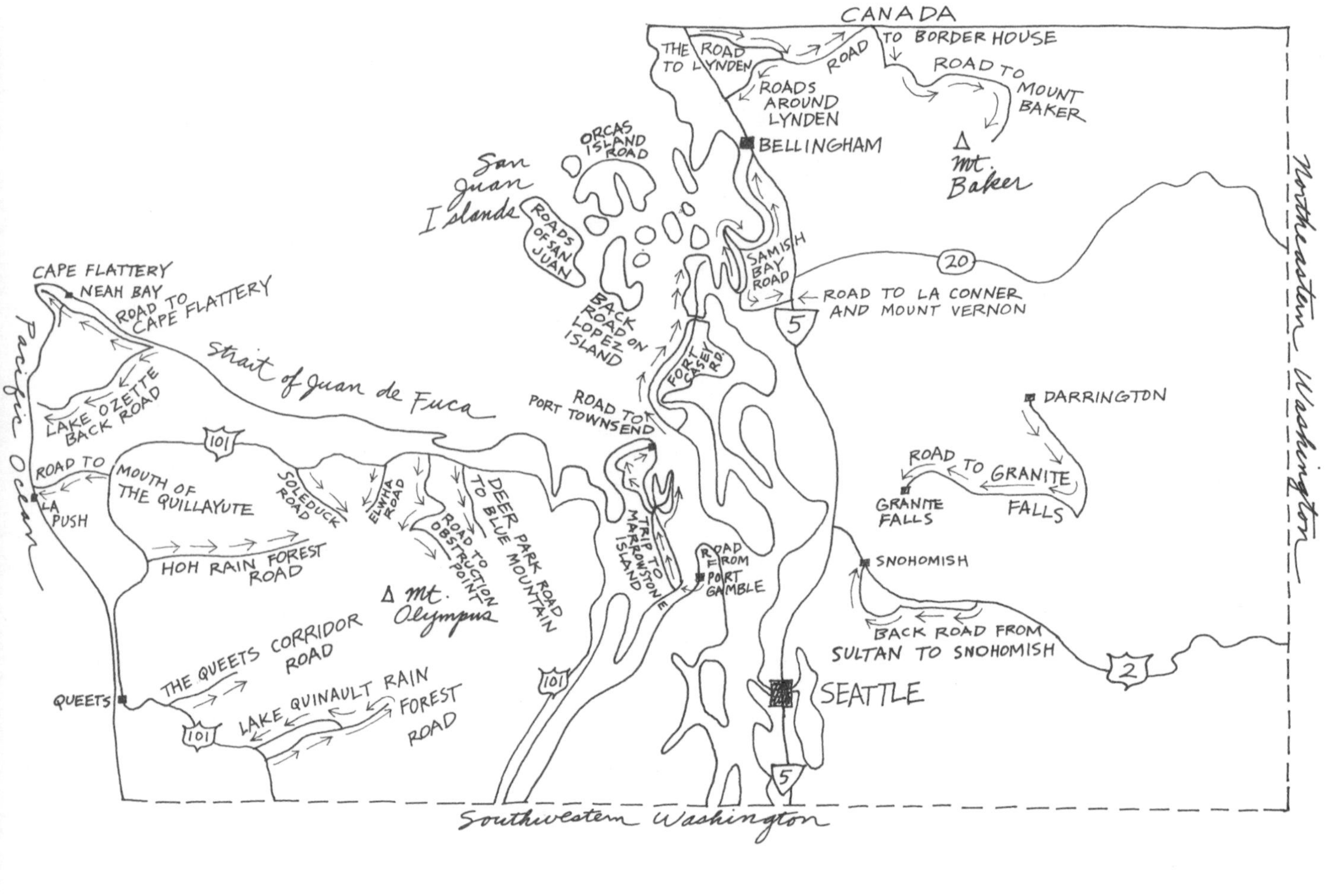
CANADA
THE ROAD TO LYNDEN
ROAD TO BORDER HOUSE
ROADS AROUND LYNDEN
ROAD TO MOUNT BAKER
Mt. Baker
BELLINGHAM
ORCAS ISLAND ROAD
San Juan Islands
ROADS OF SAN JUAN
SAMISH BAY ROAD
20
ROAD TO LA CONNER AND MOUNT VERNON
5
BACK ROAD LOPEZ ON ISLAND
FORT CASEY RD.
CAPE FLATTERY
NEAH BAY
ROAD TO CAPE FLATTERY
Pacific Ocean
Strait of Juan de Fuca
LAKE OZETTE BACK ROAD
ROAD TO PORT TOWNSEND
DARRINGTON
Northeastern Washington
101
ROAD TO MOUTH OF THE QUILLAYUTE
LA PUSH
SOLEDUCK ROAD
ELWHA ROAD
ROAD TO OBSTRUCTION POINT
DEER PARK ROAD TO BLUE MOUNTAIN
TRIP TO MARROWSTONE ISLAND
ROAD TO GRANITE FALLS
GRANITE FALLS
ROAD FROM PORT GAMBLE
SNOHOMISH
HOH RAIN FOREST ROAD
Mt. Olympus
BACK ROAD FROM SULTAN TO SNOHOMISH
2
THE QUEETS CORRIDOR ROAD
QUEETS
LAKE QUINAULT RAIN FOREST ROAD
SEATTLE
Southwestern Washington

# Northwestern Washington

I recall the rich greenness of the Olympic forest, the alpine glory of Mount Olympus, a view of Tatoosh Island off Cape Flattery bathed in sunshine, the fun of ferryboat rides among the San Juans, the neatly arranged farms of the descendants of the early Dutch settlers near Lynden, and uncooperative Mount Baker that would not come out of its cloud cover so I could draw it.

Fireweed, Snohomish County

*Lake Quinault rain forest road*

Hemlock, alder, cedar, maple, and fir are all draped with moss. Soft light filters to a forest floor blanketed with fern and oxalis. I ride on a good gravel road that is narrow in spots and has obviously been planned with the beauty of the landscape in mind rather than speed. At the end of the road foot trails begin beside clear, rushing Grave Creek.

Forest road,
Olympic National Park,
Grays and Jefferson Counties

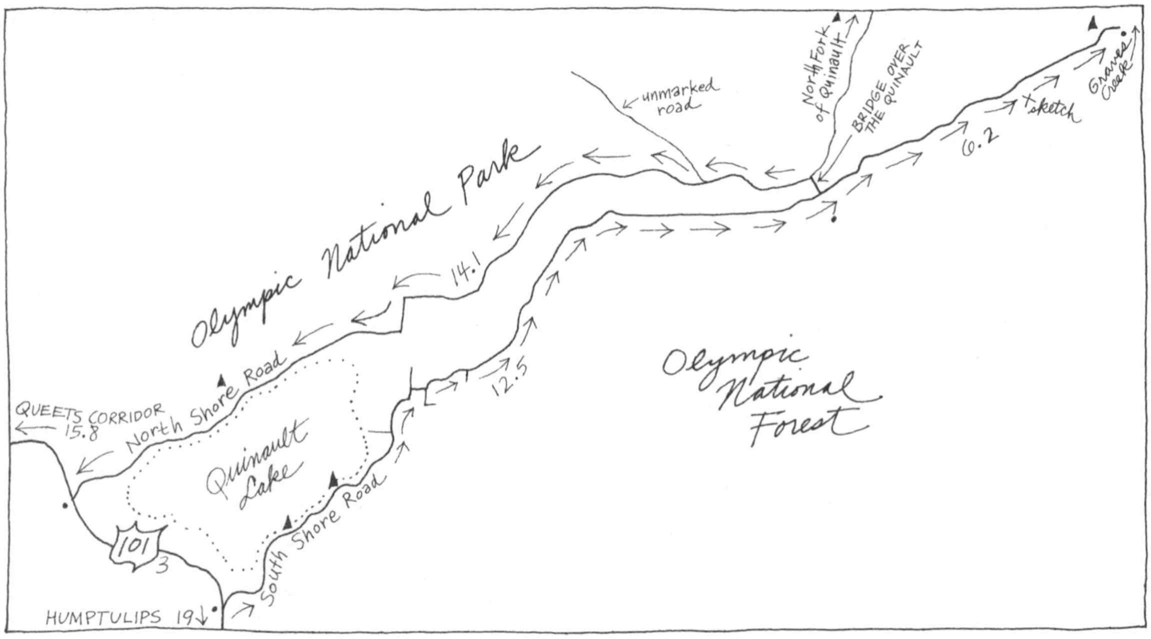

unmarked road
North Fork of Quinault
BRIDGE OVER THE QUINAULT
6.2
sketch
Graves Creek
Olympic National Park
14.1
12.5
Olympic National Forest
QUEETS CORRIDOR 15.8
North Shore Road
Quinault Lake
South Shore Road
101
3
HUMPTULIPS 19


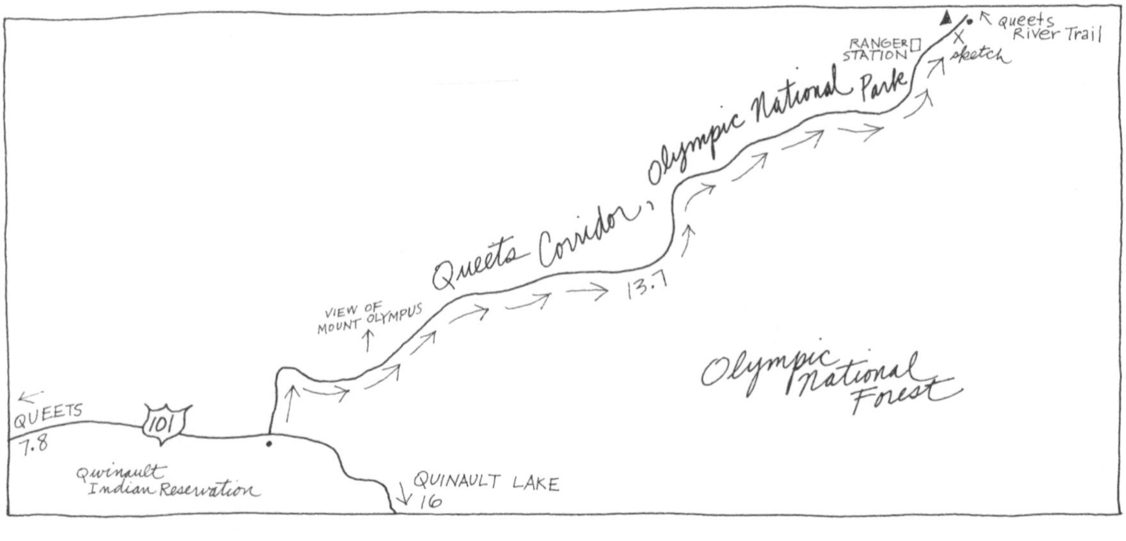

RANGER STATION
Queets River Trail
sketch
Queets Corridor, Olympic National Park
VIEW OF MOUNT OLYMPUS
13.7
Olympic National Forest
QUEETS 7.8
101
Quinault Indian Reservation
QUINAULT LAKE 16


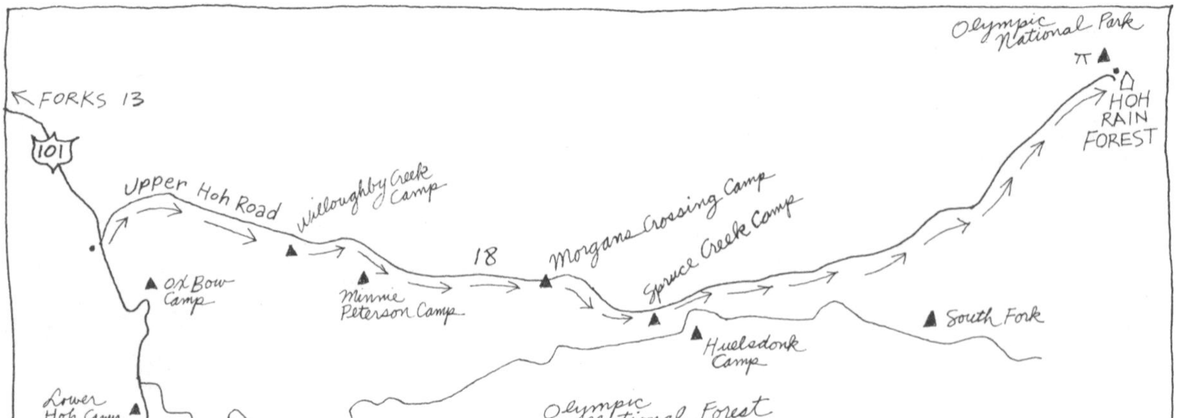

Olympic National Park
HOH RAIN FOREST
FORKS 13
101
Upper Hoh Road
Willoughby Creek Camp
18
Morgans Crossing Camp
Spruce Creek Camp
Ox Bow Camp
Minnie Peterson Camp
South Fork
Huelsdonk Camp
Lower Hoh Camp
Olympic National Forest
Lower Hoh Road
101
KALALOCH 20

## The Queets Corridor road

The road following Queets River runs through a deep rain forest. At the end of the corridor I have a fine view of the Queets. A sign at the beginning of a hike from here states, "You must ford the Queets River first before taking the trail. It is wide and rocky and you must choose a good spot since it changes from year to year. After a rainfall it might be too difficult to ford."

Trails go up the Queets River or branch off along Tshletshy Creek to the North Fork of the Quinault River.

The road to Hoh Rain Forest is another that must be experienced. At Hoh there are short walks one can take to see epiphytes (air plants) in profusion and thick draperies of club moss, giant Sitka spruce, hemlock, fir, red cedar, and red alder. All this green glory is supported by about 142 inches of rain each year in the Hoh Valley.

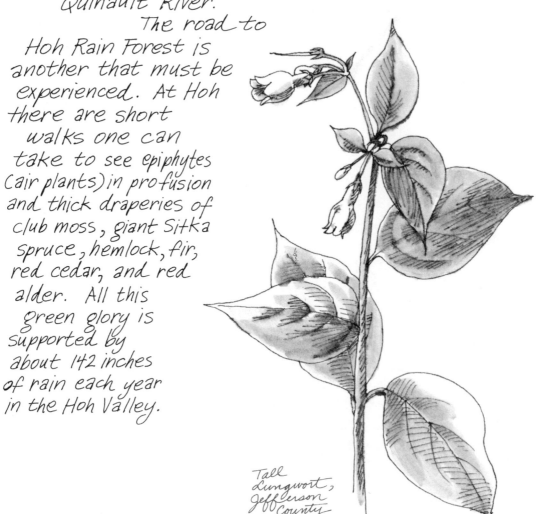

Rain forest, Queets Corridor, Jefferson County

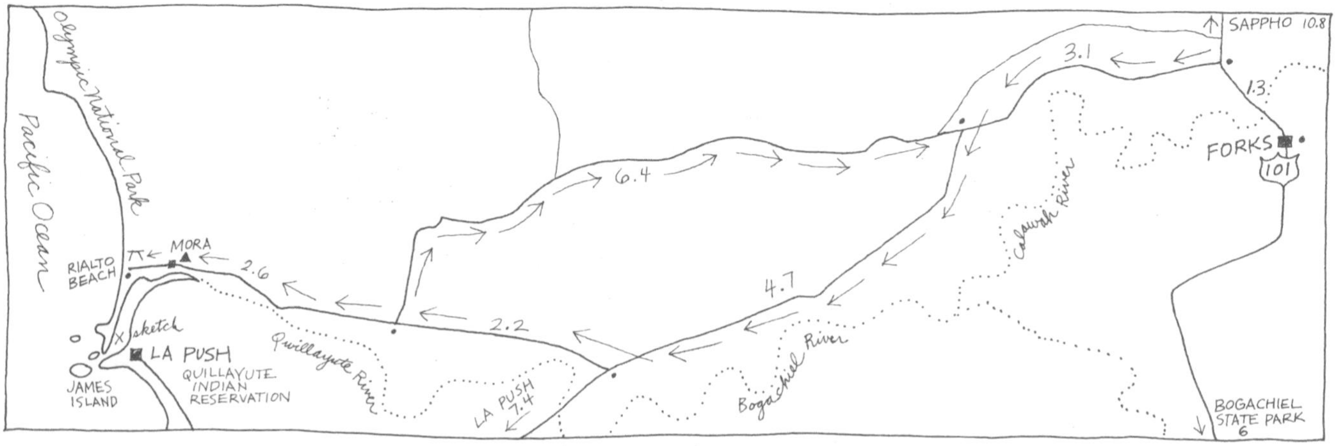
SAPPHO 10.8
3.1
1.3
FORKS
101
6.4
Olympic National Park
Pacific Ocean
Calawah River
MORA
RIALTO BEACH
2.6
4.7
2.2
x sketch
LA PUSH
QUILLAYUTE INDIAN RESERVATION
JAMES ISLAND
Quillayute River
LA PUSH 7.4
Bogachiel River
BOGACHIEL STATE PARK 6

## The road to the mouth of the Quillayute

It is a fast back road through the forest to the beach opposite La Push at the mouth of the Quillayute. The village looks inviting from the Rialto Beach side, near Mora. Once there, however, it isn't quite as picturesque, although the fishing boats and wharf activity lend some excitement to the town. I sketch James Island across the Quillayute and a fishing boat bringing in its catch.

Mora Beach has naturalist walks and trails leading to other beaches, which are separated by bold, rocky headlands.

# Lake Ozette back road

No road at all reached Ozette until about 1930.. The Scandinavians who homesteaded the area had to pack in along the Hoko River trail. Now the road follows the Hoko River and Big River to tranquil Lake Ozette. Here trail heads begin to Sand Point and to Cape Alava. Excavations are being made just north of the cape, where an Ozette Indian village was buried by mud some four hundred years ago.

Lake Ozette, Clallam County

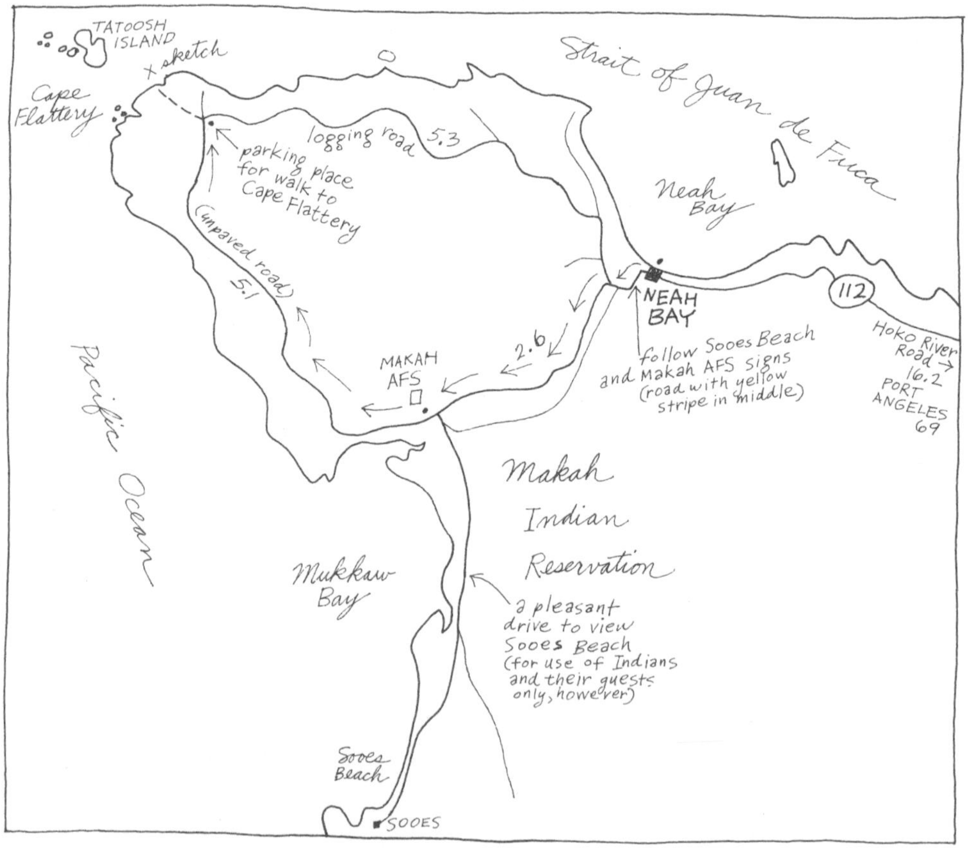
TATOOSH ISLAND
x sketch
Strait of Juan de Fuca
Cape Flattery
logging road
5.3
parking place for walk to Cape Flattery
Neah Bay
(unpaved road)
5.1
NEAH BAY
112
2.6
MAKAH AFS
follow Sooes Beach and Makah AFS signs (road with yellow stripe in middle)
Hoko River Road 16.2 →
PORT ANGELES 69
Pacific Ocean
Makah Indian Reservation
Mukkaw Bay
a pleasant drive to view Sooes Beach (for use of Indians and their guests only, however)
Sooes Beach
SOOES

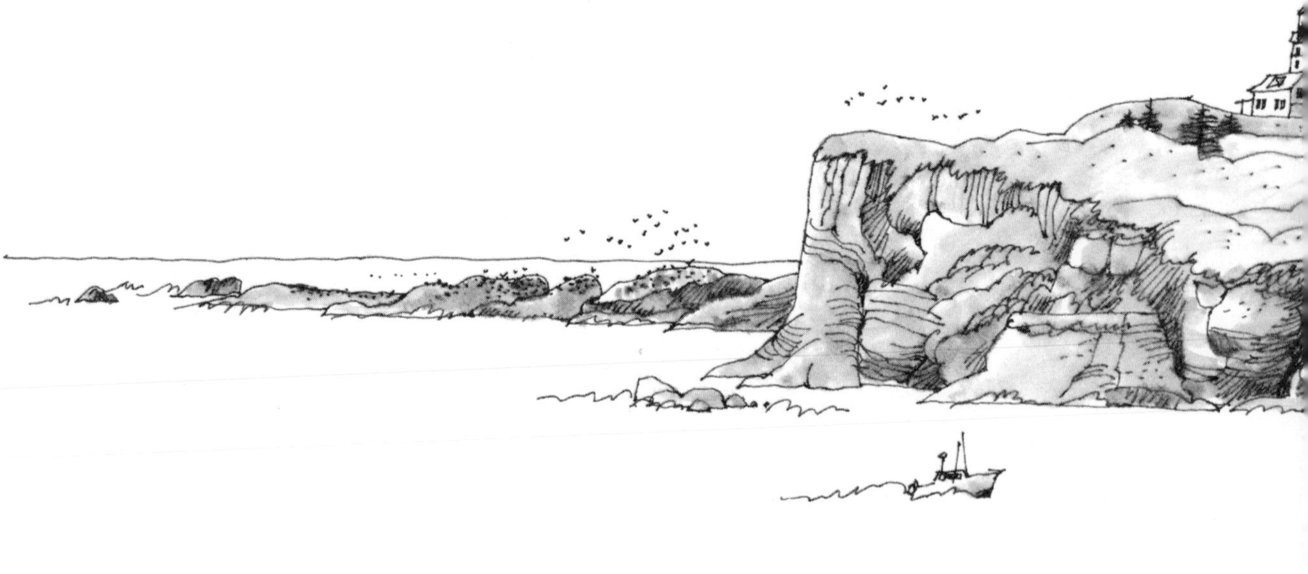

## The road to Cape Flattery

It is foggy along the Strait of Juan de Fuca; so I am surprised and pleased to find Cape Flattery in bright sunshine. The trail to the dramatic viewpoint is a root-strewn path. The roots spread out from the base of ancient red cedars and sitka spruce. Scores of boats pass by, including a black-hulled sailing ship. A young bald eagle pursued by seabirds flies to cover in the forest. Feeling a part of all the drama, I sketch the island from a cliffside perch, as Tatoosh's lighthouse horn booms a mournful cry across the sunlit sea.

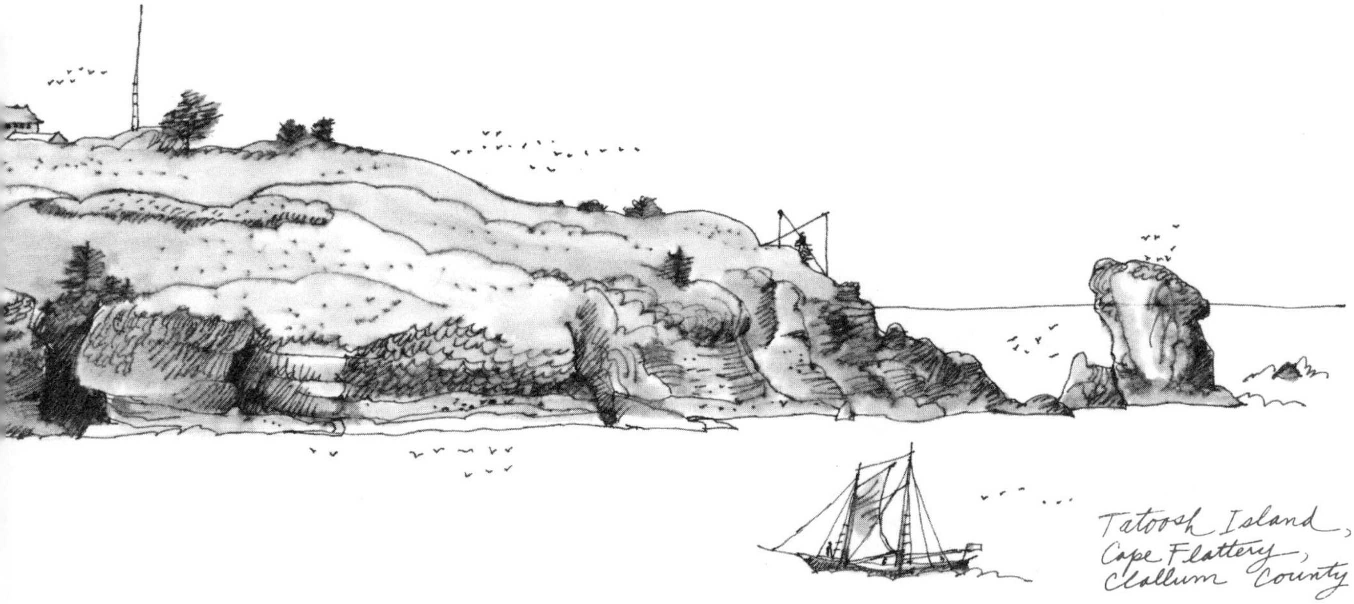

Tatoosh Island, Cape Flattery, Clallum County

## The road to Obstruction Point

The road to Soleduck, the road along the Elwha River, and the road to Hurricane Ridge are beautiful trips and easily driven. The road to Obstruction Point, which takes off from Hurricane Ridge, is bumpy and steep at times. There are astonishing vistas to enjoy, including an expansive view of Puget Sound with snow-capped Mount Baker on the horizon.

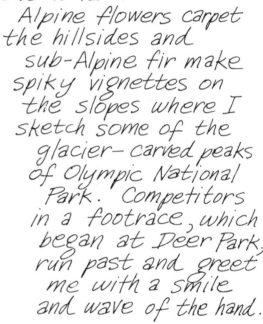

Alpine flowers carpet the hillsides and sub-Alpine fir make spiky vignettes on the slopes where I sketch some of the glacier-carved peaks of Olympic National Park. Competitors in a footrace, which began at Deer Park, run past and greet me with a smile and wave of the hand.

Avalanche Lily, Clallum County

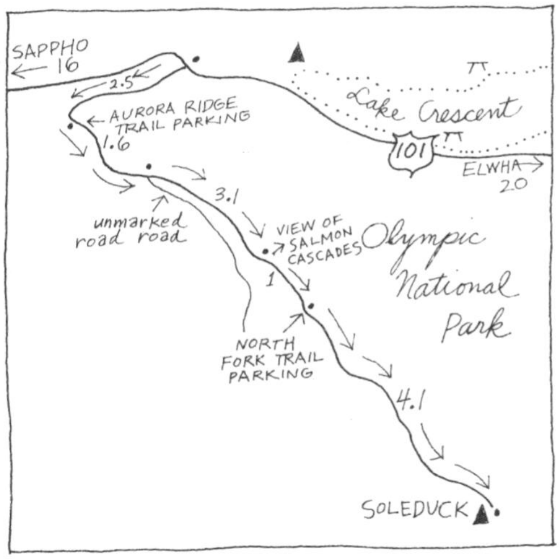
SAPPHO 16
2.5
AURORA RIDGE TRAIL PARKING
1.6
Lake Crescent
101
ELWHA 20
3.1
unmarked road road
VIEW OF SALMON CASCADES
Olympic National Park
1
NORTH FORK TRAIL PARKING
4.1
SOLEDUCK

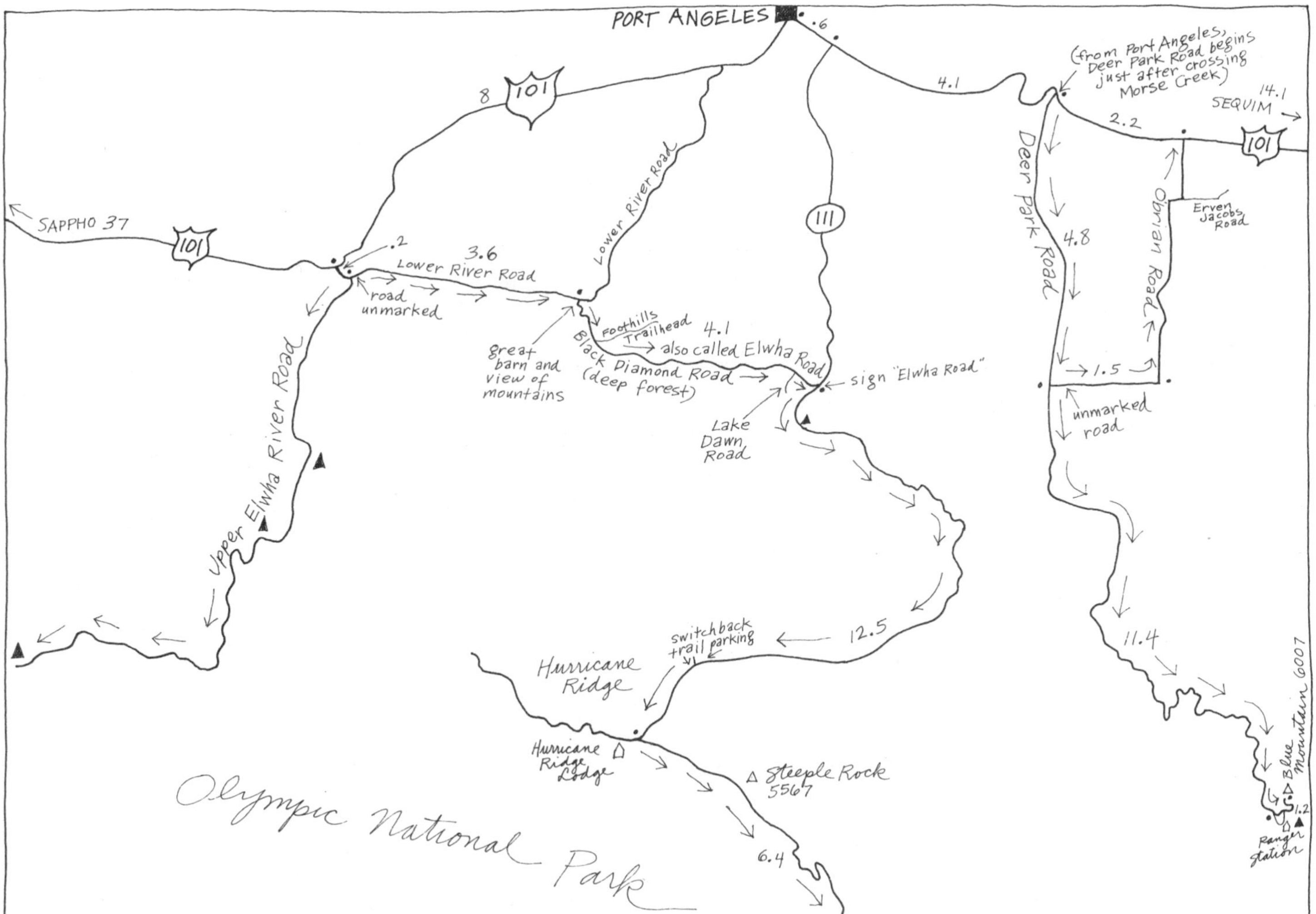
PORT ANGELES
.6
8
101
4.1
(from Port Angeles, Deer Park Road begins just after crossing Morse Creek)
14.1
SEQUIM
2.2
101
SAPPHO 37
101
Lower River Road
111
Deer Park Road
Obrian Road
Erven Jacobs Road
.2
3.6
Lower River Road
road unmarked
4.8
Foothills Trailhead
4.1
also called Elwha Road
Black Diamond Road (deep forest)
great barn and view of mountains
sign "Elwha Road"
1.5
Upper Elwha River Road
Lake Dawn Road
unmarked road
12.5
switchback trail parking
Hurricane Ridge
11.4
Blue Mountain 6007
Hurricane Ridge Lodge
Steeple Rock 5567
1.2
Ranger station
Olympic National Park
6.4
Obstruction Peak 6450
(Trails begin from here from .3 miles to 19.8 miles)
sketch X

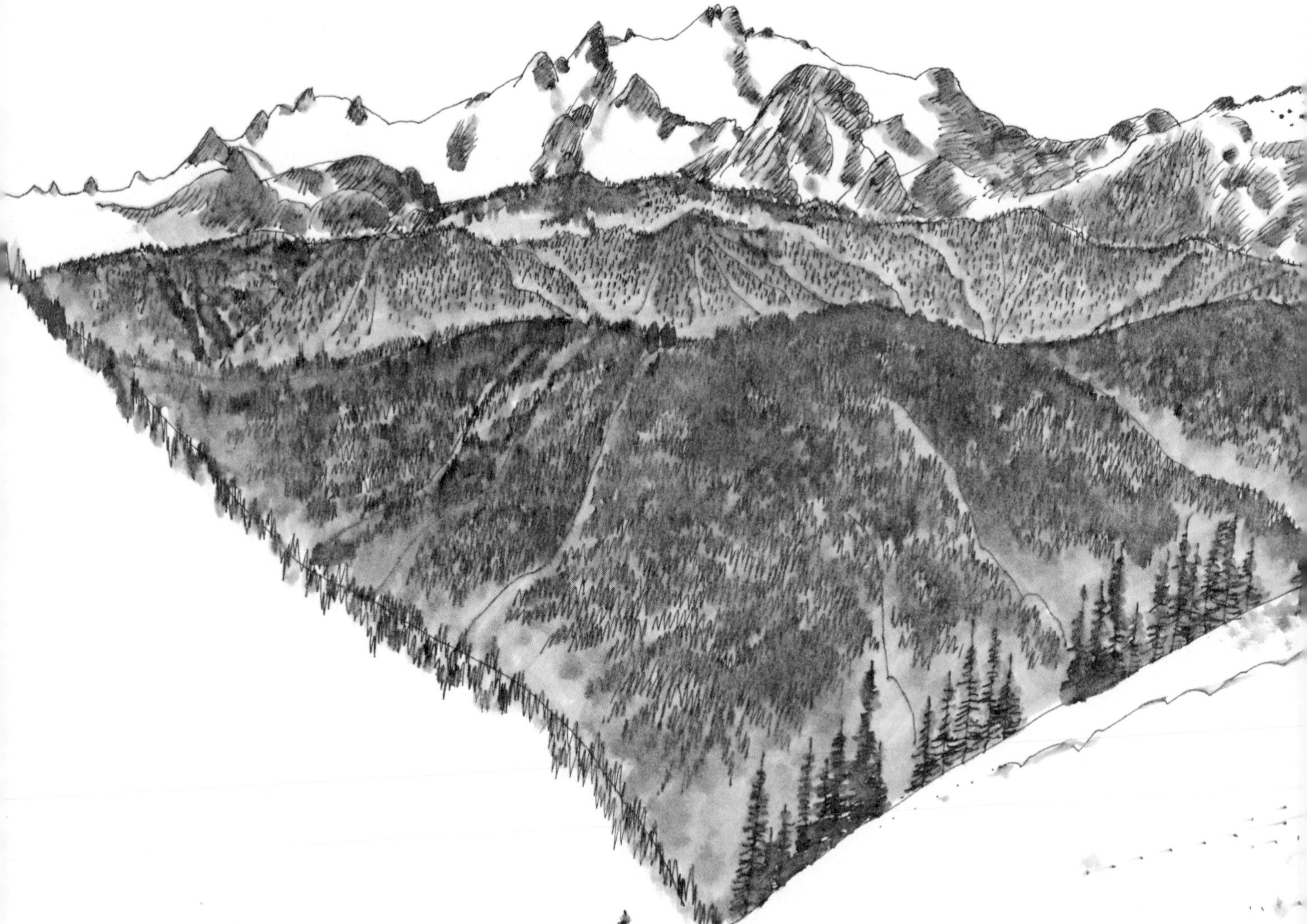

Mt. Olympus
from Obstruction Point,
Clallum County

Piper Bell, found only in Olympic National Park

Bush Cinquefoil, Blue Mountain, Olympic National Park

# Deer Park Road to Blue Mountain

The sharp, upthrust peaks of the Olympic Range are some 70 million years old but, geologically, they are considered new mountains. The serious exploration of the Olympics began in 1889 when James Christie, financed by a Seattle newspaper, led a trip into the mountains.

From time to time the passing of oncoming vehicles requires great caution on the narrow road toward the top of Blue Mountain. At the crest, on that pleasant clear day, I let time slip away and forget my own concerns, as I look out on the spaciousness of nature. In their rock crevice habitat I sketch buttery yellow cinquefoil and pale lavender piper bell, found only in Olympic National Park.

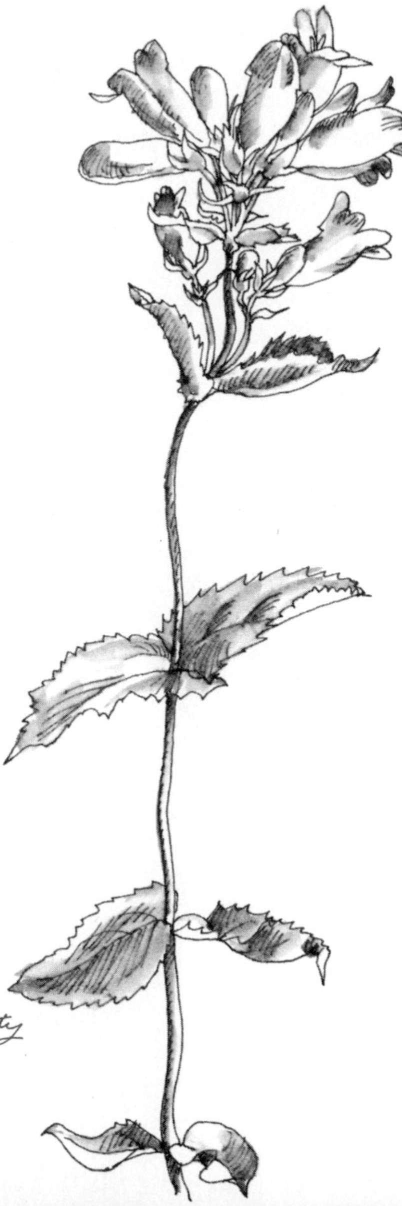

Lowbush Penstemon, Clallum County

## The road from Port Gamble

Port Gamble, a historic mill town on a bluff overlooking the Hood Canal, was built by settlers to resemble their beloved East Machias, Maine. Saint Paul's Episcopal Church, 1870, was modeled after the Congregational Church of East Machias. The steeple bell arrived by sailing vessel in 1879 and still calls people to worship on Sundays. I enjoy reading sentimental epitaphs in the shaded graveyard overlooking the canal. One reads, "Shed not for her the bitter tear / Nor give the heart to vain regret / T'is but the casket that lies here / The gem that filled it sparkles yet."

St. Paul's Church, Port Gamble, Kitsap County

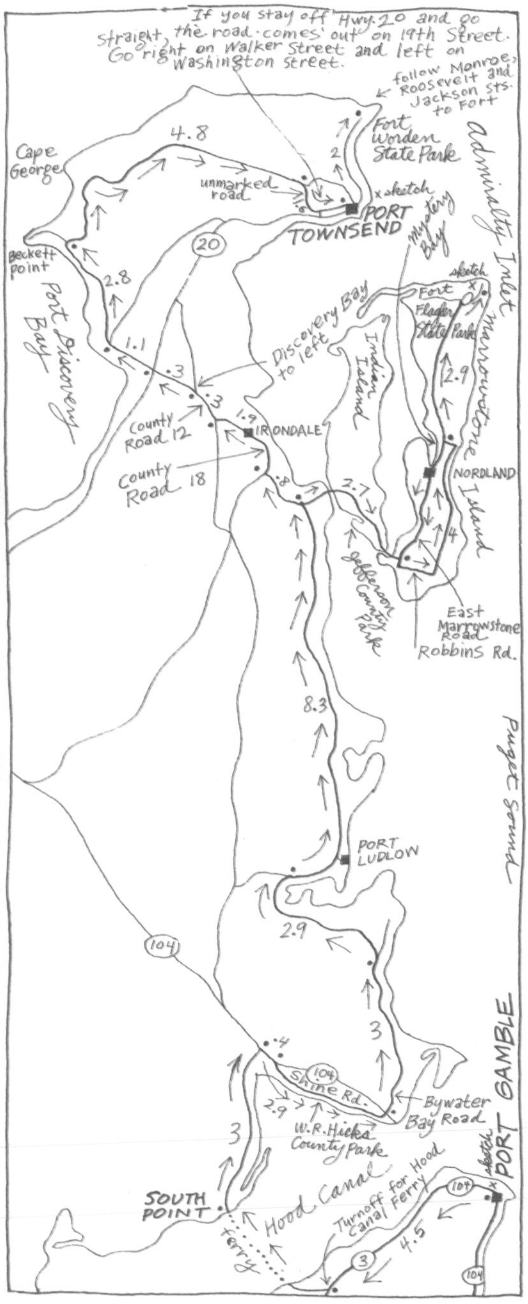
If you stay off Hwy. 20 and go straight, the road comes out on 19th Street. Go right on Walker Street and left on Washington Street.
follow Monroe, Roosevelt and Jackson Sts. to Fort
Fort Worden State Park
Admiralty Inlet
Cape George
4.8
2
unmarked road
x sketch
PORT TOWNSEND
20
Mystery Bay
Beckett point
2.8
Port Discovery Bay
sketch
Fort Flagler State Park
Marrowstone Island
Discovery Bay to left
Indian Island
1.1
.3
.3
2.9
1.9
IRONDALE
County Road 12
County Road 18
NORDLAND
.8
2.7
.4
Jefferson County Park
East Marrowstone Road
Robbins Rd.
8.3
Puget Sound
PORT LUDLOW
2.9
104
3
.4
104
Shine Rd.
Bywater Bay Road
2.9
W.R. Hicks County Park
3
PORT GAMBLE
Hood Canal
SOUTH POINT
ferry
Turnoff for Hood Canal Ferry
104
3
4.5
104

The old lighthouse, Marrowstone Island, Jefferson County

## a trip to Marrowstone Island

In 1792 Captain George Vancouver of the Royal British Navy charted the entrance to Puget Sound and found that the high bluffs of the island there looked as if they were composed of marrow stone. (The island was named after this material.) Fort Flagler State Park is situated on the north end of the island and, while there, I draw a view of the 1895 lighthouse, Puget Sound, and Mount Baker. Many of the original buildings of Fort Flagler, founded in 1887, are still standing and are part of the fascination of Marrowstone Island.

Road to Port Townsend

There is a sign, hand-painted by the ranger, at Rothschild House in Port Townsend. It says, "111 YEARS OLD. MOST ITEMS ORIGINAL. ENTRY WALL-PAPER—1891, PARLOR—1885. YOUNGEST DAUGHTER LIVED HERE 78 YEARS, LAST 36 ALONE. MR. R. OWNED GEN. STORE DOWN TOWN. 5 CHILDREN, 3 GRAND. YOUNGEST SON GAVE HOUSE TO STATE PARKS IN 1958. A NICE FAMILY MEMORIAL!"

Port Townsend was named by Captain George Vancouver in 1792 in honor of the Marquis of Townshend. It has many buildings and houses of historic interest and is picturesquely situated on a bluff overlooking the bay and Admiralty Inlet.

Fort Worden State Park nearby, with its fort buildings and old lighthouse, is also quite interesting.

Henry's original stove, Rothschild House, Port Townsend, Jefferson County

Disappearing (it swings down out of sight) Carriage gun, Fort Casey, Island County

## Fort Casey to Coupeville and Oak Harbor

Big gun emplacements overlook Admiralty Inlet and point at passing ships. While I sketch, a work party of young people are painting the guns, which glisten in their new olive gray coat. The old lighthouse is now a display center, with photographs and historical material.

There are three state parks on Whidbey Island: Fort Casey, South Whidbey, and Deception Pass.

If you pick up an Island County map you may investigate all the roads on quiet, agricultural Whidbey Island.

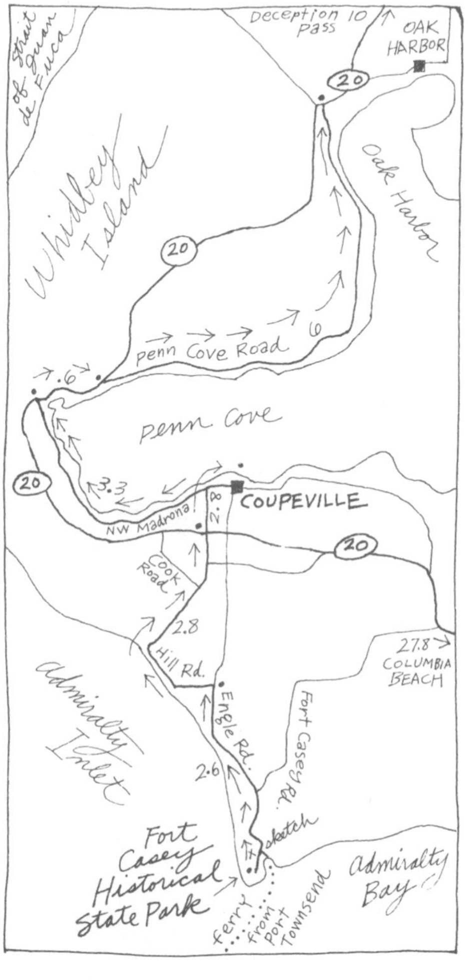

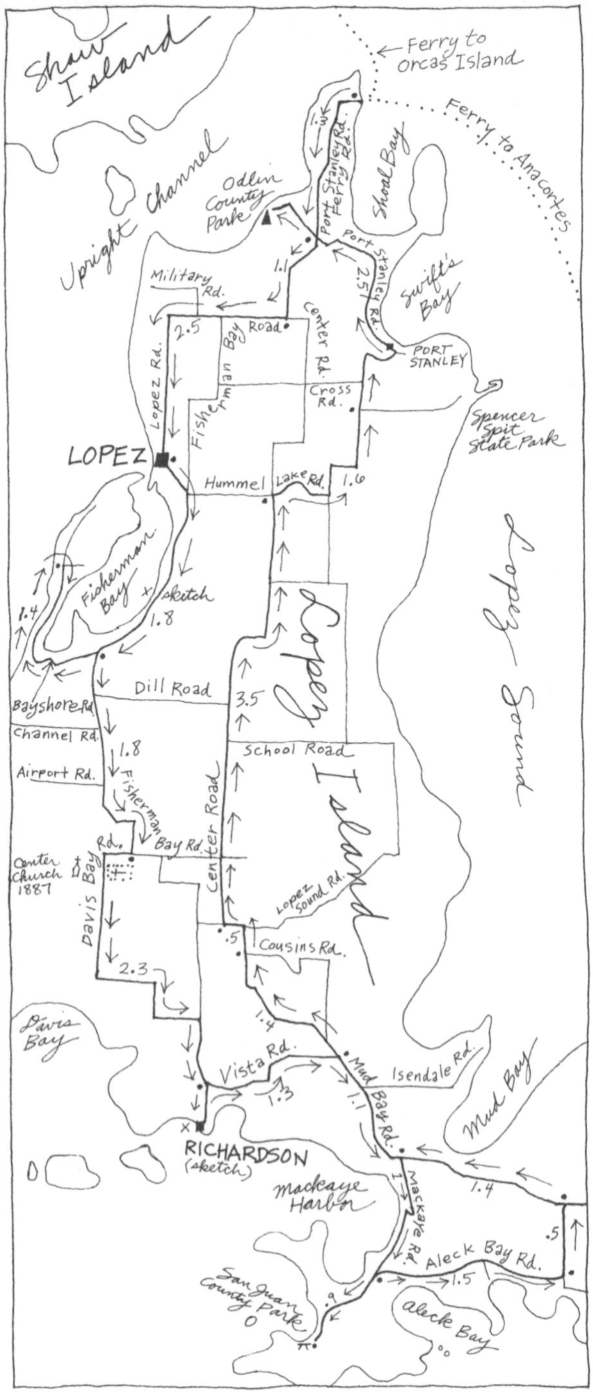
Shaw Island
Ferry to Orcas Island
Ferry to Anacortes
Upright Channel
Odlin County Park
Shoal Bay
Port Stanley Rd.
Ferry Rd.
Swift's Bay
PORT STANLEY
Military Rd.
Fisherman Bay Road
Center Rd.
Lopez Rd.
Cross Rd.
Spencer Spit State Park
LOPEZ
Hummel Lake Rd.
Fisherman Bay
sketch
Lopez Island
Lopez Sound
Dill Road
Bayshore Rd.
Channel Rd.
Airport Rd.
School Road
Center Road
Fisherman Bay Rd.
Center Church 1887
Davis Bay Rd.
Lopez Sound Rd.
Cousins Rd.
Davis Bay
Vista Rd.
Mud Bay Rd.
Isendale Rd.
Mud Bay
RICHARDSON
(sketch)
Mackaye Harbor
Mackaye Rd.
Aleck Bay Rd.
San Juan County Park
Aleck Bay

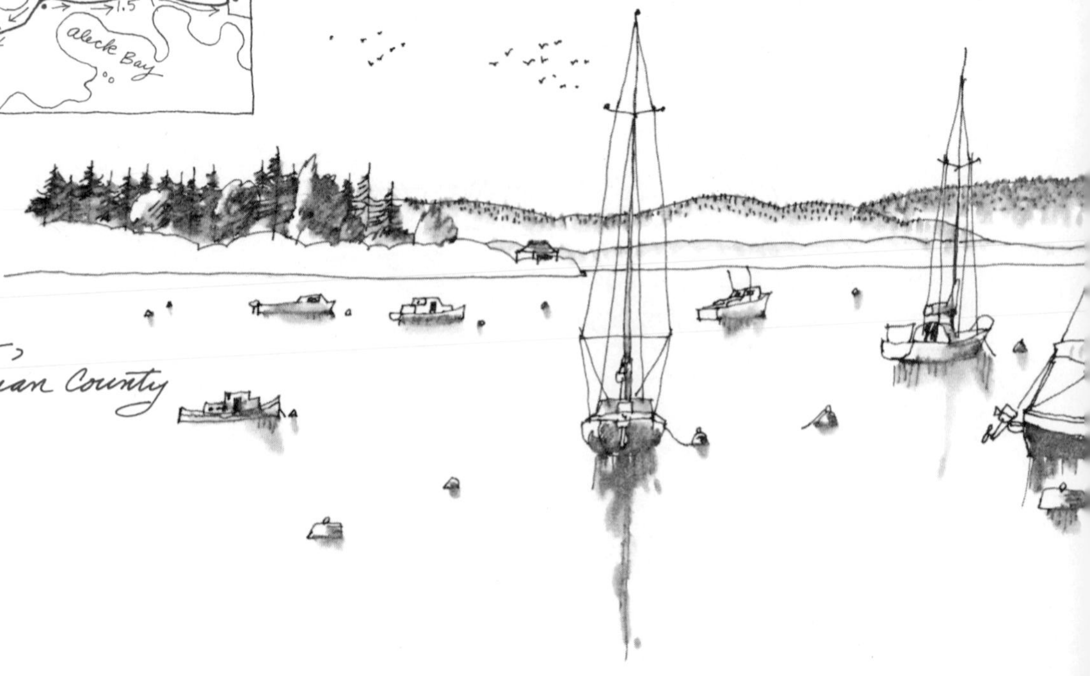

*Fisherman Bay, Lopez Island, San Juan County*

*Back road on Lopez Island*

It is incredibly calm at Fisherman Bay in the early morning. Motorboats have not started up as yet and the cries of seabirds resound across the water.

At Richardson I sketch the Richardson General Store. A friendly place, its shelves and tables are crowded with groceries, dry goods, sundries, and hardware. The village was settled by George Richardson, who established a farm there about 1870. A lively fishing port around 1900, it is now again a quiet and serene village.

Richardson General Store,
Lopez Island, San Juan County

# Orcas Island Road

On the way to Orcas Island the ferry stops at the charming, well-tended, flower-bedecked dock at Shaw Island. Nuns are arriving to open the little chapel on the pier. This island, although quite lovely, seems somewhat private, and I continue on to Orcas.

Orcas is the largest of the 172 islands that comprise the archipelago of the San Juans. I drive to the top of the 2,400-foot Mount Constitution for views of the islands and mainland beyond. A sign from the 1890s declares this to be "the finest marine view in all of North America." A stone tower at the top, built in the 1930s, was patterned after 12th-century European watchtowers. Its architect had this message engraved in metal at the site: "To him who restores, my sincere commendation. To one who would alter, eternal damnation." Ellsworth Storey, 1936.

Orcas Island ferry, San Juan County

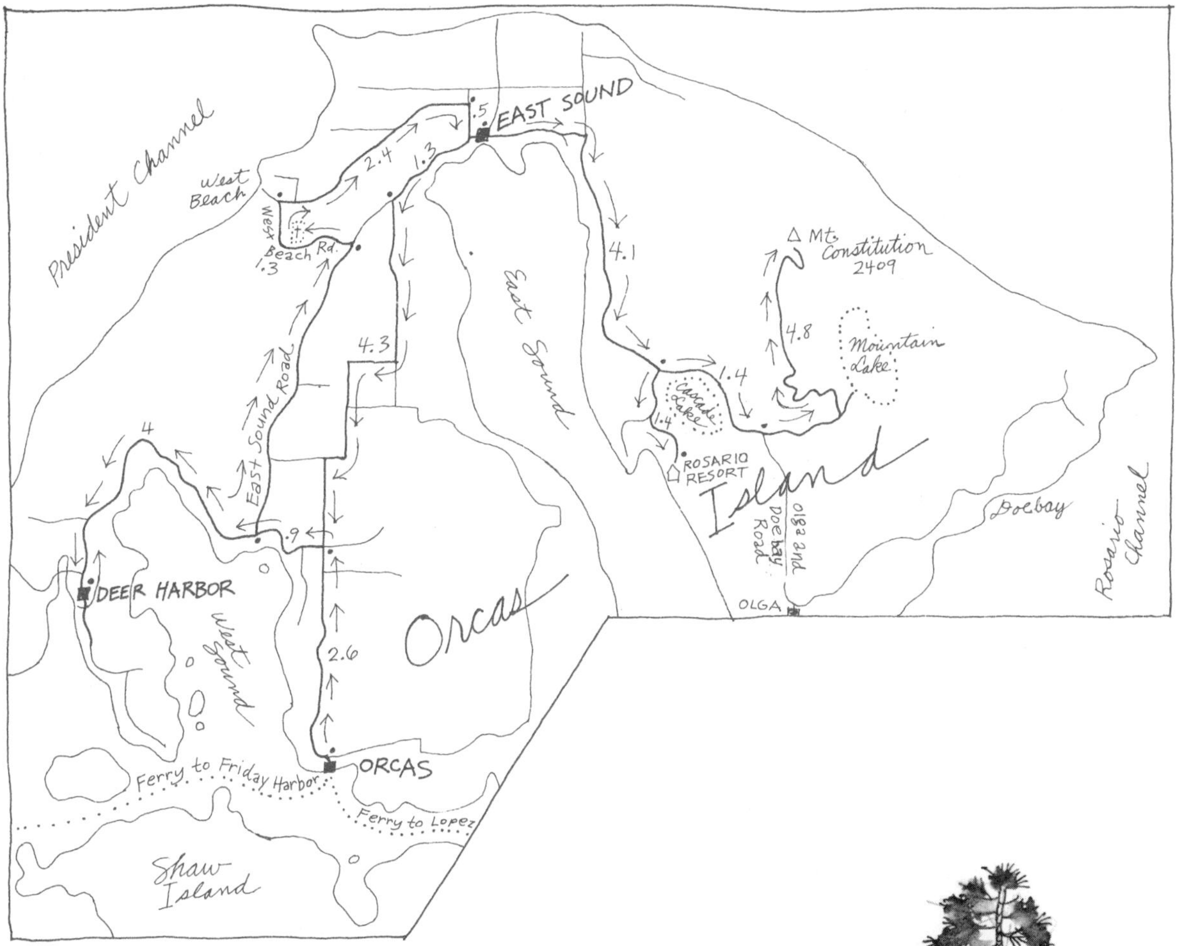
President Channel
West Beach
West Beach Rd.
1.3
2.4
1.3
.5
EAST SOUND
4.1
Mt. Constitution 2409
4.8
Mountain Lake
1.4
Cascade Lake
1.4
ROSARIO RESORT
East Sound
Island
Olga and Doe bay Road
Doebay
Rosario Channel
OLGA
4.3
East Sound Road
4
.9
DEER HARBOR
West Sound
Orcas
2.6
ORCAS
Ferry to Friday Harbor
Ferry to Lopez
Shaw Island

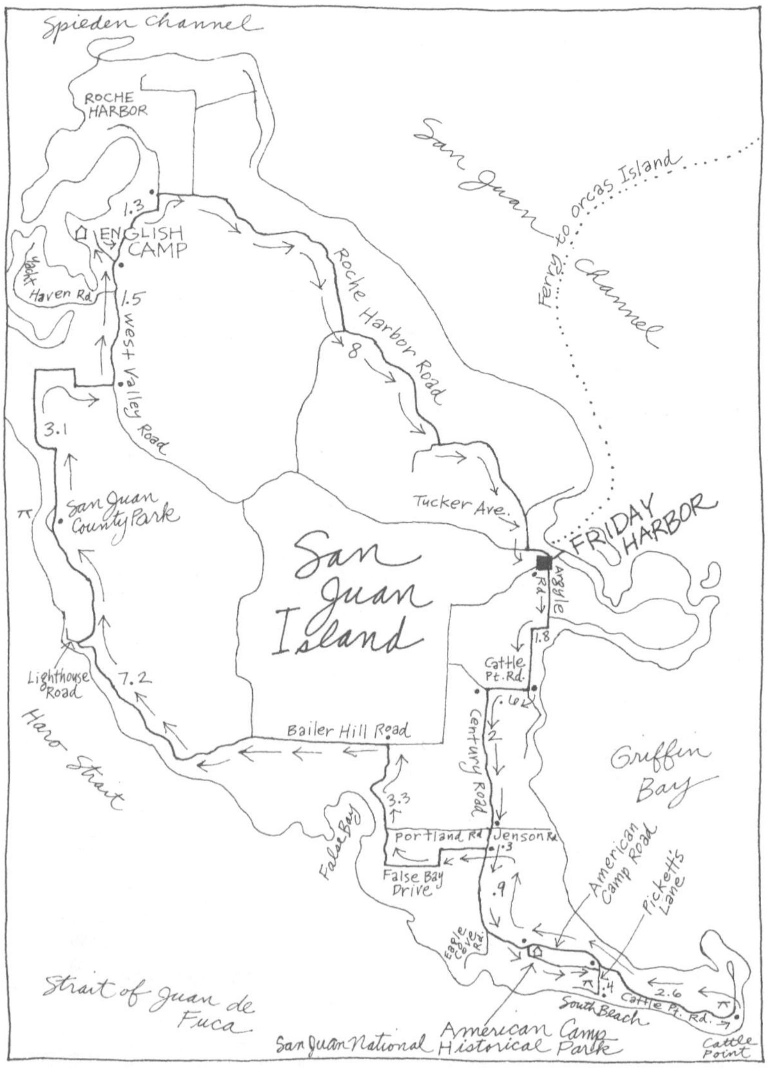
Spieden channel
ROCHE HARBOR
1.3
ENGLISH CAMP
Haven Rd
1.5
West Valley Road
3.1
San Juan County Park
Lighthouse Road
7.2
Haro Strait
Roche Harbor Road
8
San Juan Channel
Ferry to Orcas Island
Tucker Ave.
FRIDAY HARBOR
San Juan Island
Argyle Rd.
1.8
Cattle Pt. Rd.
.6
Bailer Hill Road
Century Road
2
Griffin Bay
3.3
Portland Rd
Jenson Rd
.3
False Bay
False Bay Drive
.9
American Camp Road
Pickett's Lane
.4
2.6
Cattle Pt. Rd.
South Beach
Cattle Point
Strait of Juan de Fuca
American Camp
San Juan National Historical Park

Fort English, San Juan Island,
San Juan County

# Roads of San Juan

At the National Park on the road around the island there is a historical display. At South Beach the shore is long and strewn with water-worn logs. Farther on is a good view of False Bay with the Olympic mountain range in the background. With the tide out, there are plenty of tide pools to inspect.

At English Camp I sketch the blockhouse built around 1860 when the old fort was in its heyday. The British flag is still flown here, respecting the peaceful settlement of a border dispute in which they declared the San Juan Islands to be American rather than Canadian land. There is a grove of magnificent maple trees nearby, and the ranger tells me that one tree that has been core-tested is over three hundred years old.

## Road to La Conner and Mount Vernon

Colorful flower baskets ornament stores along the main street of the fishing village of La Conner. I sketch the town from across the Swinomish Channel. Gaches Mansion, a twenty-two-room historic house on Second Street, is at top left in the picture, and a big blue-and-white sockeye salmon purse seiner boat is in the foreground.

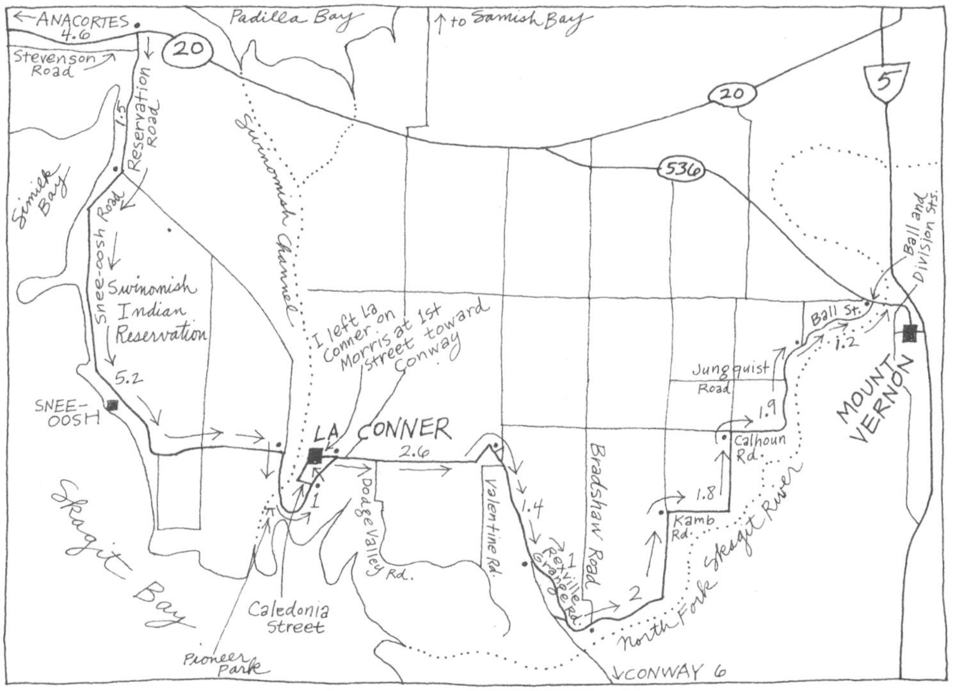


A Swinomish Indian boy, who watches me draw, tells me proudly that he has an eighteen-foot boat with which he fishes for king salmon. Just then a large pleasure boat passes with an auxiliary boat perched on it. "Lotsa cash for that," he says, "the boat on the stern is as big as mine."

The purse seiner is being readied for sea and, before I finish my drawing, its crew waves good-bye to relatives ashore as it sails away.

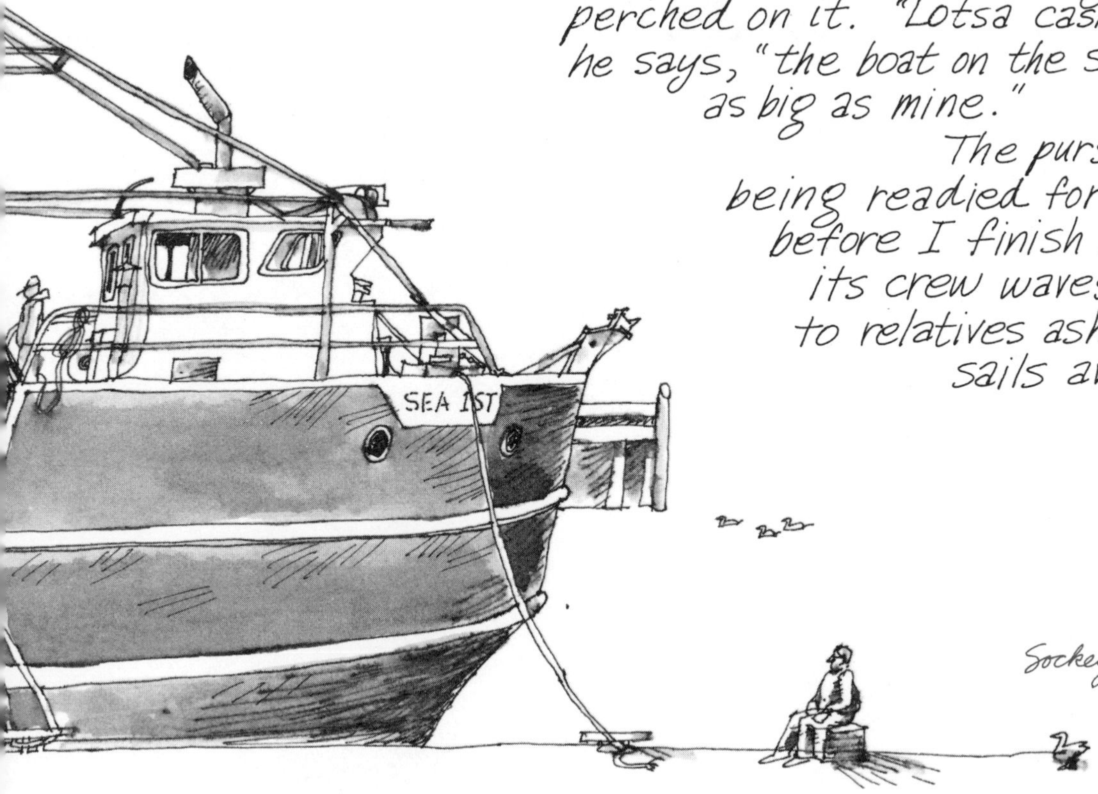

Sockeye Purse Seiner, La Conner, Skagit County

Samish Bay,
Skagit County

# Samish Bay road

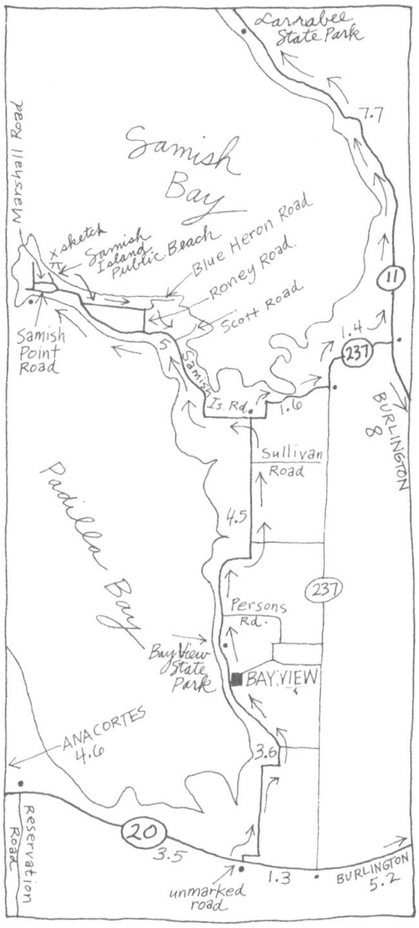


A steep wooden stairway goes to Samish Island Public Beach, which offers fifteen hundred feet of tideland for people's use. The bay is a spawning ground for the Pacific oyster, and intertidal hardshell clams and Dungeness crabs can be found at the beach at low tide.

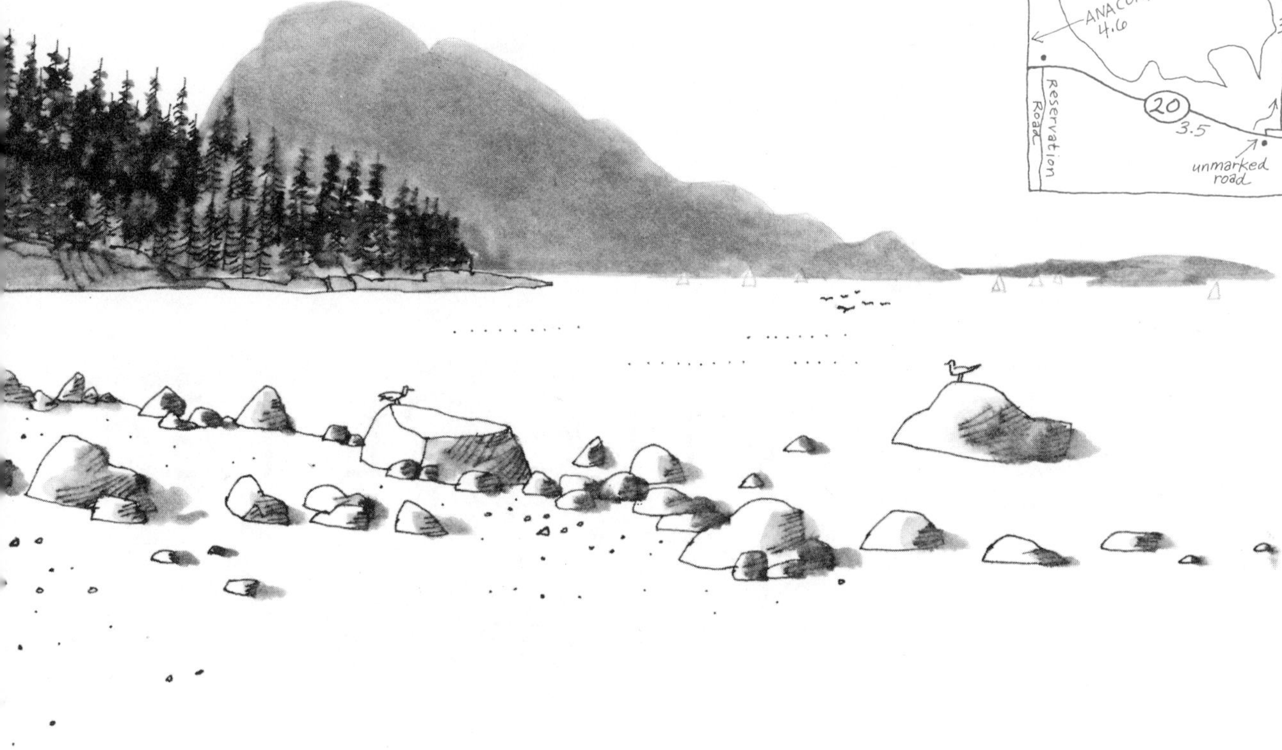

This beach of rocks and barnacles is a most tranquil place. There is the faint hum of commerce in the distance, but the cries of seabirds fill the air. A great blue heron flies by and I can hear the air rush through its wings.

McCORMICK-DEERING
PAT

# The road to Lynden

The Peace Arch in Blaine commemorates the hundred years of open border shared by Canada and the United States between 1814 and 1914. After visiting the arch and its gardens, I drive through green, rolling meadowlands to Lynden. At Hans C. Berthusen Park, an ideal picnic spot, I draw the red barn shown on the next page with its bold white markings. Hans and Lida's old stump privy stands to the right of the barn. On the left is a 1906 threshing machine. Old tractors and antique farm machinery are arriving for Lynden's annual threshing bee and each engine makes its own "pock pock" sound.

I sketch a McCormick-Deering W61 tractor from the thirties, nicknamed "The Outhouse" after its boxlike homemade cab.

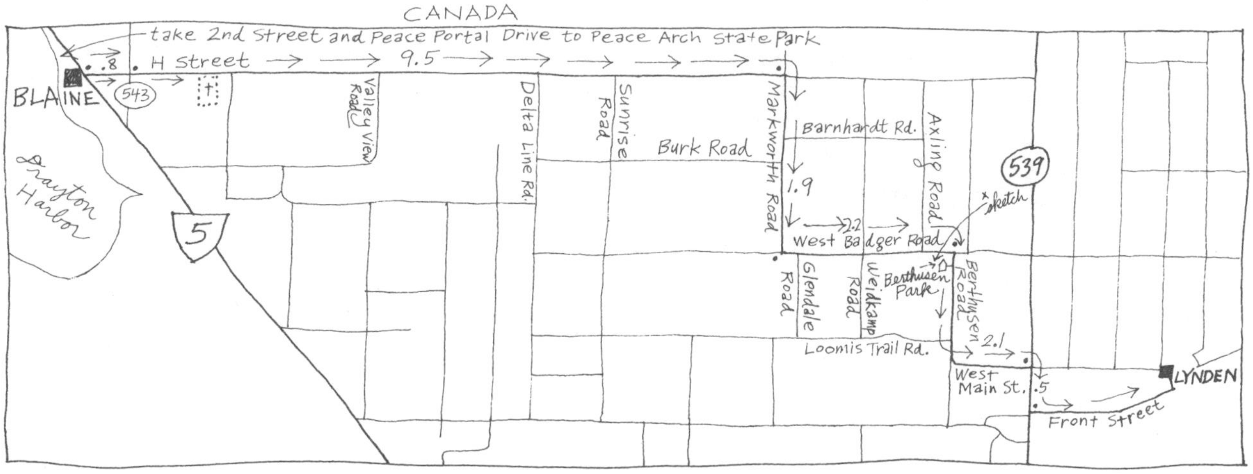


"The Outhouse",
Lynden, Whatcom County

*Berthusen Barn, Lynden, Whatcom County*

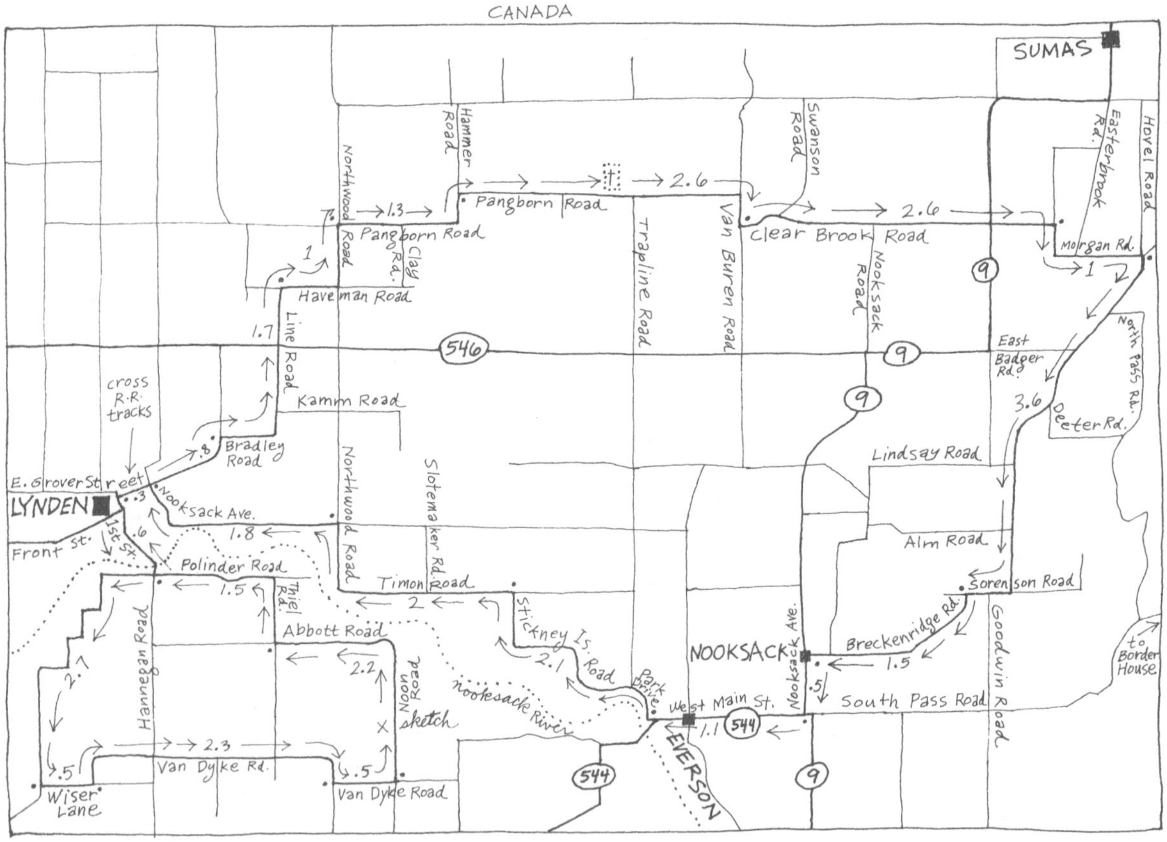

CANADA
SUMAS
LYNDEN
NOOKSACK
EVERSON
Pangborn Road
Clear Brook Road
Haveman Road
Kamm Road
Bradley Road
E. Grover Street
Nooksack Ave.
Front St.
1st St.
Polinder Road
Timon Road
Abbott Road
Van Dyke Rd.
Van Dyke Road
Wiser Lane
Hannegan Road
Northwood Road
Line Road
Hammer Road
Trapline Road
Van Buren Road
Swanson Road
Nooksack Road
Easterbrook Rd.
Hovel Road
Morgan Rd.
East Badger Rd.
North Pass Rd.
Deter Rd.
Lindsay Road
Alm Road
Sorenson Road
Breckenridge Rd.
Goodwin Road
South Pass Road
West Main St.
Stickney Is. Road
Park Drive
Slotemaker Rd.
Clay Rd.
Thiel Rd.
Noon Road
nooksack River
sketch
cross R.R. tracks
to Border House
546
544
9

## Roads around Lynden

The Dutch heritage of Lynden's settlers is reflected in the tidy character of its homes and farms. The neatness is enhanced by rows of flowers in gardens and window boxes. Big, handsome barns dot the green landscape. I sketch the graceful yellow-and-white Dykstra brothers' 1930s milking barn, which towers over the original barn. The new metal milking barn (not as picturesque) is to the left, out of my picture.

The Dykstra brothers' Barn, Whatcom County

## *The road to Border House*

This route touches the Canadian border, although no legal road continues from here into Canada. The proprietor of Border House has many a whimsical display for the enjoyment of visitors. The wagon and milk cans in my drawing are painted red, white, and blue. All the birds pictured are alive except the owl. A tour of the quaint, Greek Revival-style house includes a peek at the Teddy Roosevelt room, where he is supposed to have spent the night.

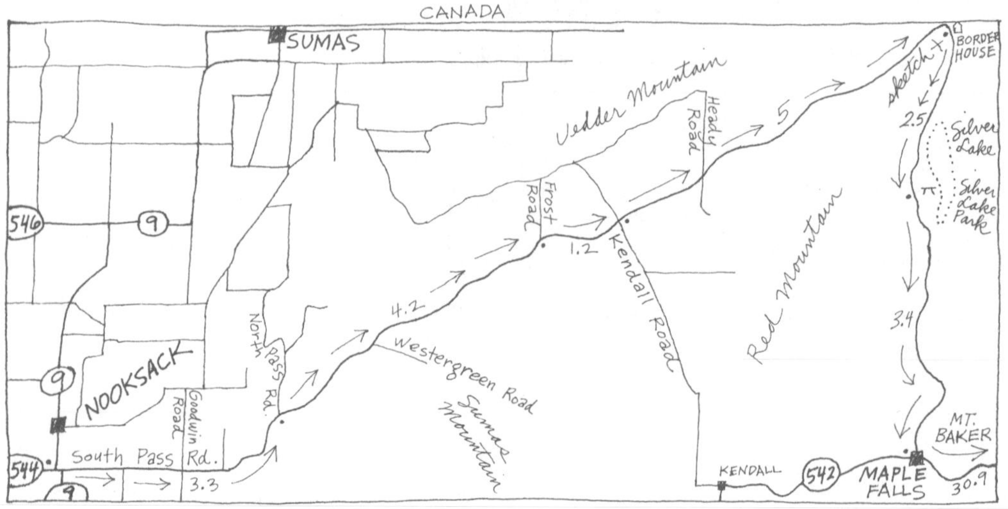


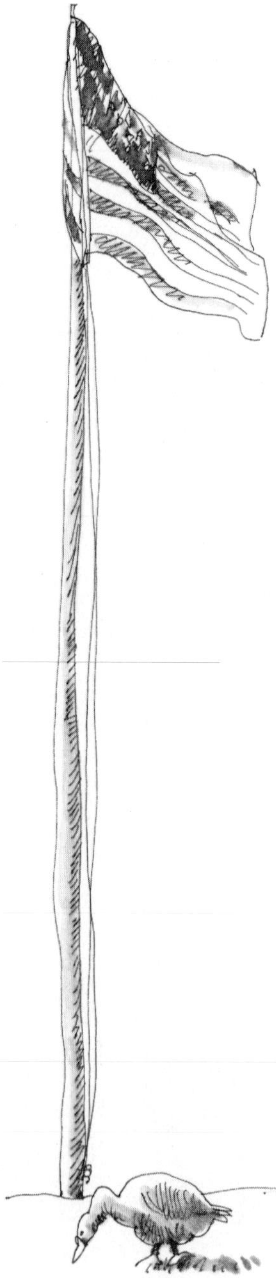

*Sign at Border House, Whatcom County*

Historical
Border House
BUILT IN 1902

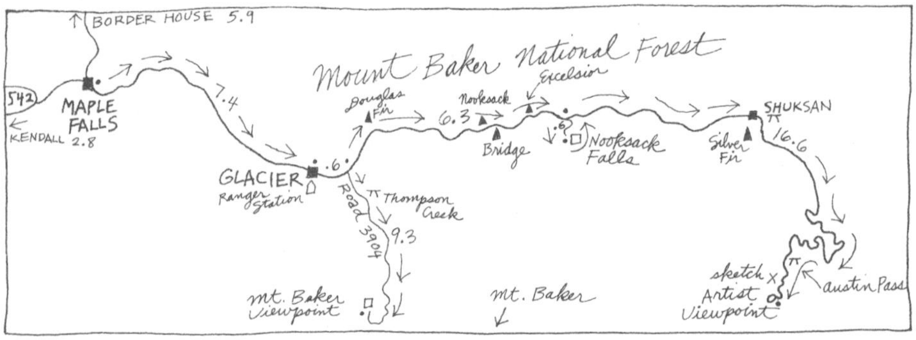
BORDER HOUSE 5.9
Mount Baker National Forest
542
MAPLE FALLS
KENDALL 2.8
7.4
Douglas Fir
Nooksack
Excelsior
6.3
Bridge
Nooksack Falls
SHUKSAN
Silver Fir
16.6
GLACIER
Ranger Station
.6
Road 3904
Thompson Creek
9.3
mt. Baker Viewpoint
mt. Baker
sketch
Artist Viewpoint
austin Pass

# The road to Mount Baker

A wet gravel road banked with snow leads to Artist Point, which is supposed to provide a good view of Mount Baker. Once there, I am enveloped in thick, misty clouds and only occasionally does a break appear in the rolling fogbanks. I decide not to go away empty-handed, however, so here you see a drawing of the foreground. You must drive to Artist Point to put mighty Mount Baker in the background and complete my picture!

Timber line, Mt. Baker, Whatcom County

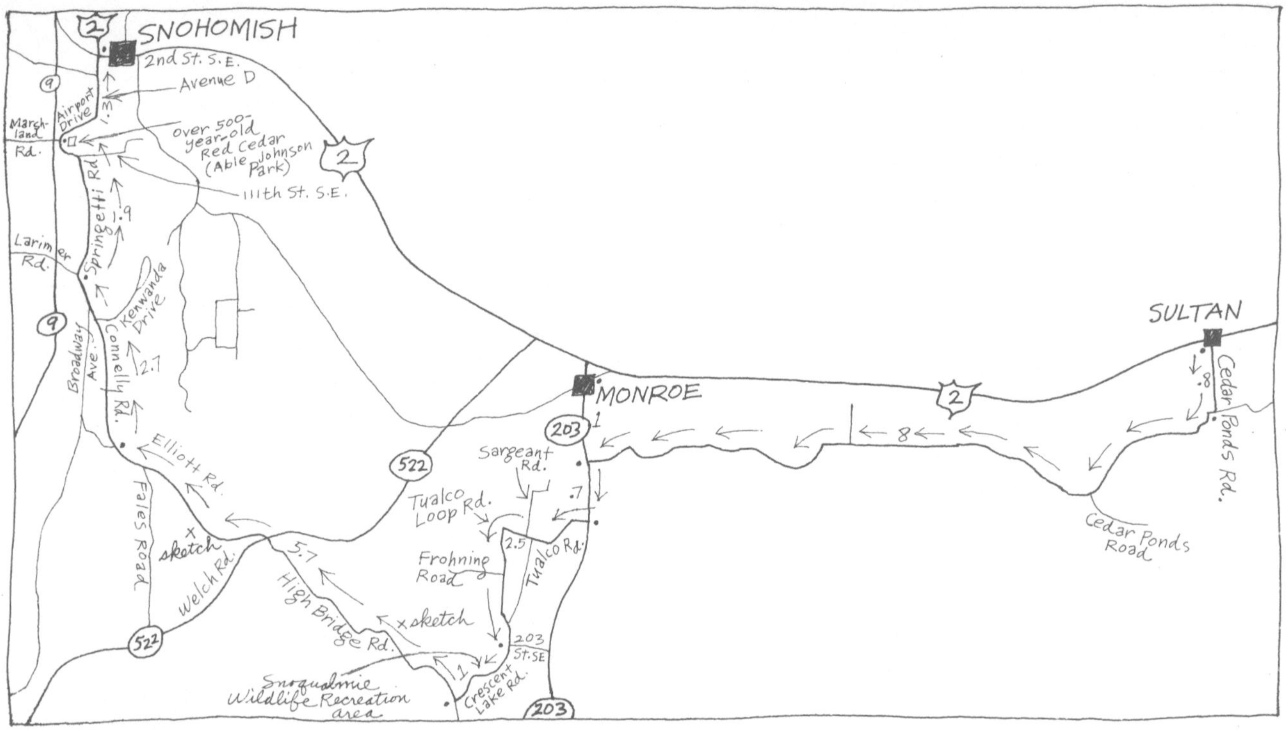


## *Back road from Sultan to Snohomish*

The road from Sultan follows the Skykomish River. From Tualco Road the scenery is green and hilly with dairy-country barns and farmhouses silhouetted against forest backgrounds. Along the way I sketch a small milking barn that has been fashioned into a house. At Ricville farm I draw a landscape encompassing most of the farm's buildings and some of the Holstein herd.

*Milking barn-house, near Monroe, Snohomish County*

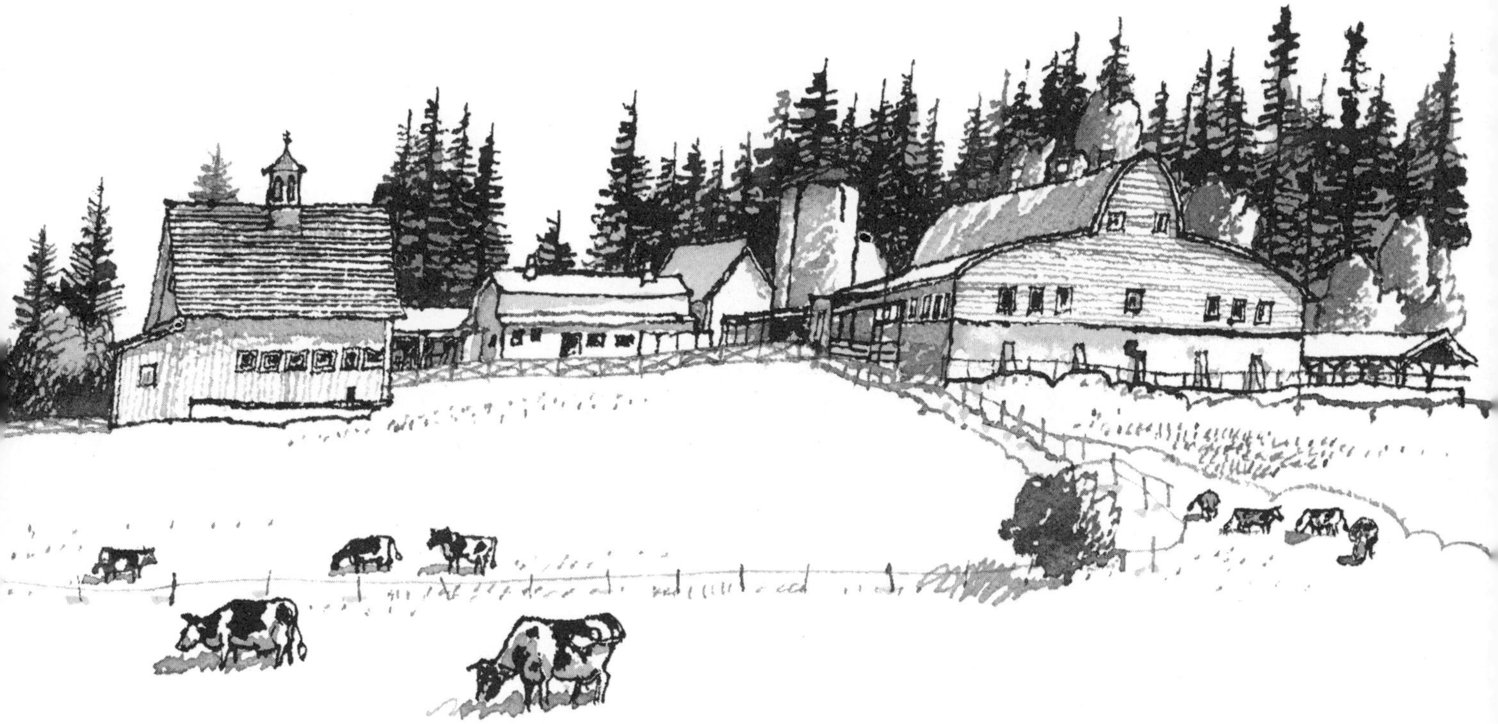

*Snohomish County farm*

Tom Thumb Grocery,
Granite Falls,
Snohomish County

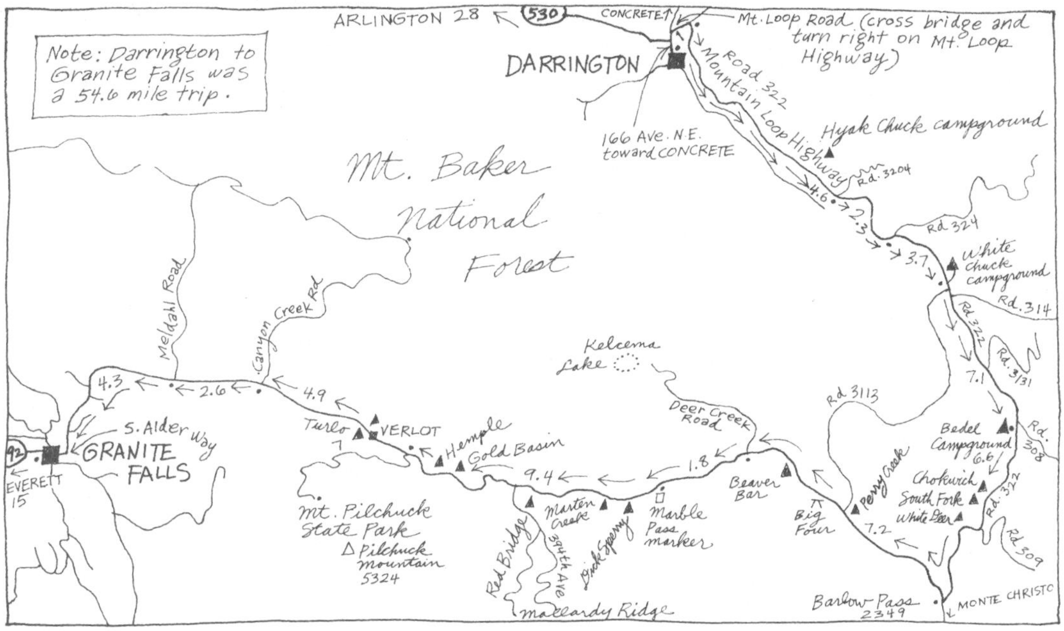


## Road to Granite Falls

From the lumber town of Darrington, this back road wanders through Mount Baker National Forest. Hemlock, big-leaf maple, vine maple, and alder flourish here. The trunks of the older white alder trees are spotted with green moss. When growing in profusion, they create incredibly intricate patterns in the forest. At Granite Falls I enjoy visiting the busy Tom Thumb Grocery and sketching its aging facade.

Self Heal (purple flowers), Snohomish County

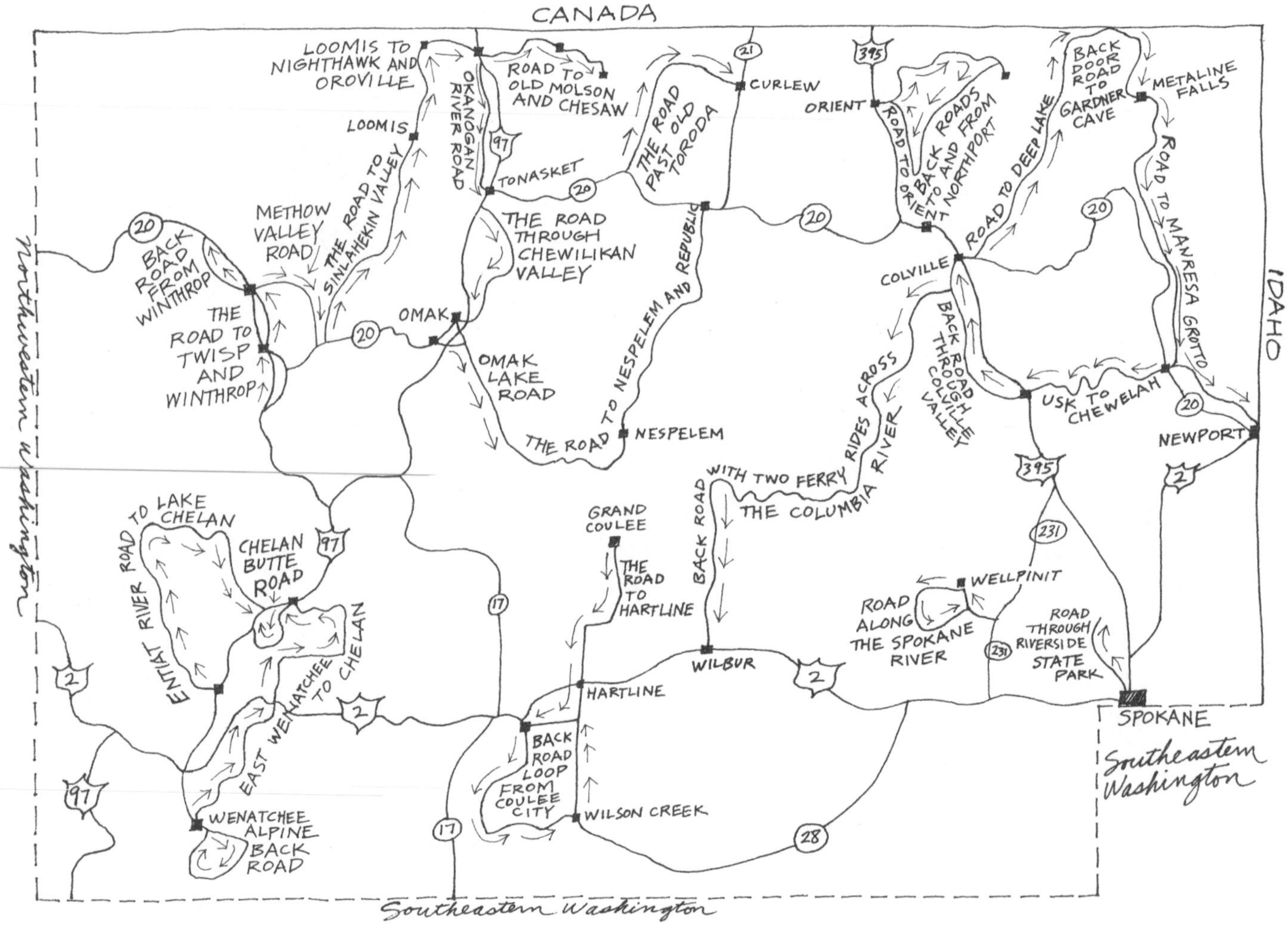
CANADA
IDAHO
Northwestern Washington
Southeastern Washington
Southeastern Washington
LOOMIS TO NIGHTHAWK AND OROVILLE
LOOMIS
OKANOGAN RIVER ROAD
ROAD TO OLD MOLSON AND CHESAW
TONASKET
THE ROAD PAST OLD TORODA
CURLEW
ORIENT
ROAD TO ORIENT
BACK ROADS TO AND FROM NORTHPORT
ROAD TO DEEP LAKE
BACK DOOR ROAD TO GARDNER CAVE
METALINE FALLS
ROAD TO MANRESA GROTTO
METHOW VALLEY ROAD
THE ROAD TO SINLAHEKIN VALLEY
BACK ROAD FROM WINTHROP
THE ROAD TO TWISP AND WINTHROP
THE ROAD THROUGH CHEWILIKAN VALLEY
OMAK
OMAK LAKE ROAD
THE ROAD TO NESPELEM AND REPUBLIC
NESPELEM
COLVILLE
BACK ROAD THROUGH COLVILLE VALLEY
BACK ROAD WITH TWO FERRY RIDES ACROSS THE COLUMBIA RIVER
USK TO CHEWELAH
NEWPORT
ROAD TO LAKE CHELAN
ENTIAT RIVER
CHELAN BUTTE ROAD
EAST WENATCHEE TO CHELAN
WENATCHEE ALPINE BACK ROAD
GRAND COULEE
THE ROAD TO HARTLINE
HARTLINE
BACK ROAD LOOP FROM COULEE CITY
WILSON CREEK
WILBUR
WELLPINIT
ROAD ALONG THE SPOKANE RIVER
ROAD THROUGH RIVERSIDE STATE PARK
SPOKANE
20
21
395
97
2
17
28
231

# Northeastern Washington

I remember the broad glacially formed valleys and their majestic rivers, the Methow, Okanogan, Similkameen, Kettle, Sanpoil, Pend Oreille, the great Columbia, and others.

I recall orchards bulging with apples; the deep forests of pine, fir, and larch; the lakes of silver hue; and vast wheat fields awaiting harvest, all this along the intriguing back roads of northeastern Washington.

Pearly Everlasting (white flowers), Chelan County

*Washington apples, Chelan county*

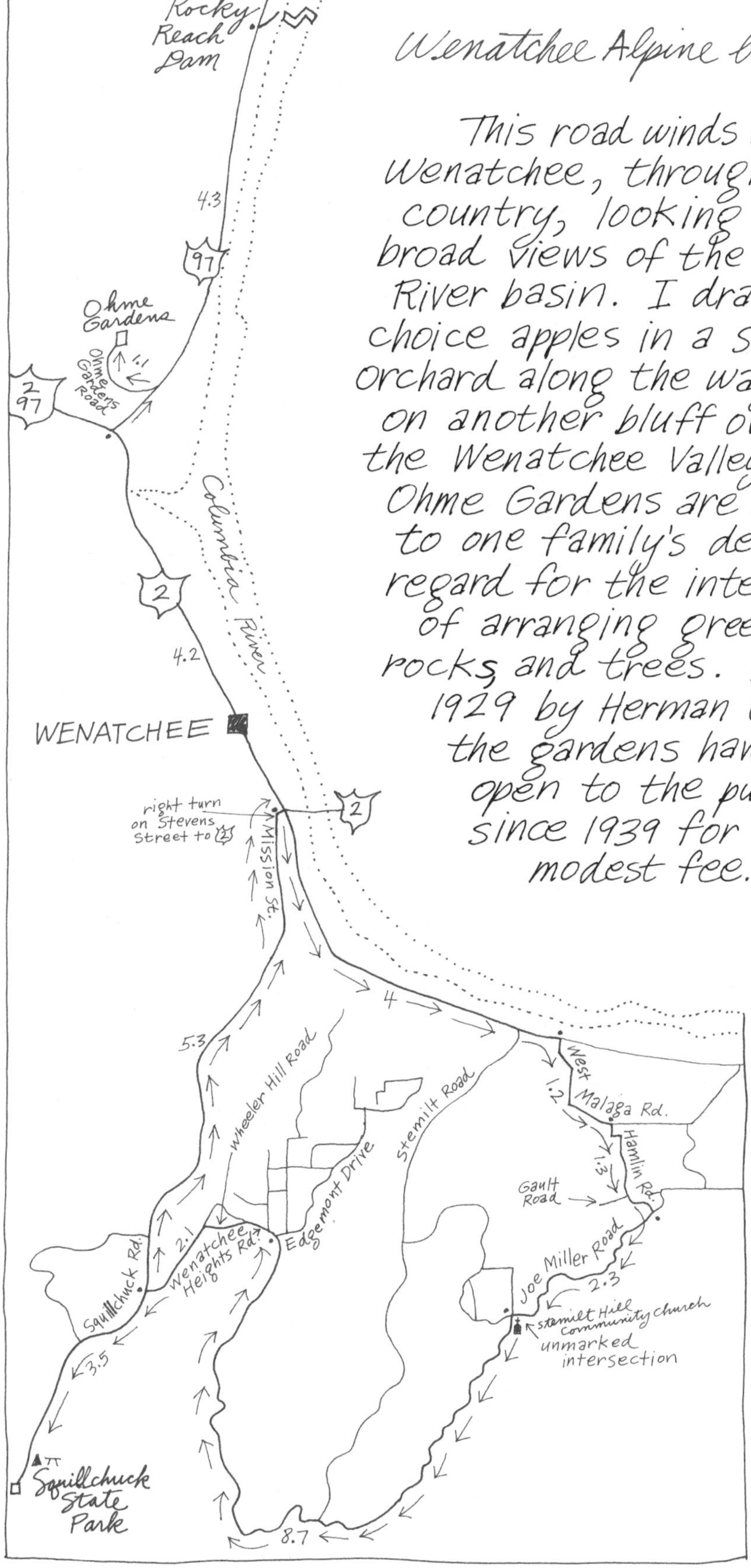

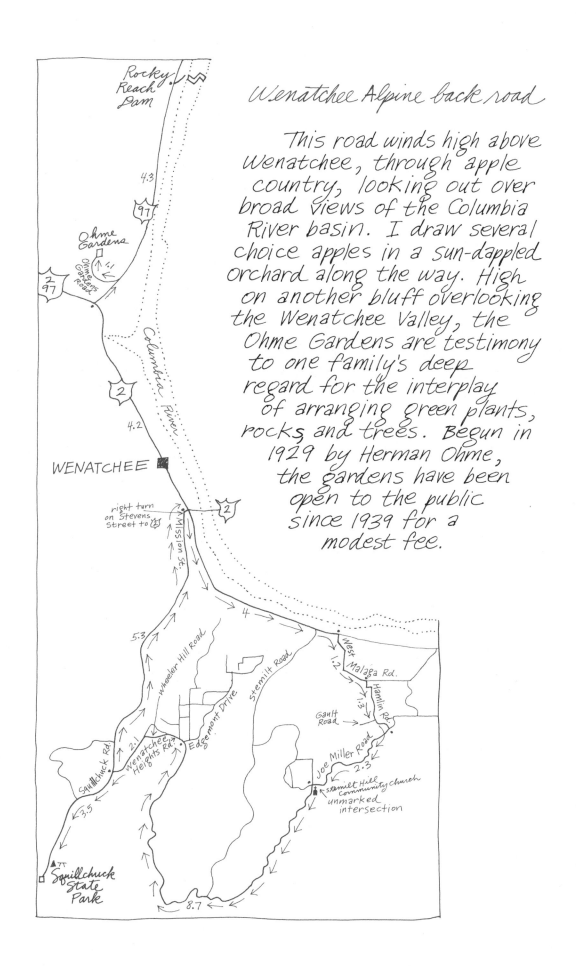

## Wenatchee Alpine back road

This road winds high above Wenatchee, through apple country, looking out over broad views of the Columbia River basin. I draw several choice apples in a sun-dappled orchard along the way. High on another bluff overlooking the Wenatchee Valley, the Ohme Gardens are testimony to one family's deep regard for the interplay of arranging green plants, rocks, and trees. Begun in 1929 by Herman Ohme, the gardens have been open to the public since 1939 for a modest fee.

Log interior,
St. Andrews Church,
Chelan, Chelan County

# East Wenatchee to Chelan

There are expansive views along this road of Wenatchee and the Columbia River. Ahead are the purple-hued bluffs of Badger Mountain. Once you have gone over the mountain and through McGinnis Canyon, the road affords a dramatic view of the farming area around Waterville. The sky darkens in the distance as rain threatens, yet the wheat fields are drenched in the afternoon sun.

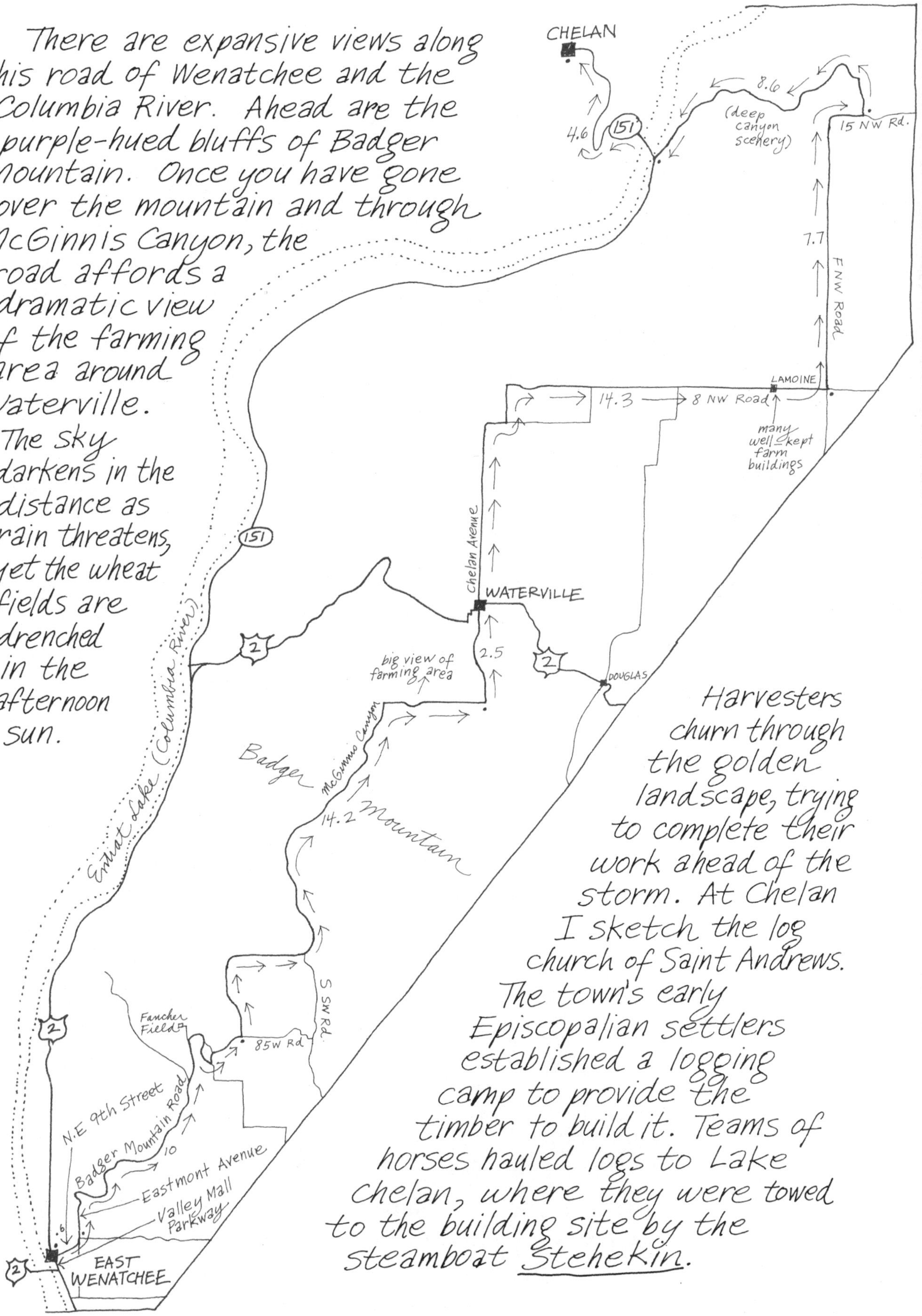


Harvesters churn through the golden landscape, trying to complete their work ahead of the storm. At Chelan I sketch the log church of Saint Andrews. The town's early Episcopalian settlers established a logging camp to provide the timber to build it. Teams of horses hauled logs to Lake Chelan, where they were towed to the building site by the steamboat <u>Stehekin</u>.

View of Columbia River from Chelan Butte, Chelan County

## Chelan Butte Road

Very soon this road offers a grand view of the Lake Chelan region. It is a narrow dirt road and slow going at times; however, the vistas from Chelan Butte lookout tower are well worth the trip. Colorful hang gliders take off from the slope below the tower, one glider circling up and up until it is only a speck in the sky. My fingers tingle as I watch this extraordinary performance, and I feel particular pleasure in having both feet securely planted upon the earth. With the Cascades as a backdrop, I continue on a primitive but picturesque road that winds past rolling fields of grain and the Columbia River shimmering in sunshine.

# Entiat River Road to Chelan

Peach, pear, and apple orchards decorate the banks a good way along the Entiat River, then pine forest and more rustic mountain scenery take over. At the 6,600-foot elevation there is a viewpoint of great mountains with snow-topped Glacier Peak looming highest. The descent then begins to Lake Chelan, a road lined with wild flowers such as tansy, fireweed, Indian paintbrush, lupine, stonecrop, and yarrow.

Chelan County
apple orchard

Old Witte Homestead
near Winthrop,
Okanogan County

The road to Twisp and Winthrop

I follow the Methow River for some miles, paralleling highways 153 and 20. Between Twisp and Winthrop I sketch the old Witte Homestead, the Methow placidly flowing past its back door. A broad field of green alfalfa is in the foreground and the mountains of the Okanogan National Forest grace the skyline.

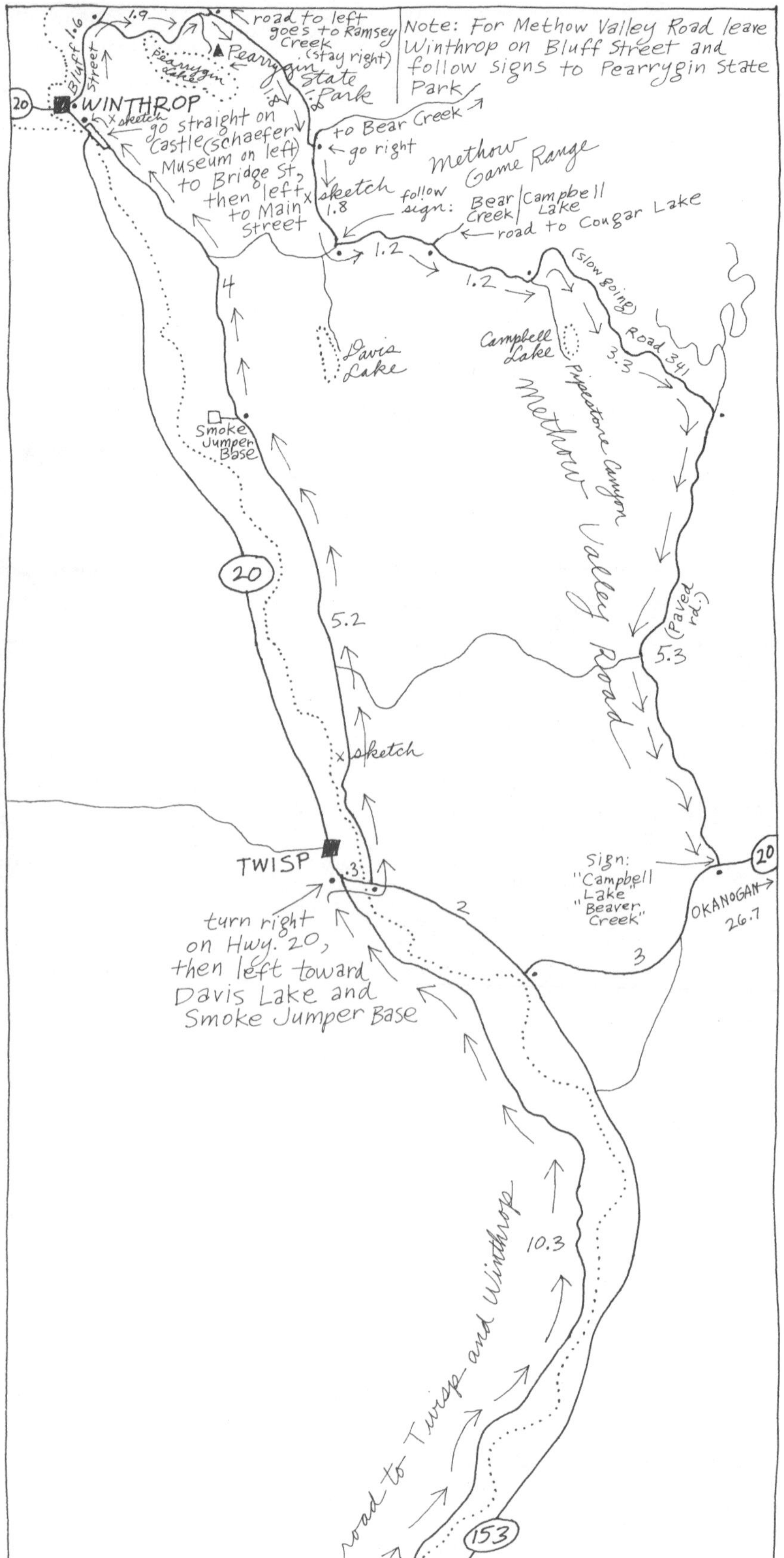

Note: For Methow Valley Road leave Winthrop on Bluff Street and follow signs to Pearrygin State Park
road to left goes to Ramsey Creek (stay right)
Pearrygin State Park
Pearrygin Lake
Bluff Street
1.6
1.9
20
WINTHROP
x sketch
go straight on Castle (Schaefer Museum on left) to Bridge St, then left to Main Street
to Bear Creek
go right
Methow Game Range
x sketch
1.8
follow sign: Bear Creek | Campbell Lake
road to Cougar Lake
1.2
1.2
(slow going)
Road 341
Davis Lake
Campbell Lake
Pipestone Canyon
Methow Valley Road
3.3
4
Smoke Jumper Base
20
5.2
(Paved rd.)
5.3
x sketch
TWISP
.3
turn right on Hwy. 20, then left toward Davis Lake and Smoke Jumper Base
2
3
Sign: "Campbell Lake" "Beaver Creek"
20
OKANOGAN 26.7
10.3
The road to Twisp and Winthrop
153
CARLTON
methow River Bridge
unmarked road
PATEROS 23

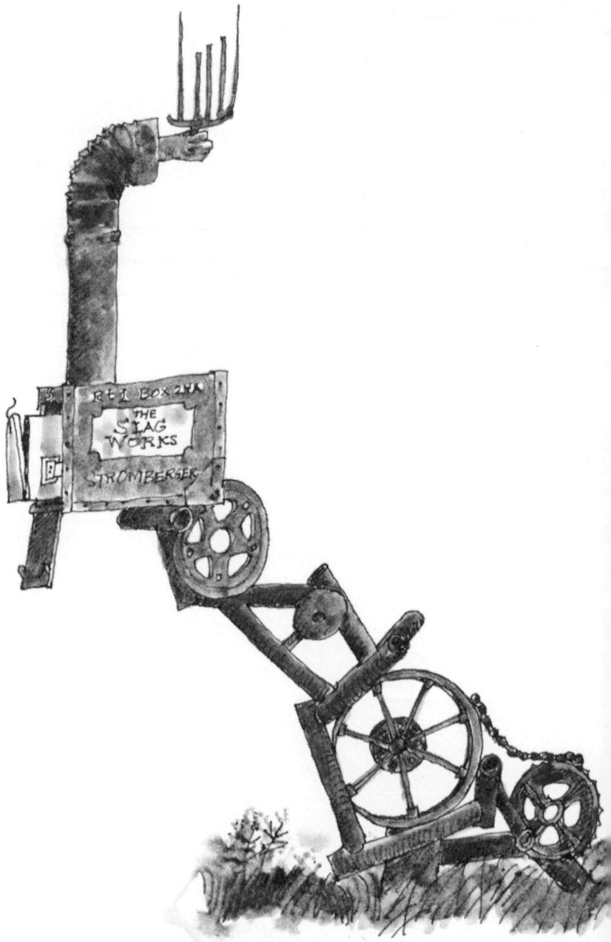

RT 1 BOX 24A
THE SLAG WORKS
STROMBERGER

Seen along the road to Winthrop, Okanogan County

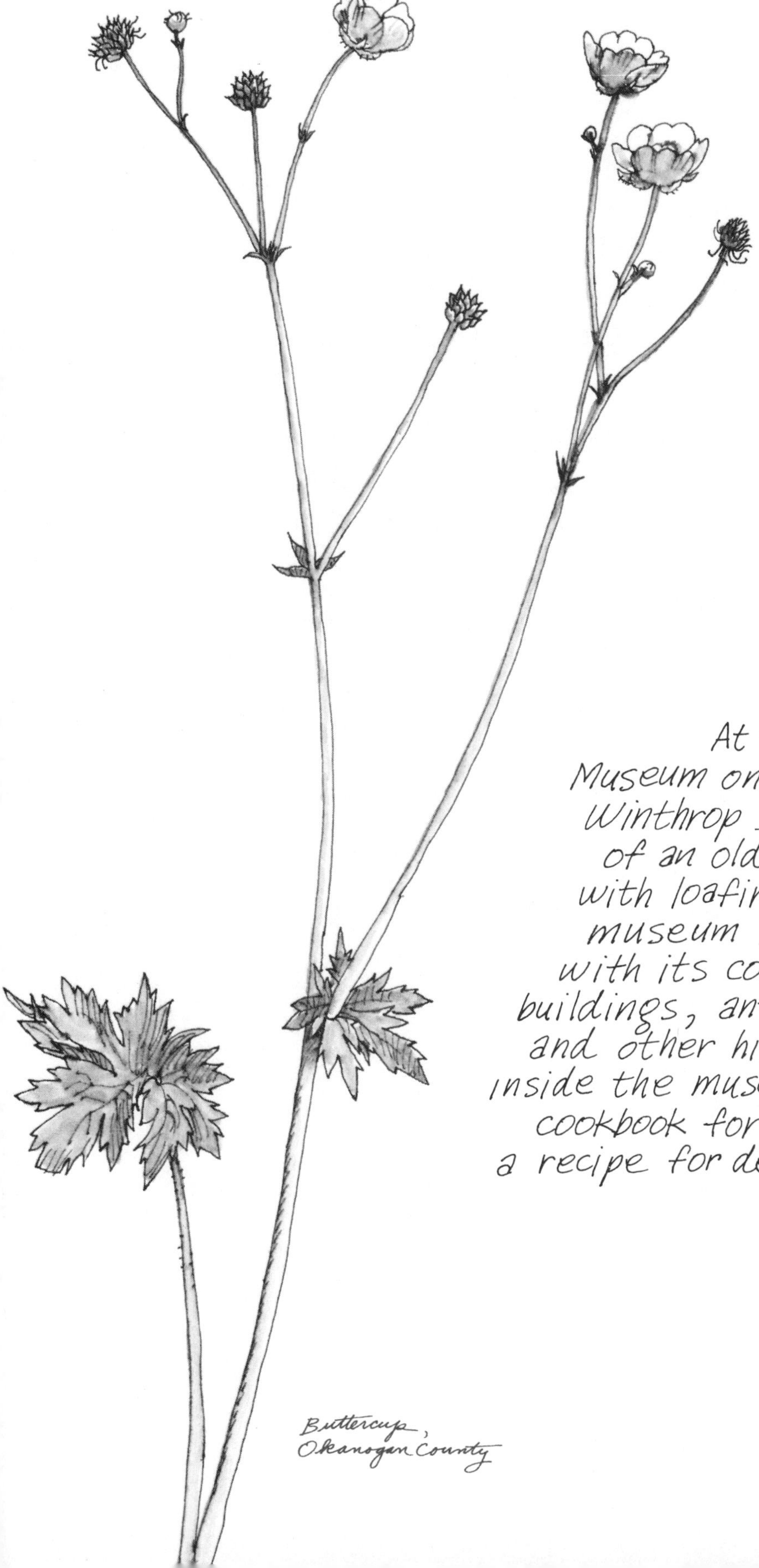

At the Simon Schaefer Museum on Castle Avenue in Winthrop I draw the facade of an old log house complete with loafing homesteader. The museum is an entertaining stop with its collection of old buildings, antique farm equipment, and other historical items. And inside the museum I find a rare cookbook for sale, which includes a recipe for deep fried pigs' ears.

Buttercup,
Okanogan County

ALL ABOARD
FOR DEAD LAKE, SODA CR.,
ROCK CR., ROBINSON CR. AN
POINTS EAST TRAIN LEAVES
6:33 AM DAILY EXCEPT SUNDAY
SKIN BURGE, CONDUCTO

*Old homesteader's cabin, Winthrop, Okanogan County*

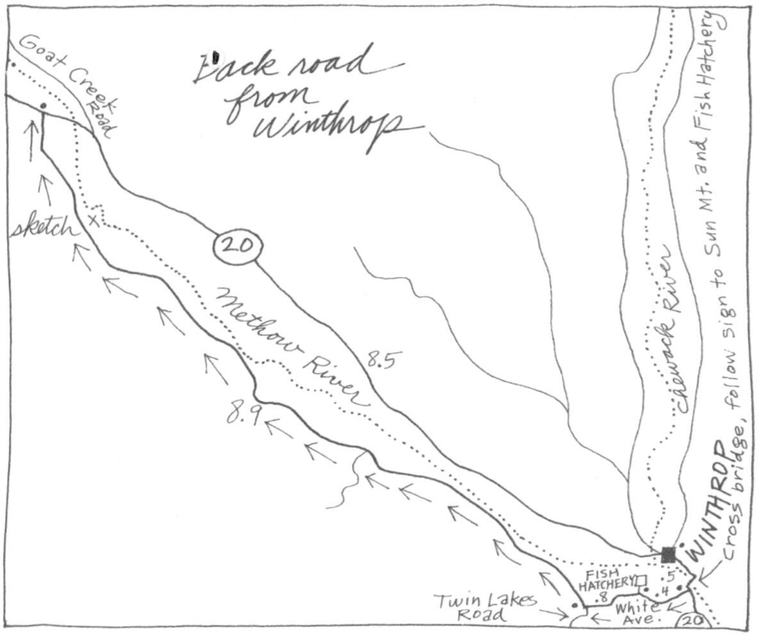

Back road from Winthrop
Goat Creek Road
sketch
20
Methow River
8.5
8.9
Chewack River
WINTHROP
Cross bridge, follow sign to Sun Mt. and Fish Hatchery
FISH HATCHERY
5
4
8
Twin Lakes Road
White Ave.
20

## Back road from Winthrop

The road follows the Methow River through farming land and into primitive pine forest. Emerging from the thick forest I am back in farm country again. Sprinklers spray water all around, making green alfalfa crops still greener. Along the road I draw a chocolate-colored barn filled with golden-hued hay.

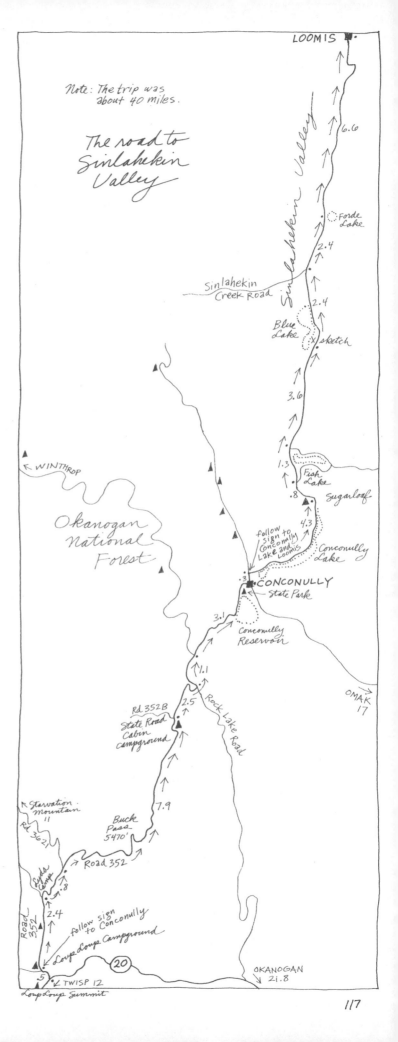

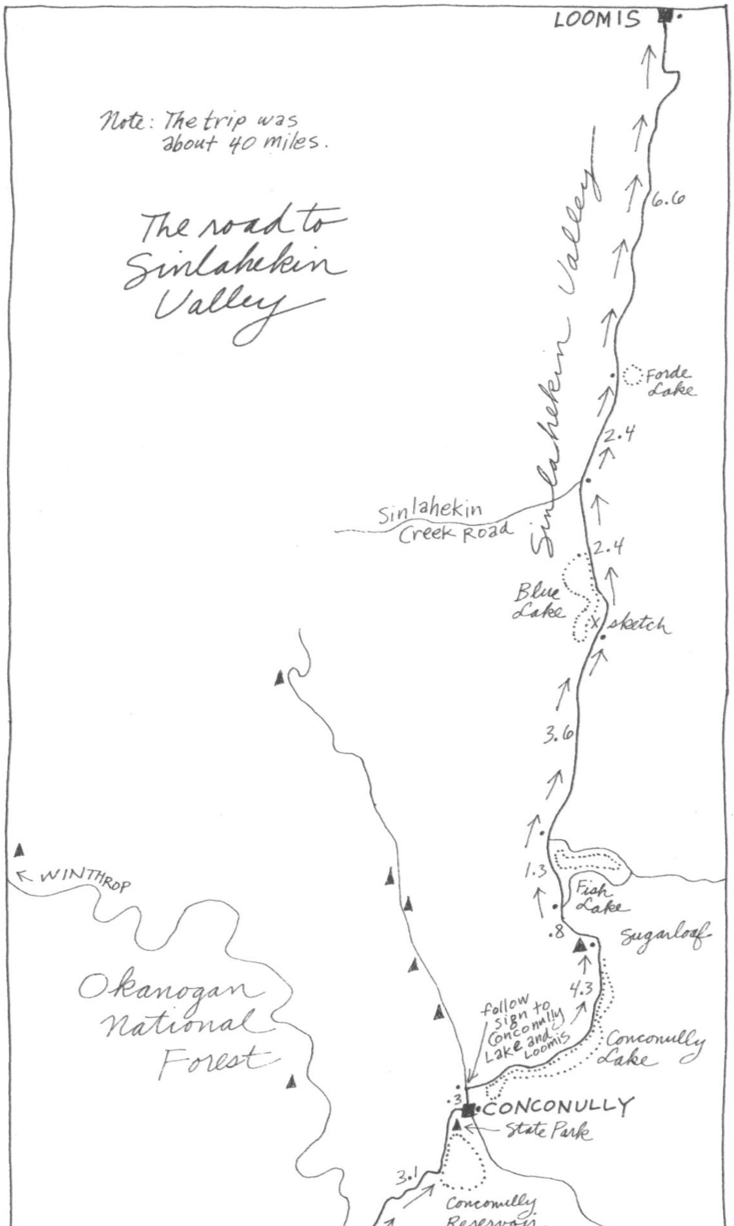

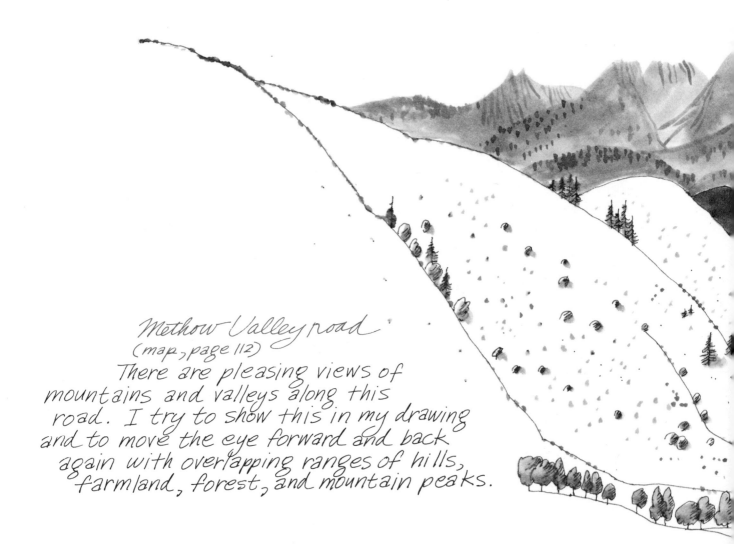

*Methow Valley road*
(map, page 112)

There are pleasing views of mountains and valleys along this road. I try to show this in my drawing and to move the eye forward and back again with overlapping ranges of hills, farmland, forest, and mountain peaks.

View of Methow Valley near Winthrop, Okanogan County

## The road to Sinlahekin Valley (map, page 117)

A good gravel road leads me through thick fir and pine forest to an old mining town once known as Salmon City. The more poetic name for this locale—Conconully—has survived. Translated from the Indian, it means "the beautiful land of the bunch grass flats."

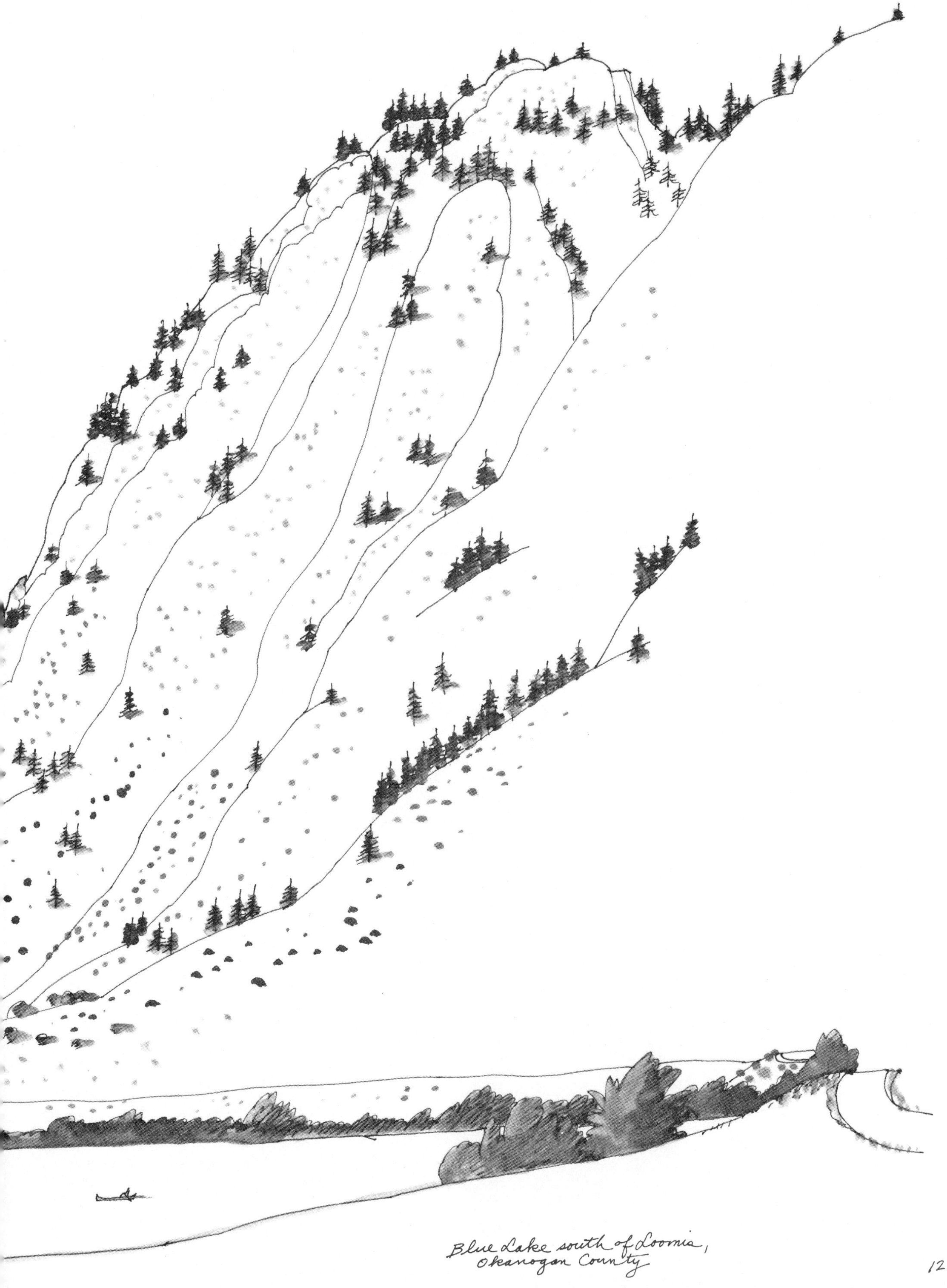

Blue Lake south of Loomis,
Okanogan County

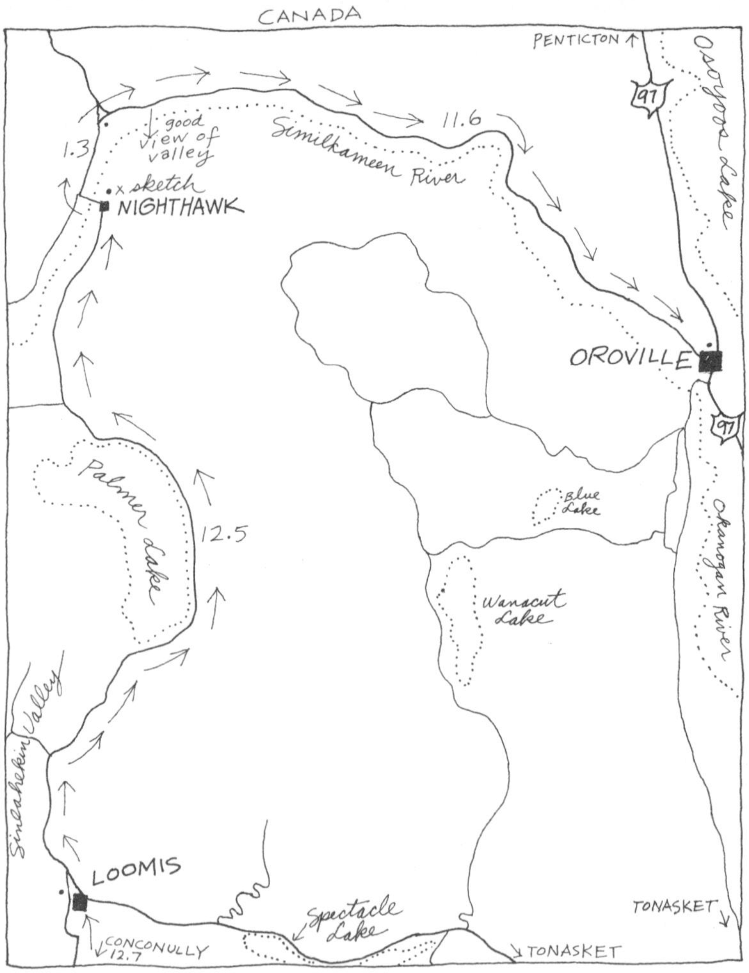

The Pink House, Nighthawk, Okanogan County

## Loomis to Nighthawk and Oroville

Rock-faced mountains, dotted with pines and firs, abruptly rise in a colorful blend of blue, gray, purple, and ocher from Sinlahekin Valley north of Loomis. Apple orchards grow at one end of Palmer Lake, while green grass carpets the southern end of the valley.

At the almost deserted mining town of Nighthawk I sketch the Pink House. It had once been a lively hostelry and perhaps even a place of questionable repute, I was told by local folks. The old store and post office and the former hotel are still there and occupied. Discoveries of precious metal in the early 1890s made both Loomis and Nighthawk booming mining towns. The boom ended in a few years, but the scenic beauty of the valley remains.

The road to Oroville follows the Similkameen River, where gold was panned in 1857.

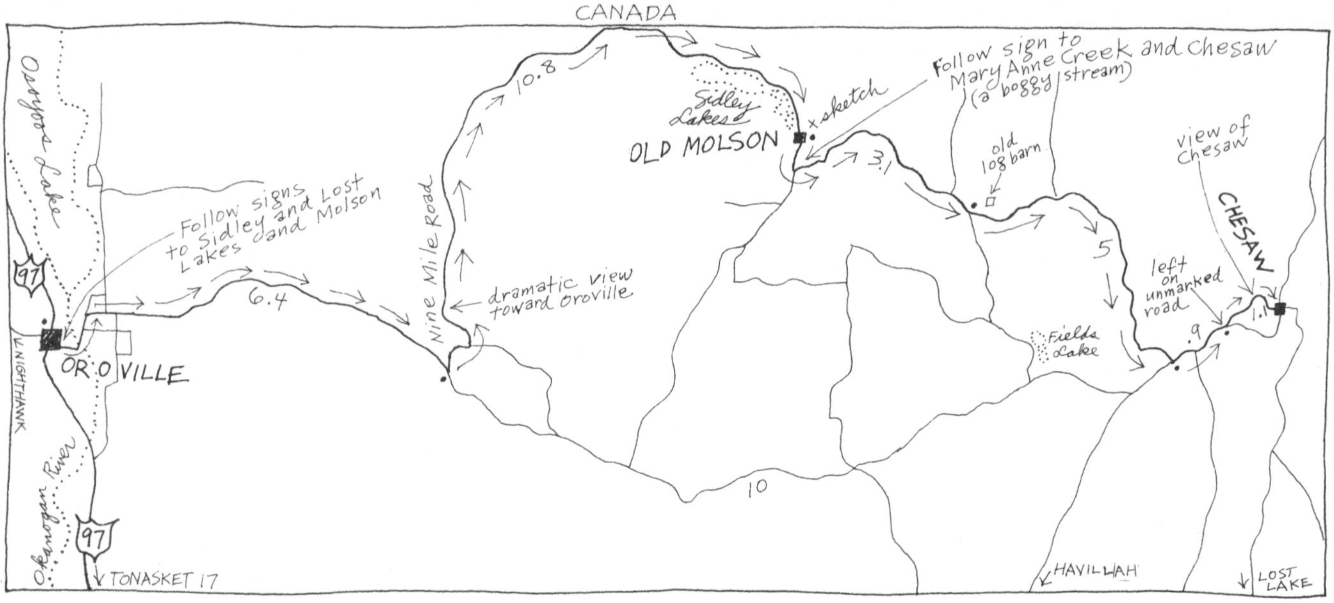


## *Road to Old Molson and Chesaw*

The road parallels the Canadian border for almost a mile and later passes Sidley Lakes before entering Old Molson. Originally the town had a doctor, veterinarian, attorney, and a milliner; a drugstore, meat market, creamery, restaurant, furniture store, grocery store, harness shop, newspaper, and garage. When Kohrdt's Garage closed its doors for the last time in 1941, that was the end of Old Molson—except, of course, for the collection of early buildings, equipment, and memorabilia that remains there today.

Chesaw, too, has some of the same flavor. This town, once center of a mining district of over five hundred, claims it is named in honor of a Chinese miner named Joe Chee Saw.

OKANOGAN COUNTY HISTORICAL SOCIETY
OLD MOLSON
WELCOME FOLKS TO OLD MOLSON FOUNDED IN 1900. SHE WAS A LIVELY MINING CAMP UNTIL A FARMER CLAIMED THE WHOLE TOWN WAS PART OF HIS HOMESTEAD. WHILE THE DISPUTE RAGED, DISGUSTED CITIZENS FOUNDED NEW MOLSON HALF-A-MILE NORTH. PEOPLE, BUSINESSES, THE POST OFFICE - EVERYTHING MOVED TO NEW MOLSON. ITS RAILROAD STATION ELEV 3706 WAS THE HIGHEST IN THE STATE. THE ORIGINAL MOLSON FADED AWAY, BUT ITS MEMORIES LINGER IN THESE WEATHER-WORN BUILDINGS.
NO DOUBLE PARKING 3 HOUR PARKING LIMIT
DEPENDABLE CHAMPION
ZEROLENE
FOR MOTOR CARS
AVOID PENALTY REPORT TO CUSTOMS VEHICLES ENTERING


*Old Molson, Okanogan County*

YE OLDE MOLSON
-1900-
MOLSON POST OFFICE
STATE
BANK
COPENHAGEN

## Okanogan River road

Countless apple trees, branches laden with red and yellow fruit, a forest of wooden poles supporting them, adorn the green banks of the Okanogan River. There are also grassy meadows, river views, farms, and sparsely wooded bluffs along the way to Tonasket.

Okanogan River Valley,
Okanogan County

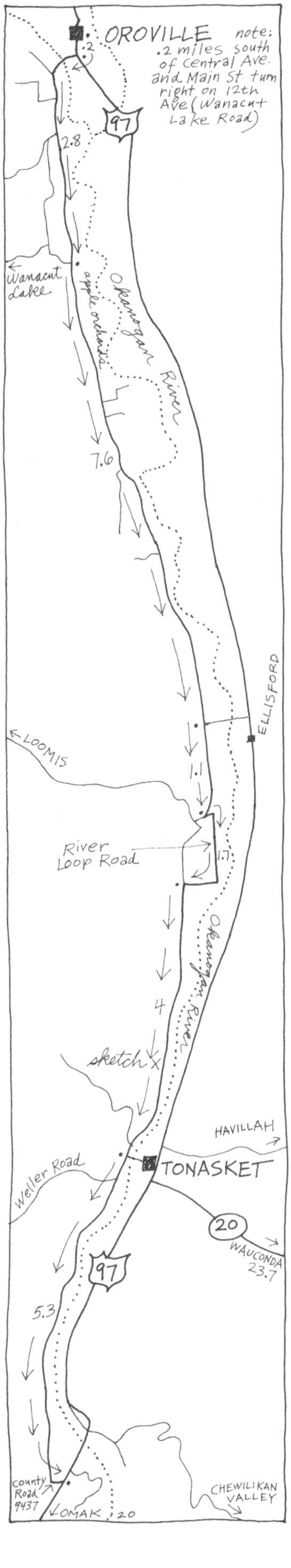

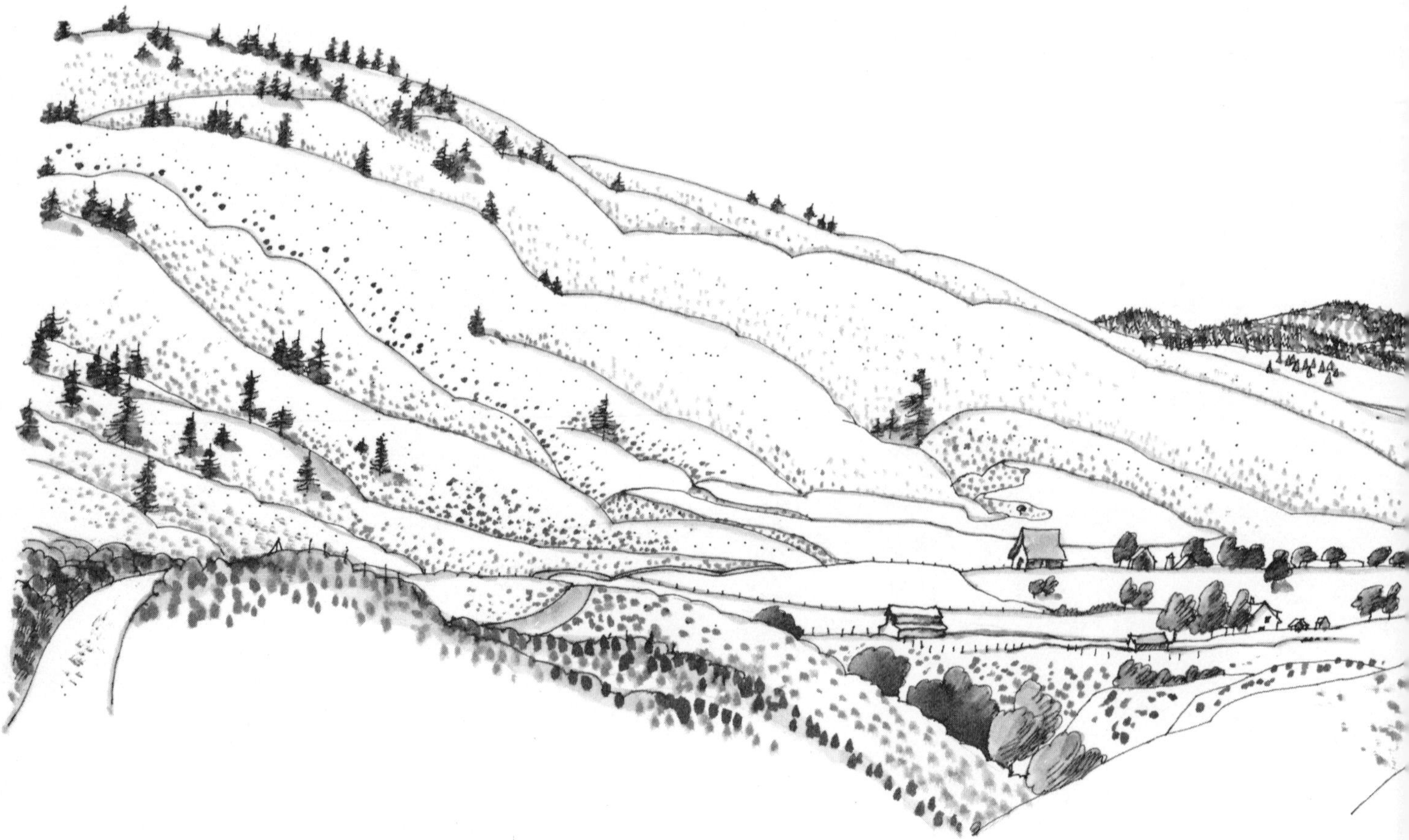

## The road through Chewilikan Valley

Driving through rocky, sparse pine, and sagebrush country, I delight in the spectacular view of the Okanogan River winding its way through McLaughlin Canyon. On July 29, 1858, 149 miners led by James McLaughlin were ambushed by Indians in the canyon. One miner, Francis Wolff by name, could not control his horse. It galloped off without him in the direction of the ambushing Indians. He had packed $2,000 in gold dust on the creature and was determined not to lose it, so with great danger to himself, he managed to get the horse back in time (from the records of the Museum of Okanogan Historical Society). I sketch this grand view of quiet Chewilikan Valley. It has its own special beauty, with gray green sagebrush dotting the hills, golden grain crops in the valley, and distant dark green forest.

Chewilikan Valley,
Okanogan County

*Lupine, Okanogan County*

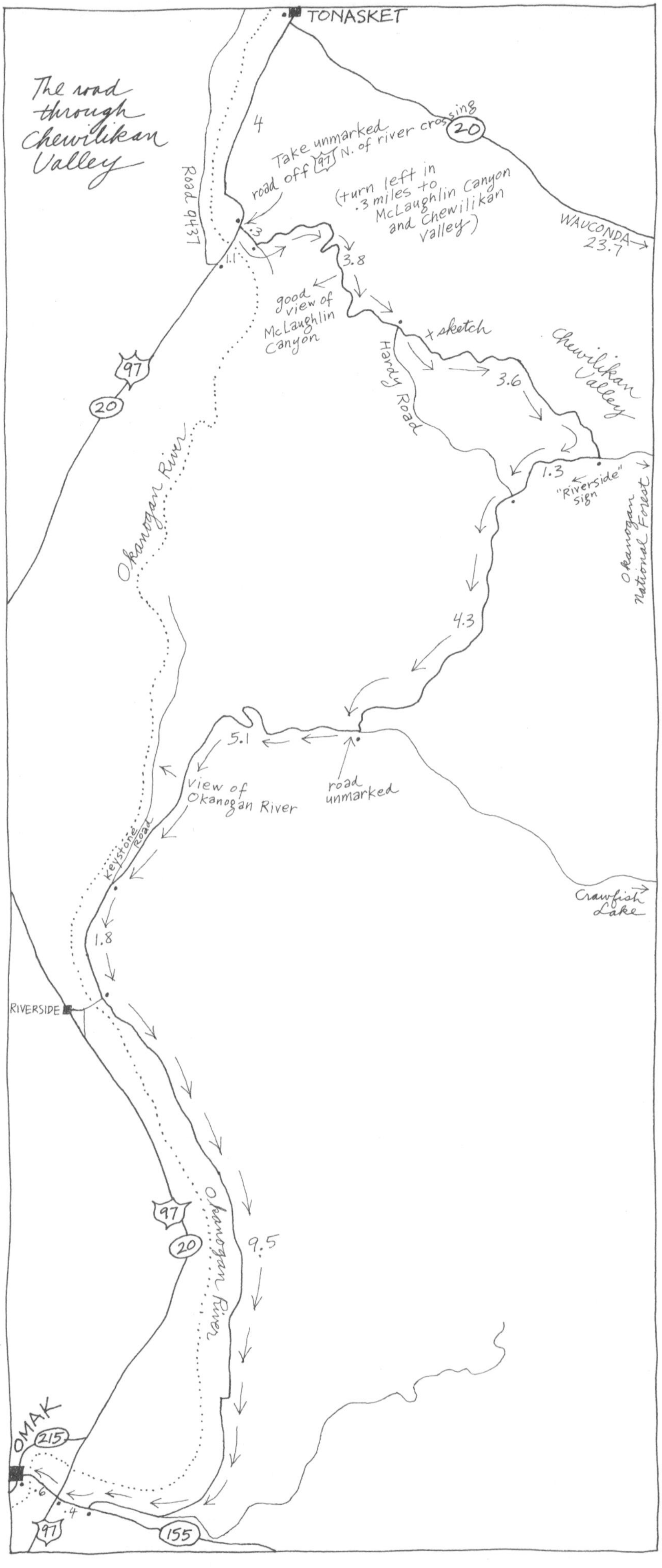
TONASKET
The road through Chewilikan Valley
4
20
Take unmarked road off 97 N. of river crossing
Road 9437
(turn left in .3 miles to McLaughlin Canyon and Chewilikan Valley)
WAUCONDA 23.7
.3
1.1
3.8
good view of McLaughlin Canyon
+sketch
Hardy Road
Chewilikan Valley
3.6
97
20
Okanogan River
1.3
"Riverside" sign
Okanogan National Forest
4.3
5.1
road unmarked
View of Okanogan River
Keystone Road
Crawfish Lake
1.8
RIVERSIDE
97
20
Okanogan River
9.5
OMAK
215
.6
.4
97
155

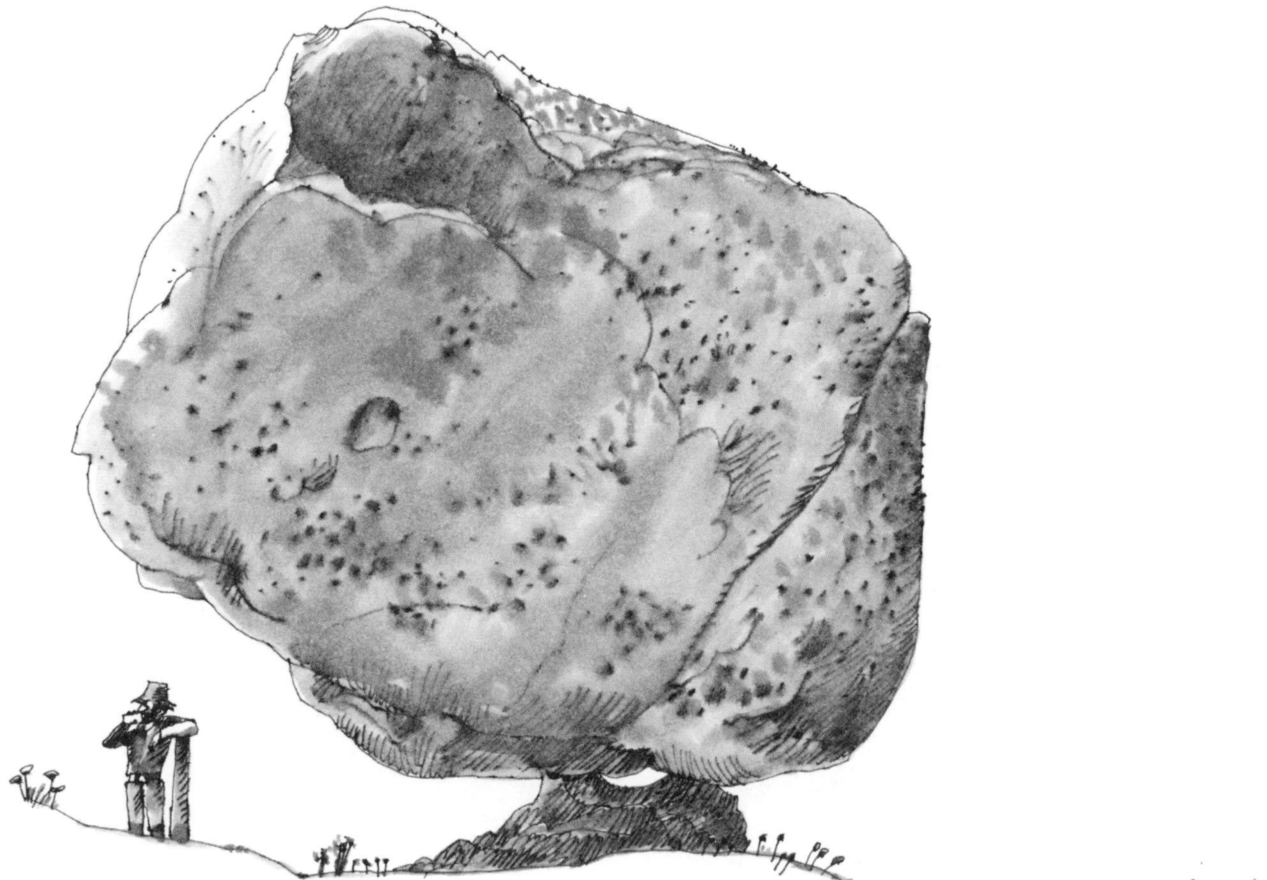

Balanced Rock,
Kartar Valley,
Okanogan County

Omak Lake,
Okanogan County

Omak Lake Road

Attesting to Okanogan County's great geological variety, here at Omak Lake massive rock formations jut majestically upward from the blue green water. Along Kartar Valley Road I sketch Balanced Rock to the buzzing of bees and grasshoppers. At Goose Lake there are plenty of ducks among the bulrushes, and on the road cows plump themselves down and have to be nudged up and along.

# The road to Nespelem and Republic

There is a dramatic view of the Columbia River along this back road to Nespelem. Once in town I visit the grave of Chief Joseph, the famous war leader of the Nez Percé Indians in the 1870s. He led his people fifteen hundred miles through Montana wilderness toward Canada, but was captured at the border by the United States Army. Finally sent to Colville Reservation, he ended his days in 1904 at Nespelem. Lettered on his gravestone is his Indian name, HIN-MAH-TOO-YAH-LAT-KEHT, "Thunder rolling in the mountains."

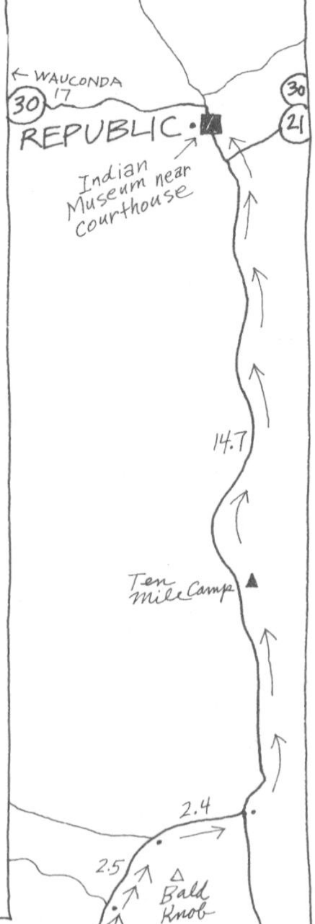


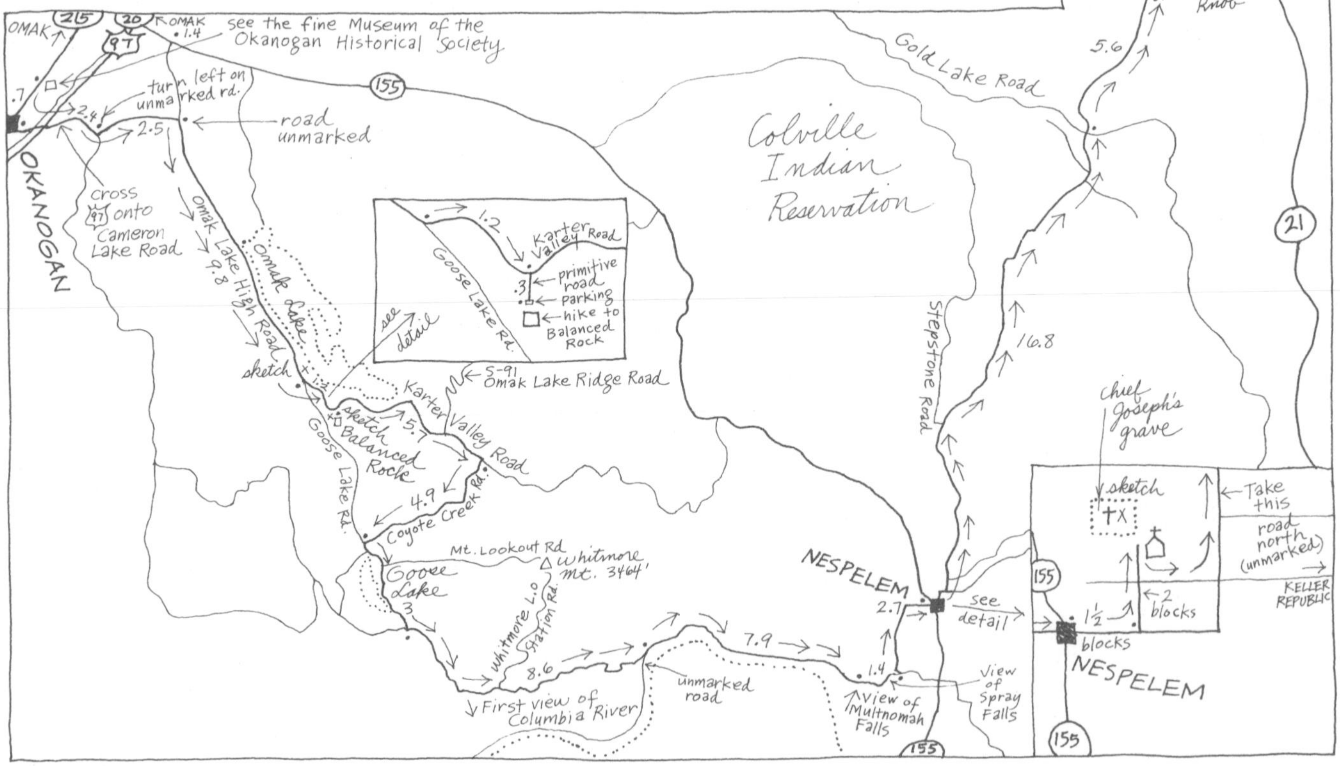

*Headstone at Nespelem, Okanogan County*

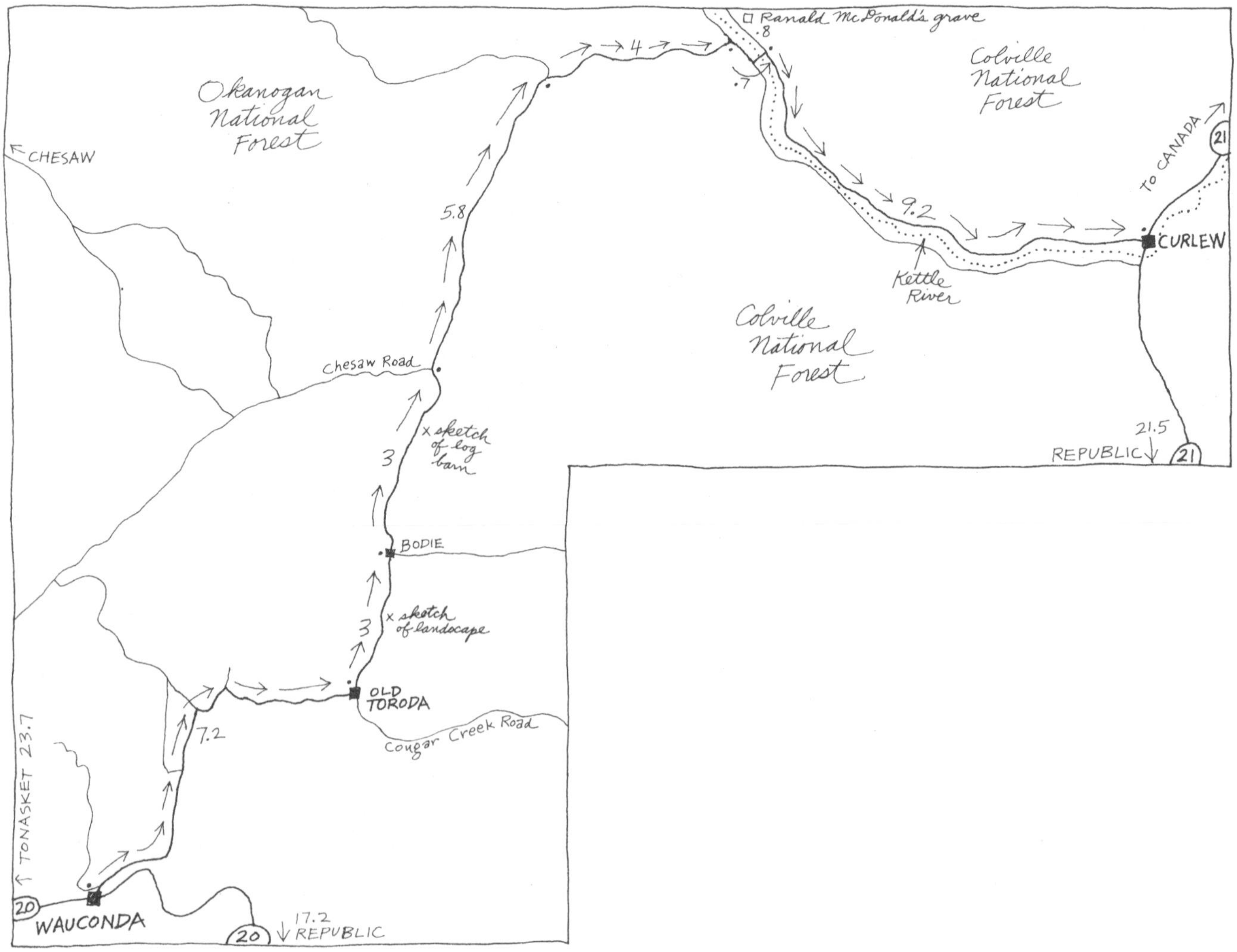
Ranald McDonald's grave
Okanogan National Forest
Colville National Forest
Colville National Forest
CHESAW
TO CANADA
21
CURLEW
Kettle River
Chesaw Road
x sketch of log barn
BODIE
x sketch of landscape
OLD TORODA
Cougar Creek Road
TONASKET 23.7
7.2
5.8
4
.8
.7
9.2
3
3
21.5
REPUBLIC
20
WAUCONDA
17.2
REPUBLIC
20

## The road past Old Toroda

There are log homesteads at Old Toroda and a ghost town at Bodie. I sketch a swayback log house along the road, then discover a big log barn to draw at Single Shot Ranch a few miles past Bodie. Log barns and farmhouses give a quaint early American look to this narrow agricultural valley. Later, in Ferry County, during a very pretty drive along the Kettle River, I witness fly-fishermen trying their luck in the free-flowing stream. This brings me, finally, to the hamlet of Curlew.

Farm near Old Toroda, Okanogan County

Log barn north of Bodie, Okanogan County

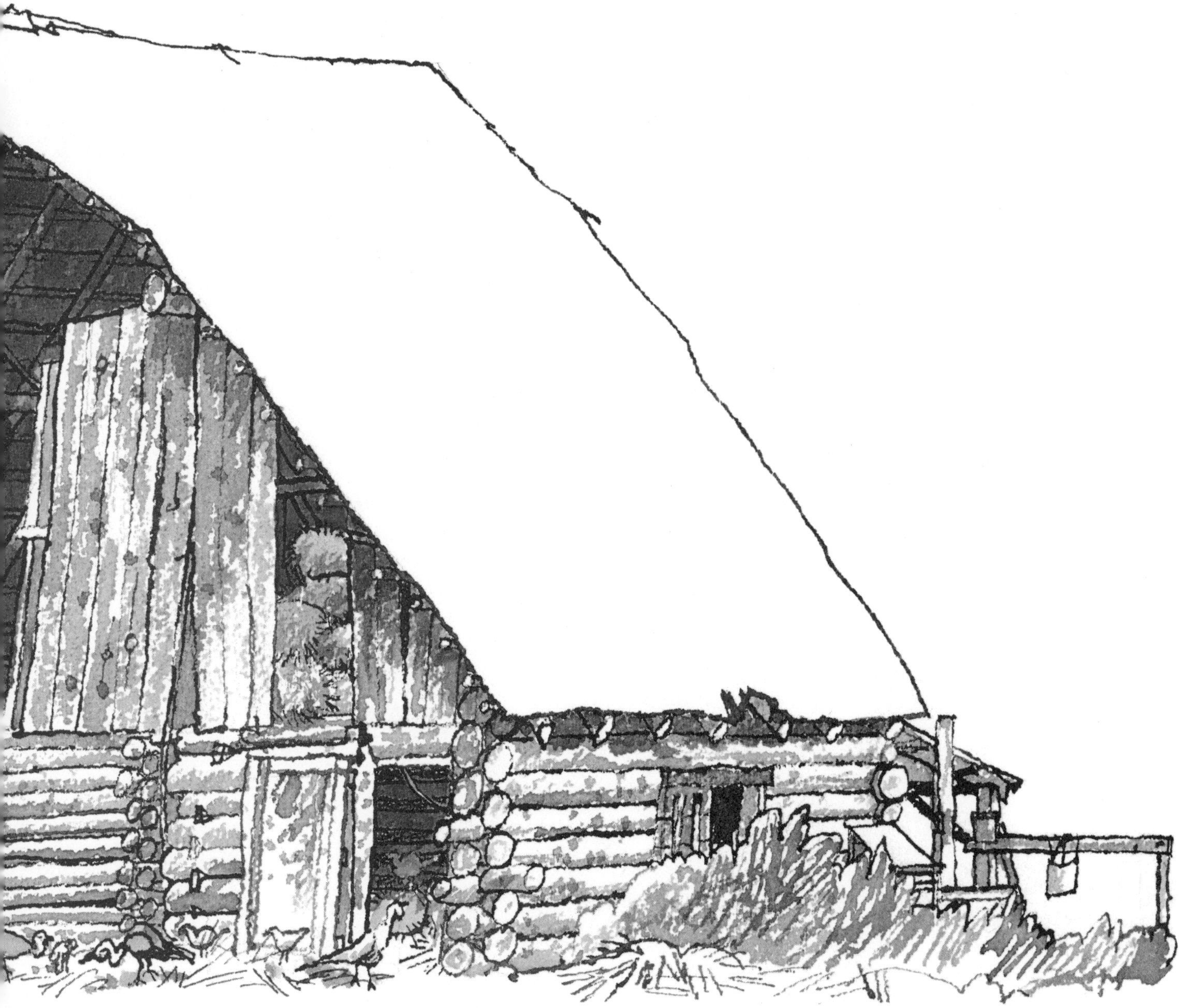

## Back roads to and from Northport 

From Orient, a back road goes past Little Pierre and Pierre Lakes. A fisherman at Pierre tells me he has fished cutthroat trout there since the 1930s. As he speaks, a great blue heron flies by chased by a hawk. Releasing plaintive cries all the while, the heron makes great maneuvers to escape the hawk. The road continues through thick forest, emerging eventually at Northport.

From Northport the scenery changes to views of the Columbia River and inland farms and woods. At Snag Cove I sketch the vast Franklin D. Roosevelt Lake portion of the Columbia River. Stalks of woolly mullein decorate the foreground of the picture.

Snag Cove,
Franklin D. Roosevelt Lake,
(Columbia River), Stevens County

Back road to and from Northport
Back road to Orient
American Fork
Limestone Road
Limestone Road
Limestone Rd.
Elbow Lake
stay on road to Elbow Lake and Northport
Kiel Ridge Road
Kiel Ridge Rd.
Flat Creek Road
Crown Creek Rd.
Sheep Creek
Sheep Creek Rd.
Flagstaff Lookout Road
unmarked road
NORTHPORT
go right toward Sheep Creek and Elbow Lake
Fisher Creek Road
Mineral Mountain Road
Pierre Lake
Little Pierre Lake
First Thought Lookout Road
cross river, turn right
ORIENT
Kettle River
Pierre Lake Road
Kettle River Rd.
Snag Cove Campground
Columbia River
sketch
Flat Creek Rd.
Franklin D. Roosevelt Lake
KETTLE FALLS
395
25
20
12.6
6.6
3
.8
9.9
4.7
2.3
5
12.2
4
6.1
3.8
35
M.P.H.

ORIENT
WEATHER STATION
OBSERVE ROCK:
If it is SWINGING,
WIND is BLOWING.
If it is WHITE,
It is SNOWING.
If it is WET,
It is RAINING
If YOU CAN'T SEE ROCK
It is FOGGY

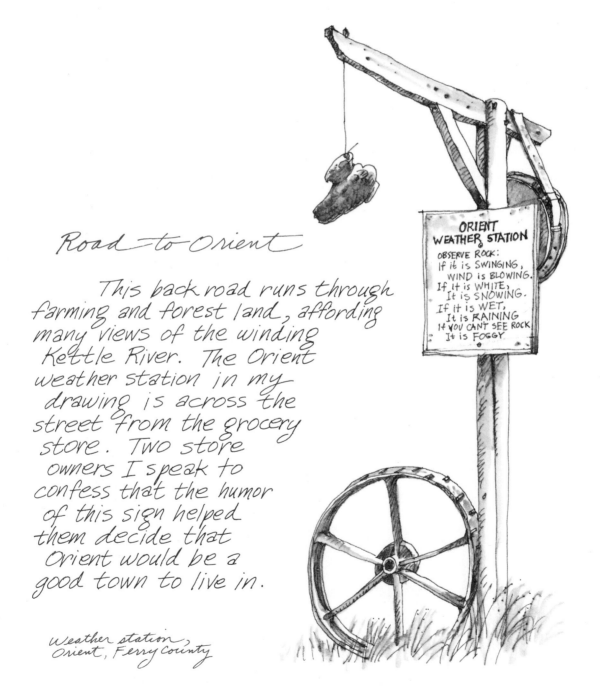

## Road to Orient

This back road runs through farming and forest land, affording many views of the winding Kettle River. The Orient weather station in my drawing is across the street from the grocery store. Two store owners I speak to confess that the humor of this sign helped them decide that Orient would be a good town to live in.

Weather station, Orient, Ferry County

# The road past Deep Lake

Attractive meadows, old homesteads, and forest scenery are found on this trip north of Colville. Deep Lake, bathed in early morning mist, conveys a mood of serenity, calm, and mystery.

Several miles farther north of Deep Lake, I sketch the 1804 Johnson homestead with its laundry spread along the fence. People settled in this valley along Deep Creek at that time to work in the local lead mines.

The old Johnson homestead,
Leadpoint, Stevens County

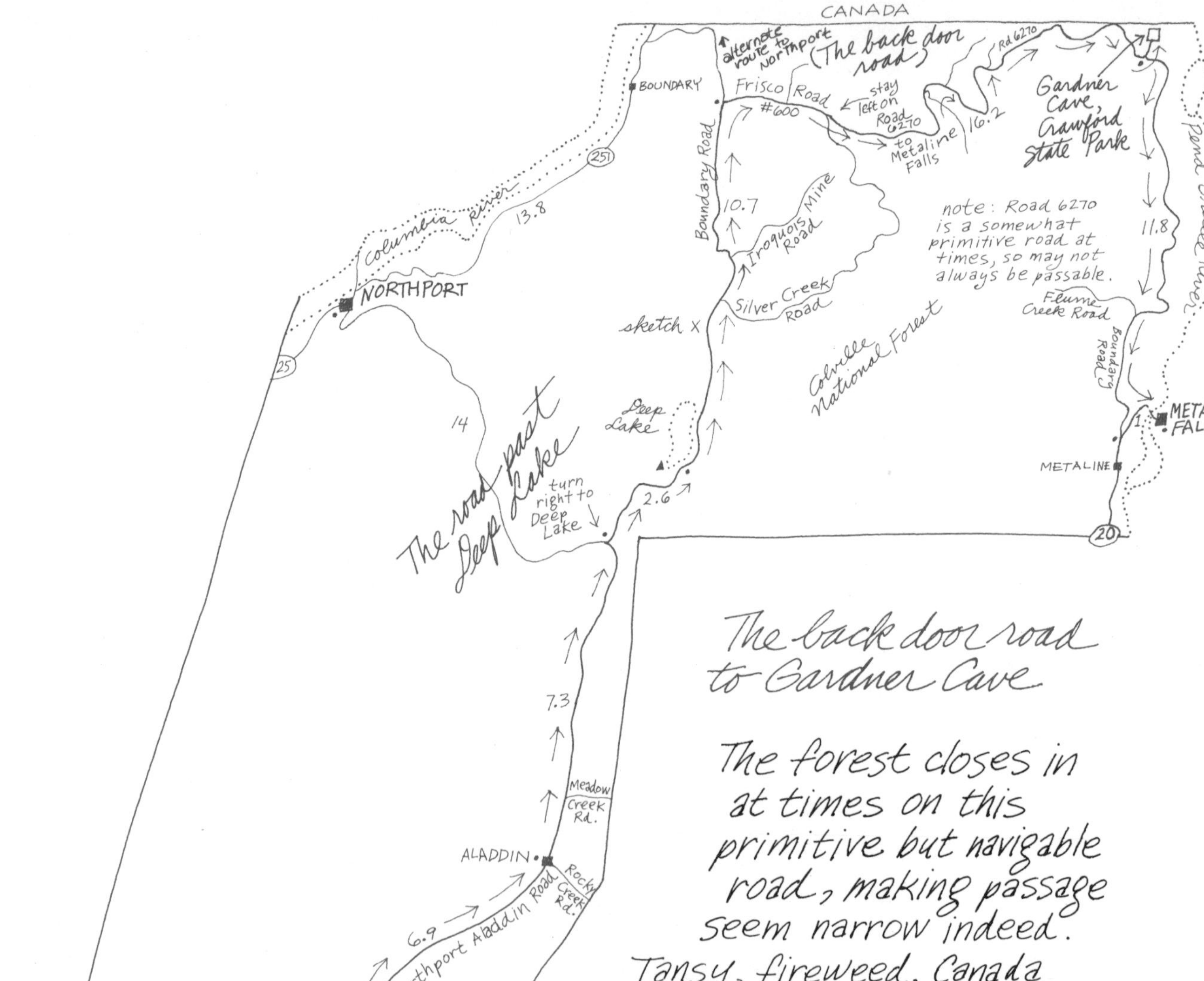


# The back door road to Gardner Cave

The forest closes in at times on this primitive but navigable road, making passage seem narrow indeed. Tansy, fireweed, Canada thistle, pearly everlasting, daisies, asters, and Indian paintbrush color the roadsides. Forest trees are red cedar, aspen, grand fir, lodgepole pine, big-leaf maple, Douglas fir, and western larch. My fingers are icy as I sketch in the 44° temperature in Gardner Cave at Crawford State Park. The profound silence of this largest limestone cavern in Washington is broken only by an occasional drip of water. I draw the column that is the wonder of this cave. It has slowly formed from the joining of stalagmites growing upward and stalactites growing downward from the cave's ceiling. At the base of the column are clear pools of water called gours (a new word for me).

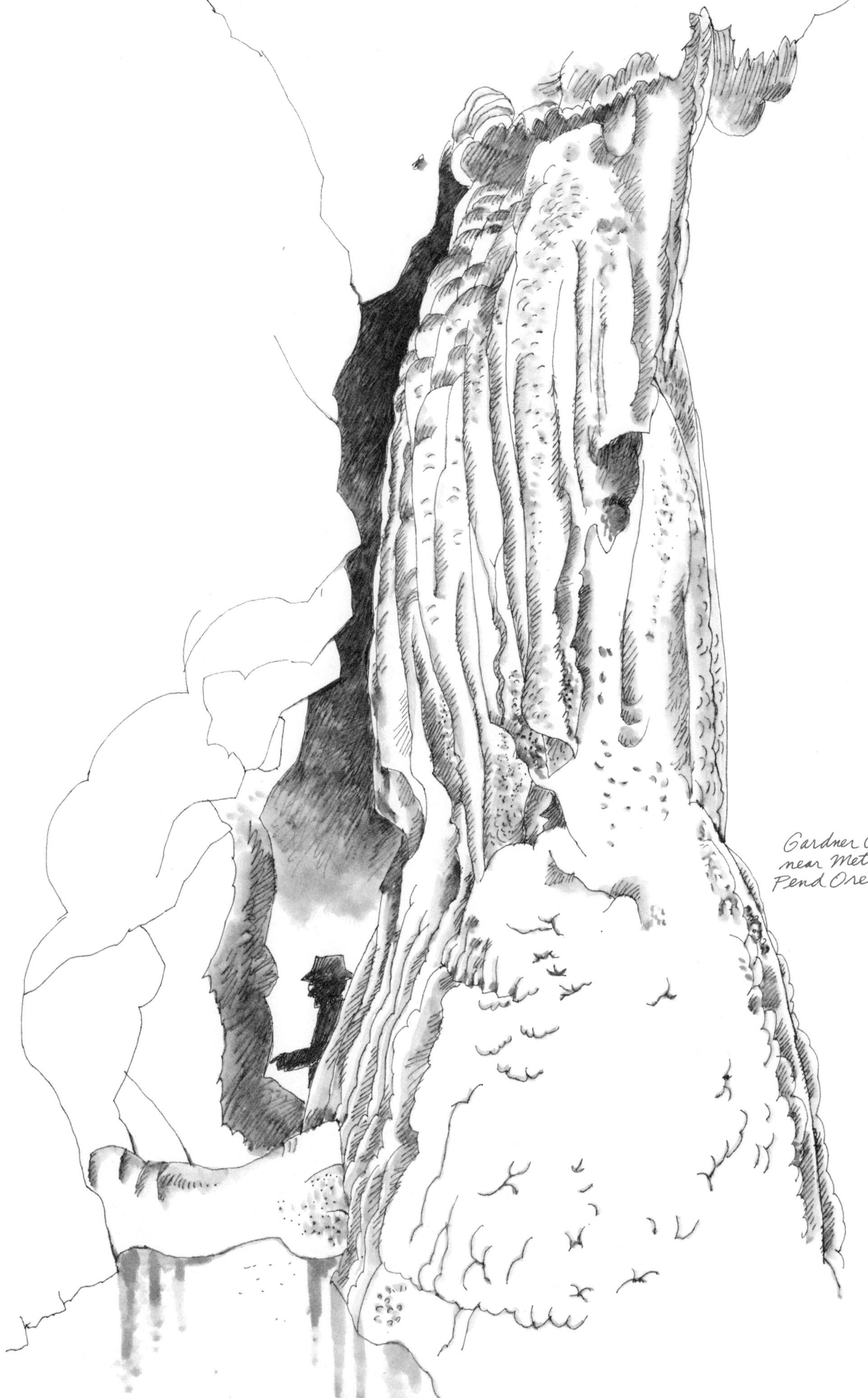

Gardner Cave
near Metal
Pend Oreille County

## Road to Manresa Grotto

From Metaline Falls, the road runs through forests, hugging the edge of the deep blue water of Sullivan Lake and south of Ione following the picturesque Pend Oreille River. At Manresa Grotto, on the Kalispel Indian Reservation, I sketch the cool gray interior of this natural cathedral formed by solid rock. Established by Catholic priest Father Dement, it is a place that inspires worship and meditation, and was revered by the Kalispel Indian tribe (despite hard rock seats).

Manresa Grotto, Pend Oreille County

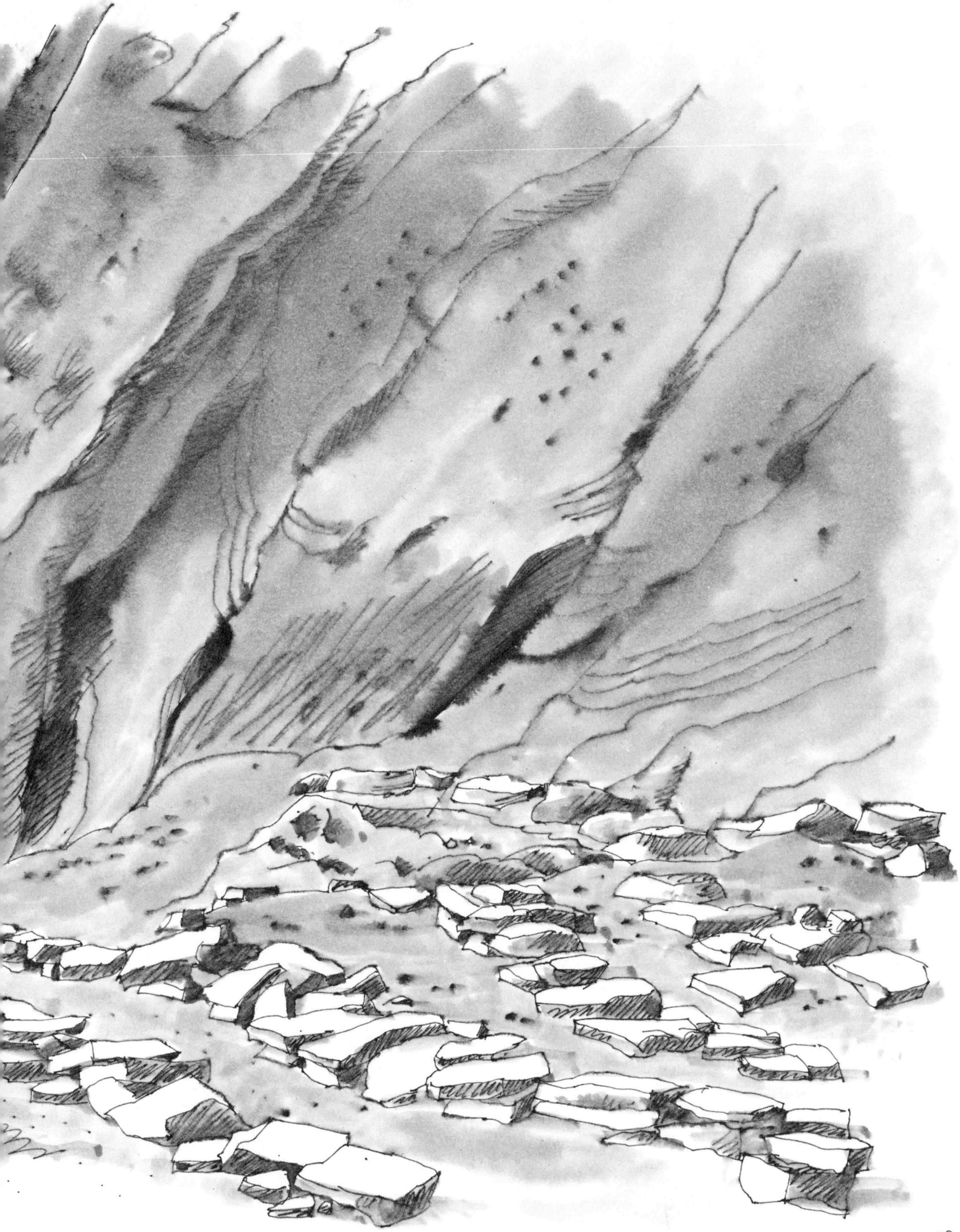

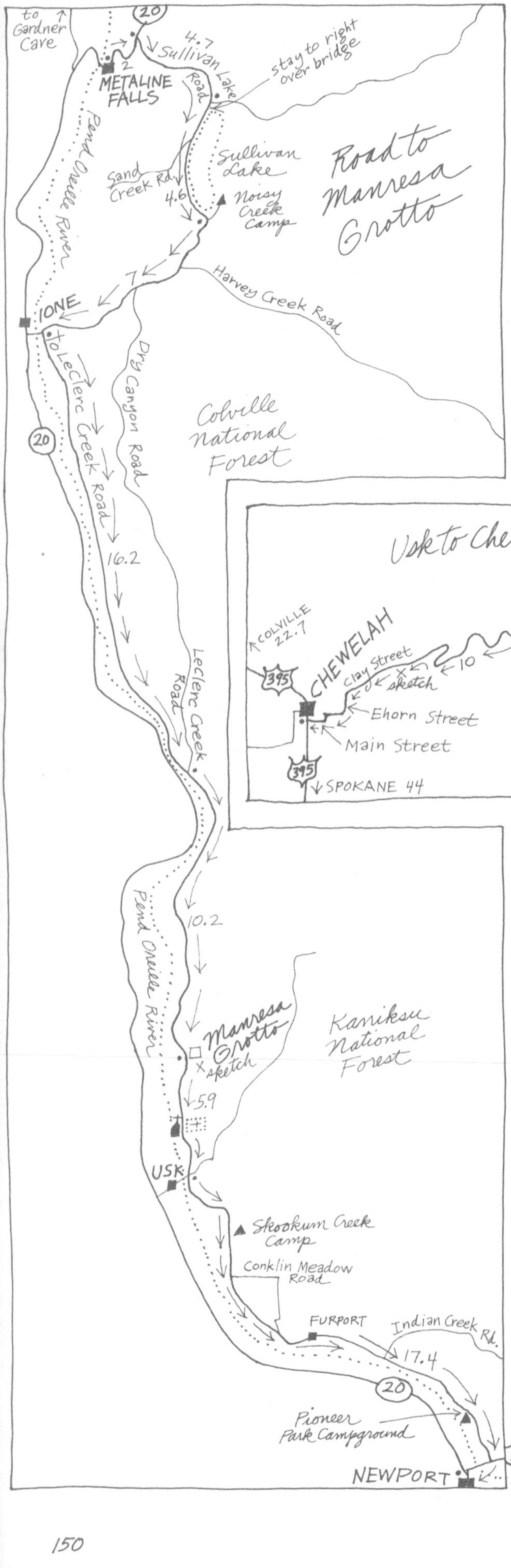
Road to Manresa Grotto
to Gardner Cave
20
4.7
Sullivan Lake Road
stay to right over bridge
METALINE FALLS
2
Pend Oreille River
Sullivan Lake
Sand Creek Rd.
4.6
Noisy Creek Camp
7
IONE
Harvey Creek Road
to Leclerc Creek Road
Dry Canyon Road
Colville National Forest
20
16.2
Leclerc Creek Road
10.2
Pend Oreille River
Manresa Grotto
sketch
Kaniksu National Forest
5.9
USK
Skookum Creek Camp
Conklin Meadow Road
FURPORT
Indian Creek Rd.
17.4
20
Pioneer Park Campground
2
NEWPORT

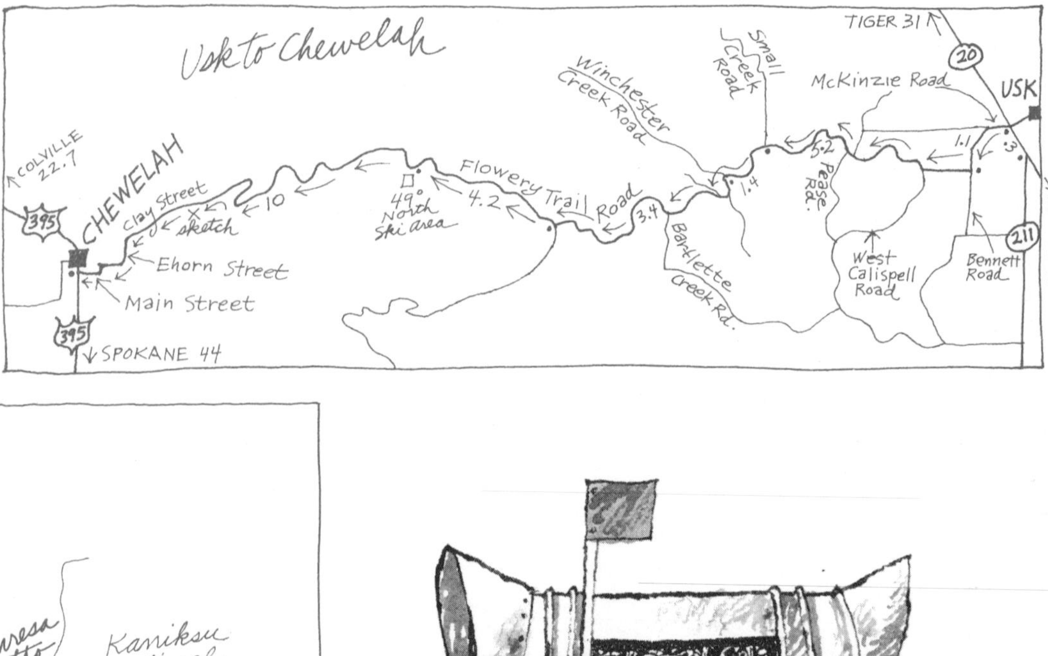
Usk to Chewelah
TIGER 31
20
Small Creek Road
Winchester Creek Road
McKinzie Road
USK
COLVILLE 22.7
CHEWELAH
395
Clay Street
sketch
10
49° North Ski area
Flowery Trail Road
4.2
3.4
1.4
5.2
Pease Rd.
1.1
3
NEWPORT 16
211
Ehorn Street
Main Street
Bartlette Creek Rd.
West Calispell Road
Bennett Road
395
SPOKANE 44

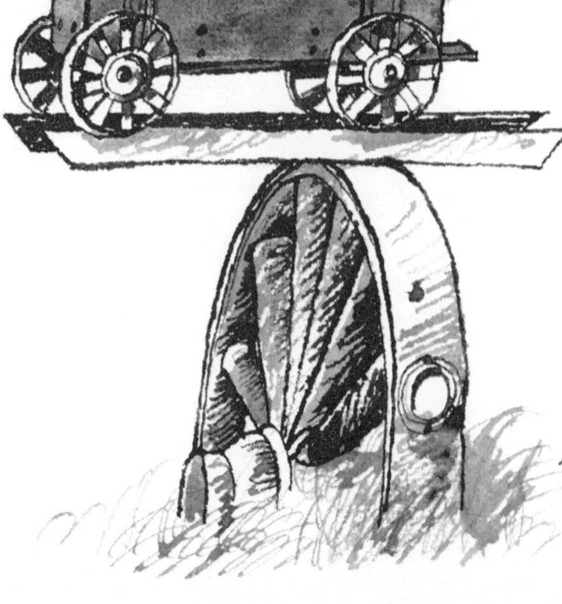

Back road mailbox

Back road musician

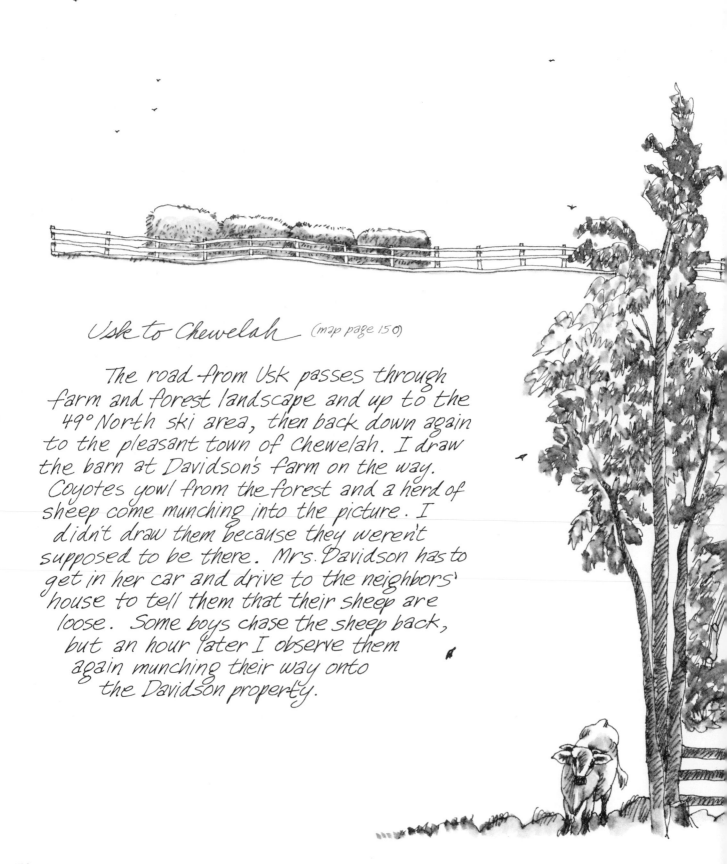

## Usk to Chewelah (map page 150)

The road from Usk passes through farm and forest landscape and up to the 49° North ski area, then back down again to the pleasant town of Chewelah. I draw the barn at Davidson's farm on the way. Coyotes yowl from the forest and a herd of sheep come munching into the picture. I didn't draw them because they weren't supposed to be there. Mrs. Davidson has to get in her car and drive to the neighbors' house to tell them that their sheep are loose. Some boys chase the sheep back, but an hour later I observe them again munching their way onto the Davidson property.

*Davidson's Farm near Chewelah, Stevens County*

## Back road through Colville Valley

There is great agricultural beauty to behold along this interesting back road—the patterns and textures of the crops, the sweeping lines of agricultural divisions. My reward for sitting quietly as I draw this farm scene is a magnificent, multicolored dragonfly that perches on my drawing board. I am extremely pleased to have inspired confidence in such an elegant member of the insect world.

Ranch in Colville Valley, Stevens County

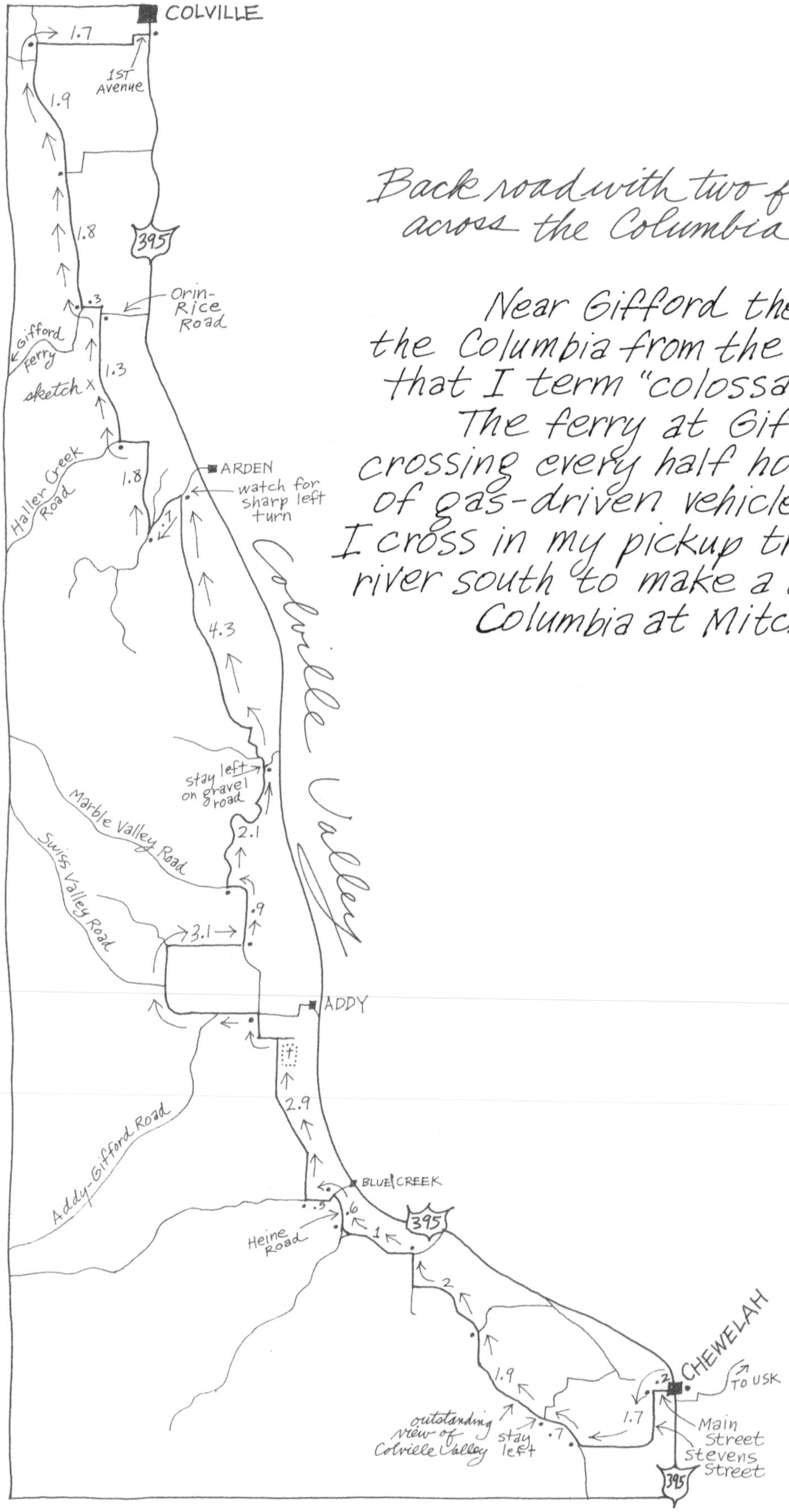


*Back road with two ferry rides across the Columbia River* (map, page 158)

Near Gifford there is a view of the Columbia from the back road I travel that I term "colossal" in my notes.
The ferry at Gifford makes a crossing every half hour with its load of gas-driven vehicles of all description. I cross in my pickup truck and follow the river south to make a drawing of the Columbia at Mitchell Point.

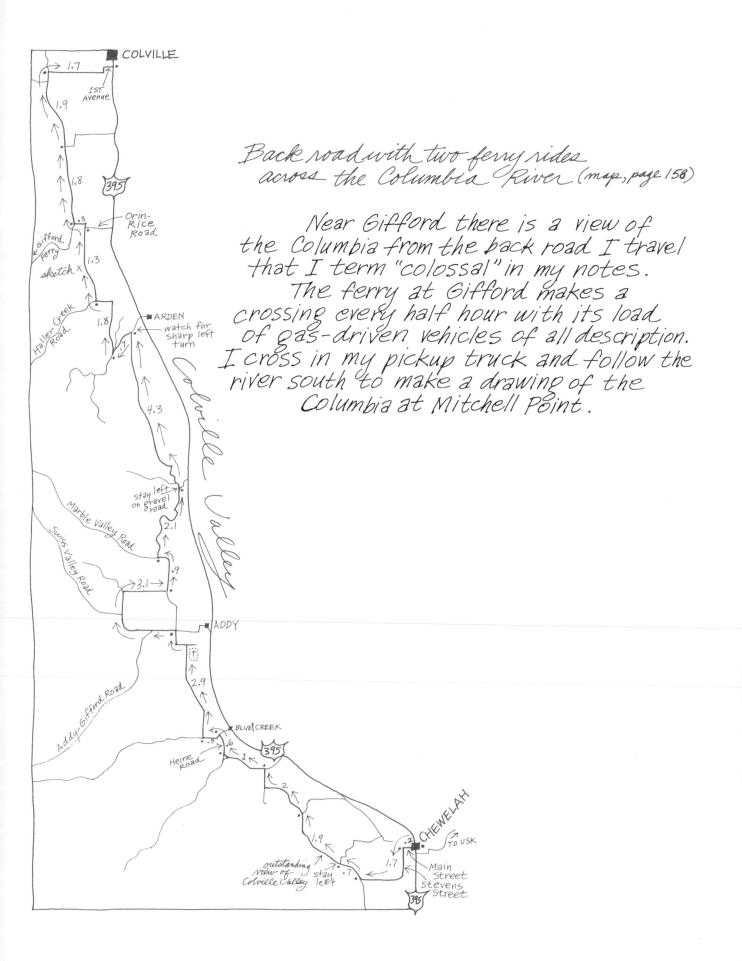

The Columbia River,
Mitchell Point,
Colville Indian Reservation,
Ferry County

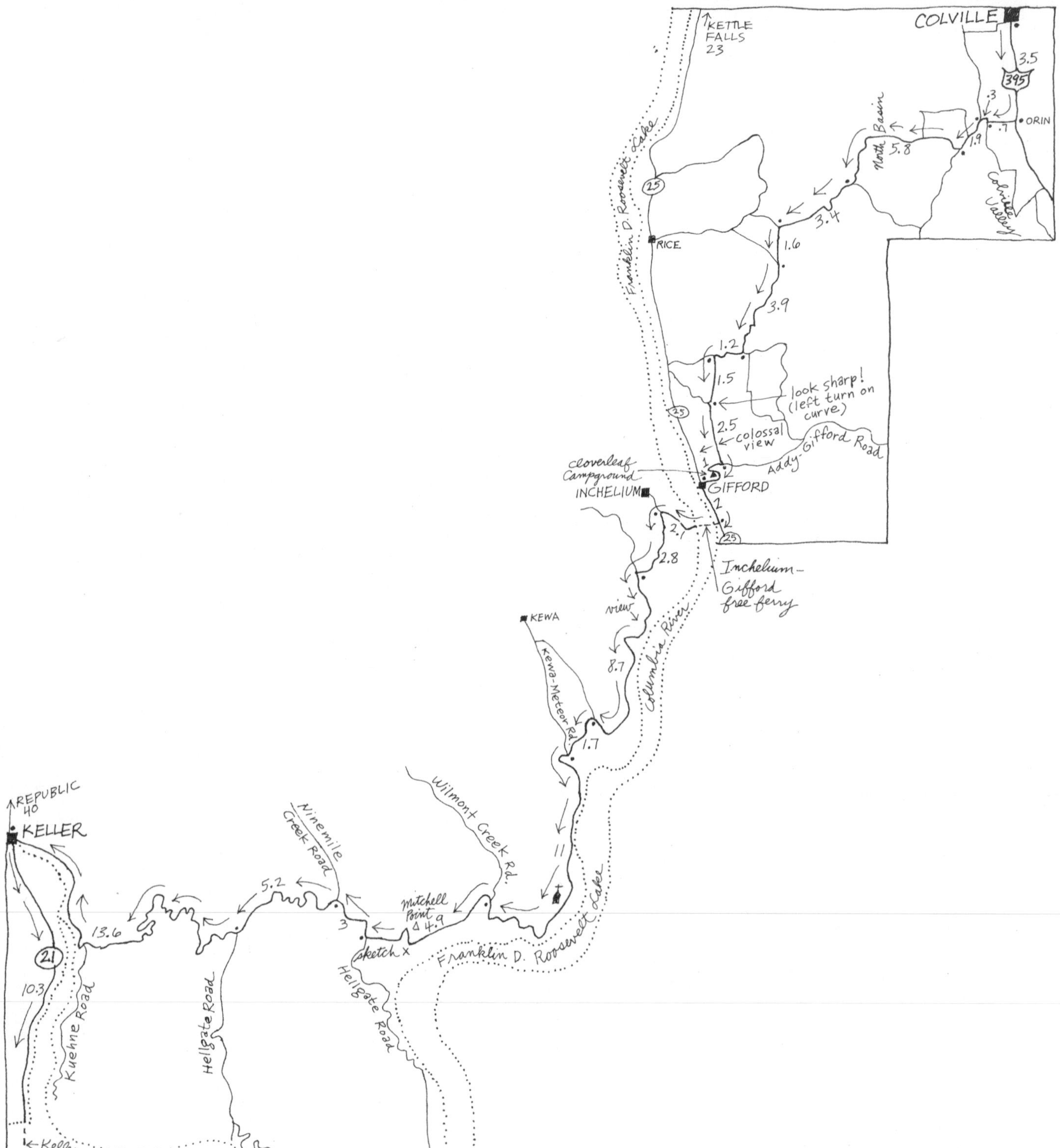
COLVILLE
KETTLE FALLS 23
3.5
395
.3
ORIN
.7
1.9
North Basin
5.8
Colville Valley
Franklin D. Roosevelt Lake
25
RICE
3.4
1.6
3.9
1.2
1.5
look sharp! (left turn on curve)
2.5
colossal view
Addy-Gifford Road
Cloverleaf Campground
INCHELIUM
GIFFORD
2
2.7
2.8
Inchelium-Gifford free ferry
KEWA
view
8.7
Kewa-Meteor Rd.
Columbia River
1.7
Wilmont Creek Rd.
11
REPUBLIC 40
KELLER
Ninemile Creek Road
5.2
Mitchell Point
4.9
3
sketch
13.6
21
10.3
Kuehne Road
Hellgate Road
Keller free ferry
Columbia River
15.5 to Wilbur

The Keller ferry ride at the end of the back road trip through Colville Indian country is delightful. I take it four times in order to make the drawing. During the eleven years two operators worked the ferry, bad weather halted its operation on only one occasion. They like their job but admit it could be a bitterly cold crossing in midwinter.

"Martha S," the ferry across Columbia River, Ferry and Lincoln Counties

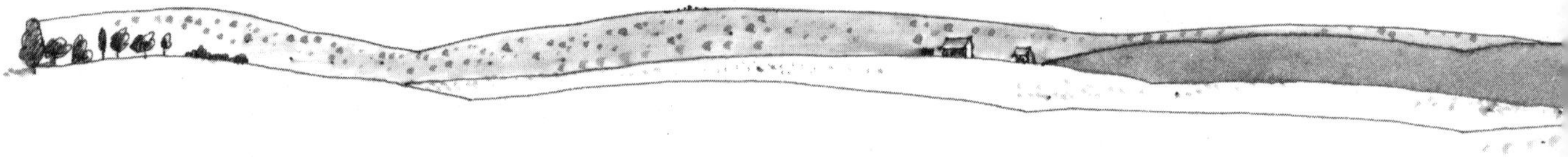

## The road to Hartline

From Grand Coulee the road winds through a rocky, sagebrush-covered draw. There is a large view of Grand Coulee dam, then a great rolling landscape plateau of wheatland all around. The horizon line is broken here and there by a lone barn, farm, and windmill and by an old silo like this one sketched near the grain elevator town of Hartline.

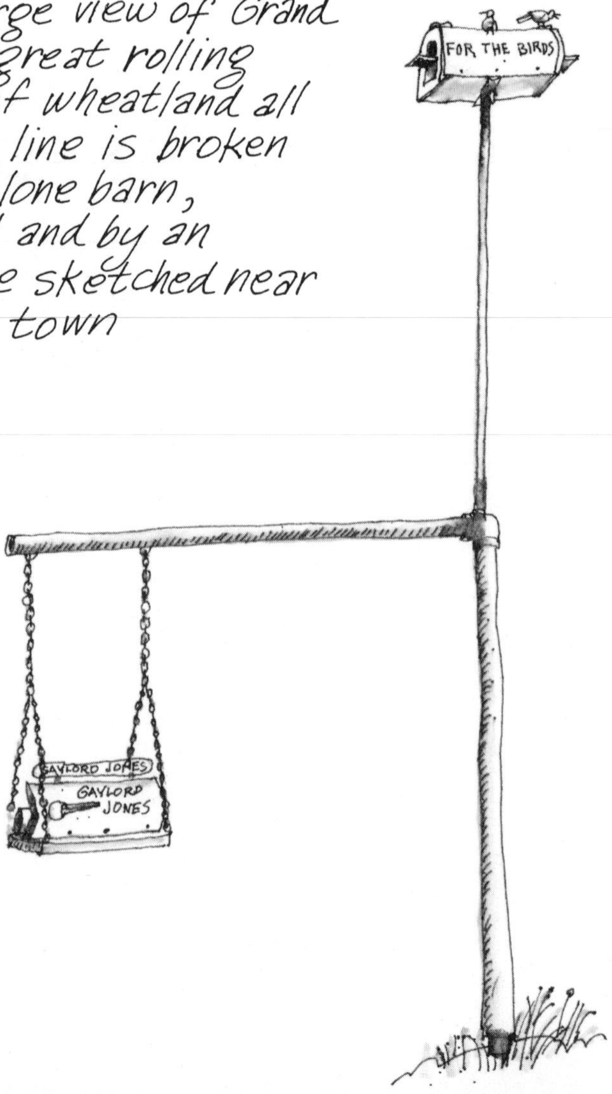


Back road mailbox

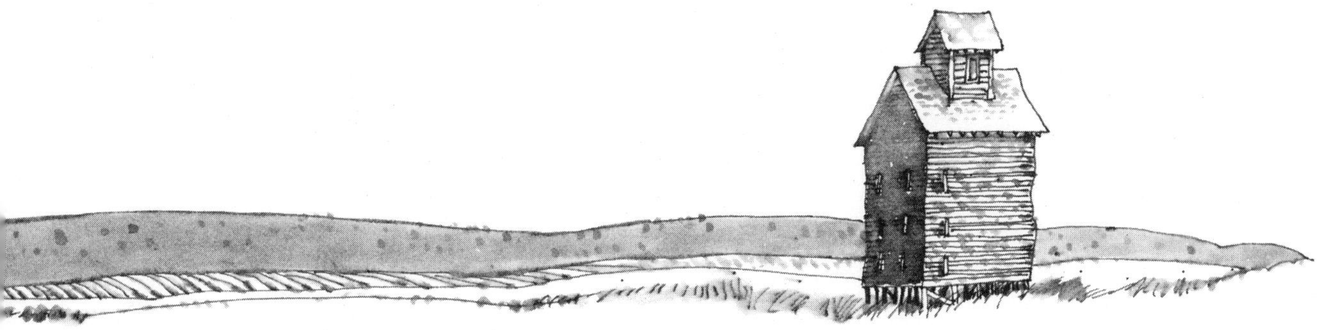

*Old silo near Hartline, Grant County*

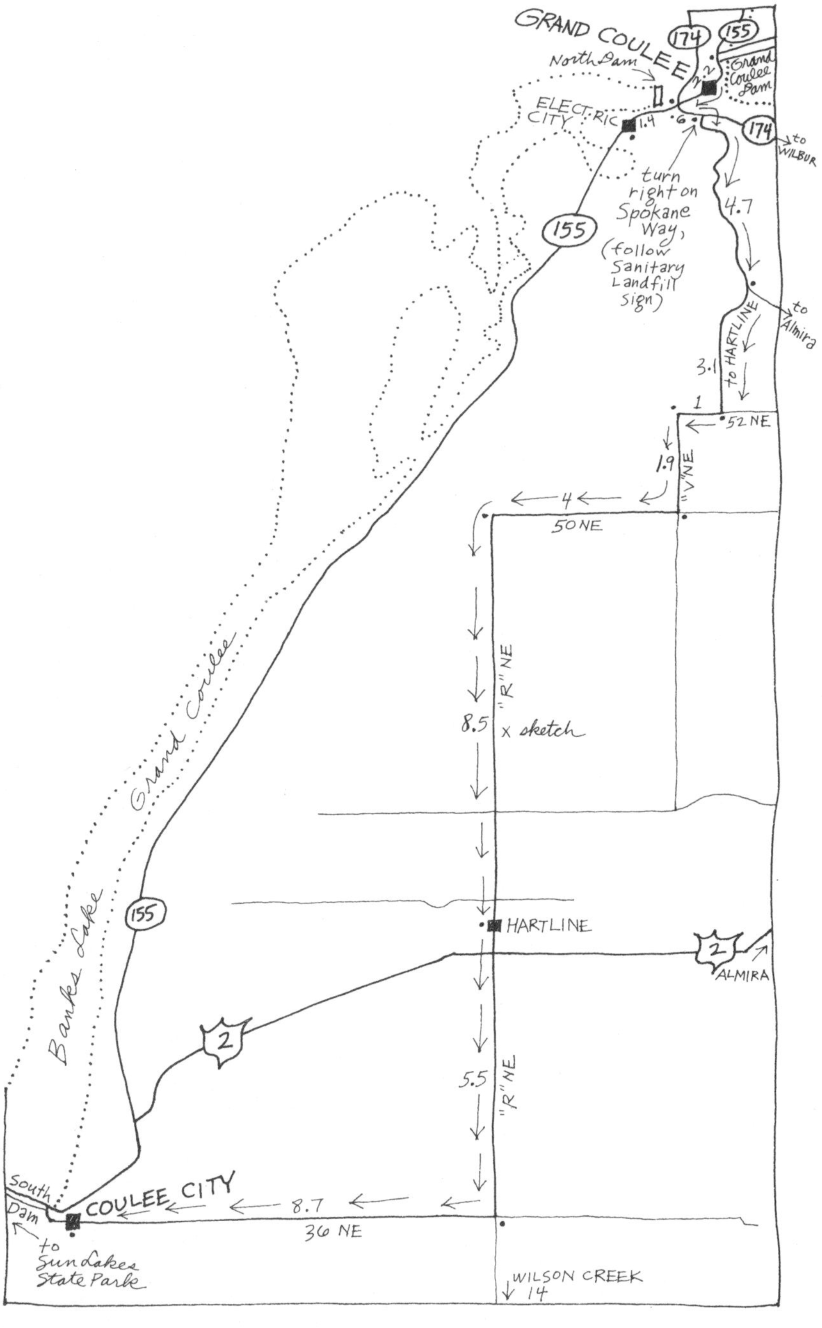

## Back road loop from Coulee City

To irrigate the farmlands of Washington, Summer Falls charges over this parapet of stone with thundering force. A hydroelectric generating facility will be placed here, a nearby notice reads. It may mean that the Falls will be eliminated, but in the meantime it is exciting to witness all that water seething, roiling, roaring, booming into Billy Clapp Lake.

The cliffs and sagebrush of Dry Coulee Road bring to mind scenery from movies of the Old West.

At Wilson Creek, where Zack Finney started the first school in 1892, and where an immigrant train arrived from Minnesota in 1901, there is a lovely shaded park just perfect for a picnic.

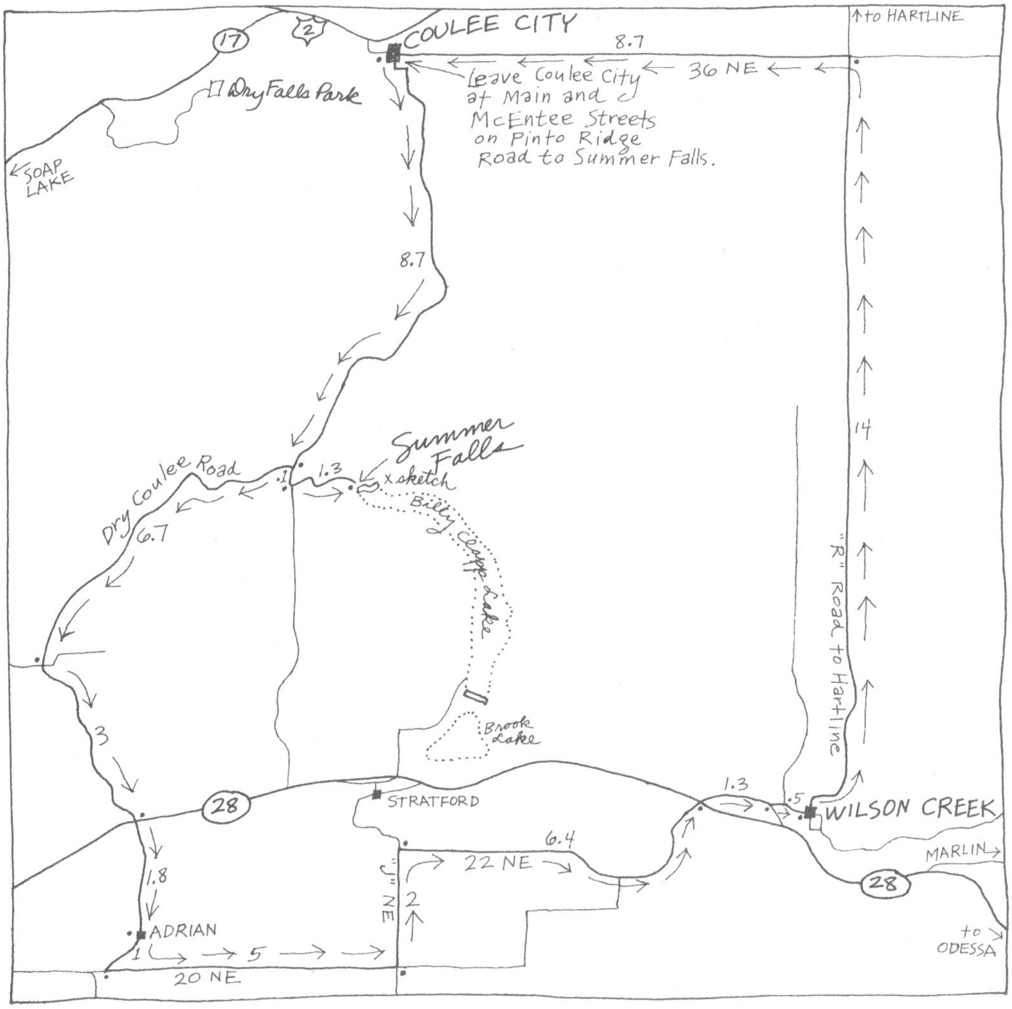


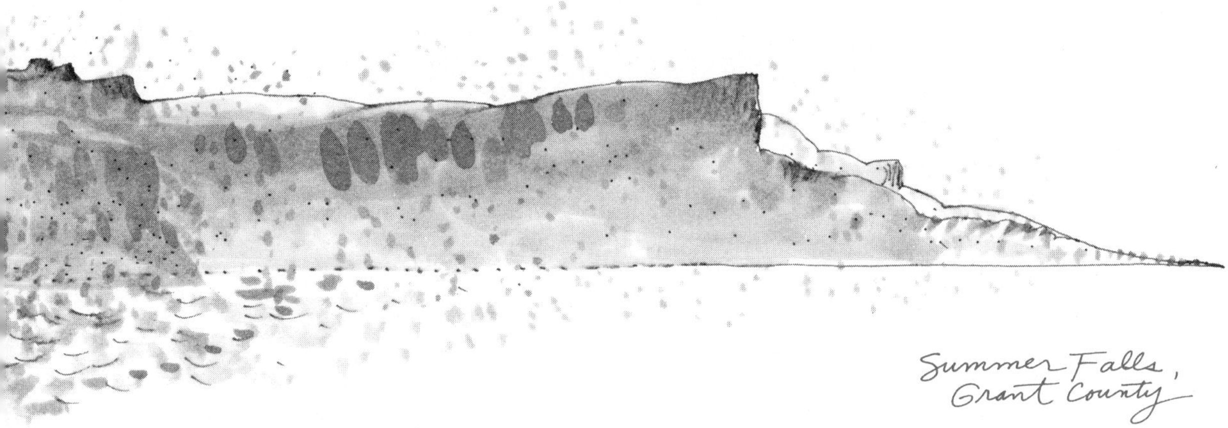

Summer Falls, Grant County

Roadside
sunflower,
Stevens County

## Road along the Spokane River

The Spokane Indian reservation road cuts through pine forest and meadow. Now I drive along the Spokane River itself and enjoy a landscape of green crops, river views, occasional farms, and roadside sunflowers in abundance.

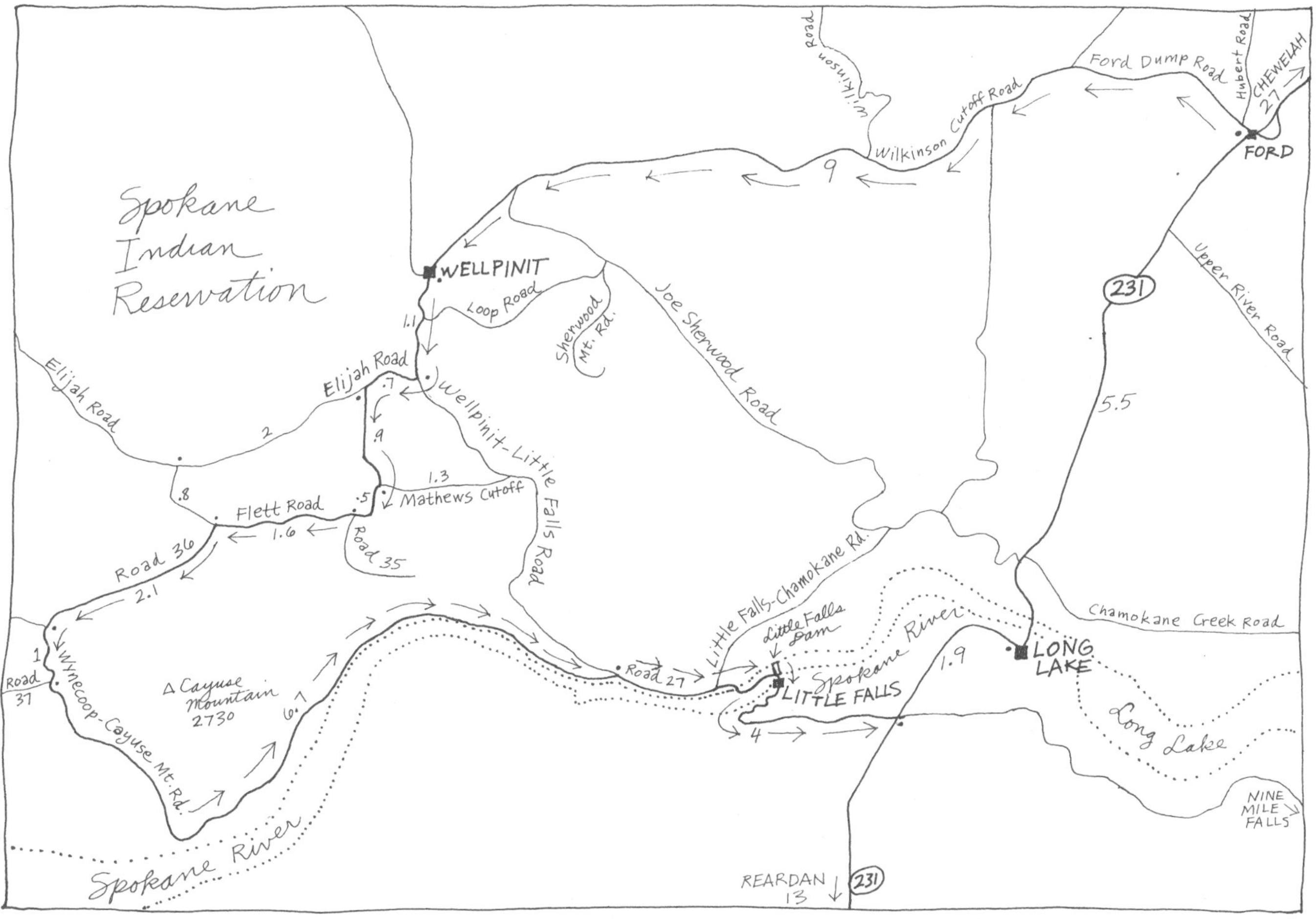

*Dalmatian Toadflax, Spokane County*

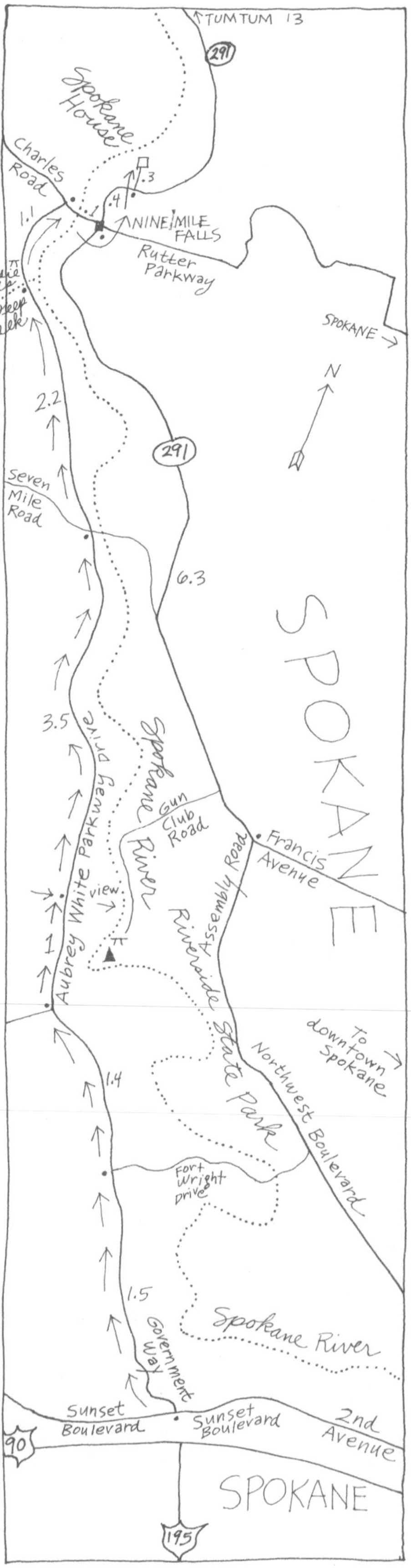

## The road through Riverside State Park

There is a splendid view of Spokane from the ridge along this forest and river road. I explore Deep Creek Canyon and find a variety of wild flowers. I make studies of two common tansy, with its bright yellow flower heads resembling golden buttons, and a yellow flower with the incredible name of Dalmatian toadflax. Spokane House Interpretive Center can be visited at the end of the trip. It is the site of an 1810 trading post and the first permanent white settlement in Washington.

Tansy, Spokane County

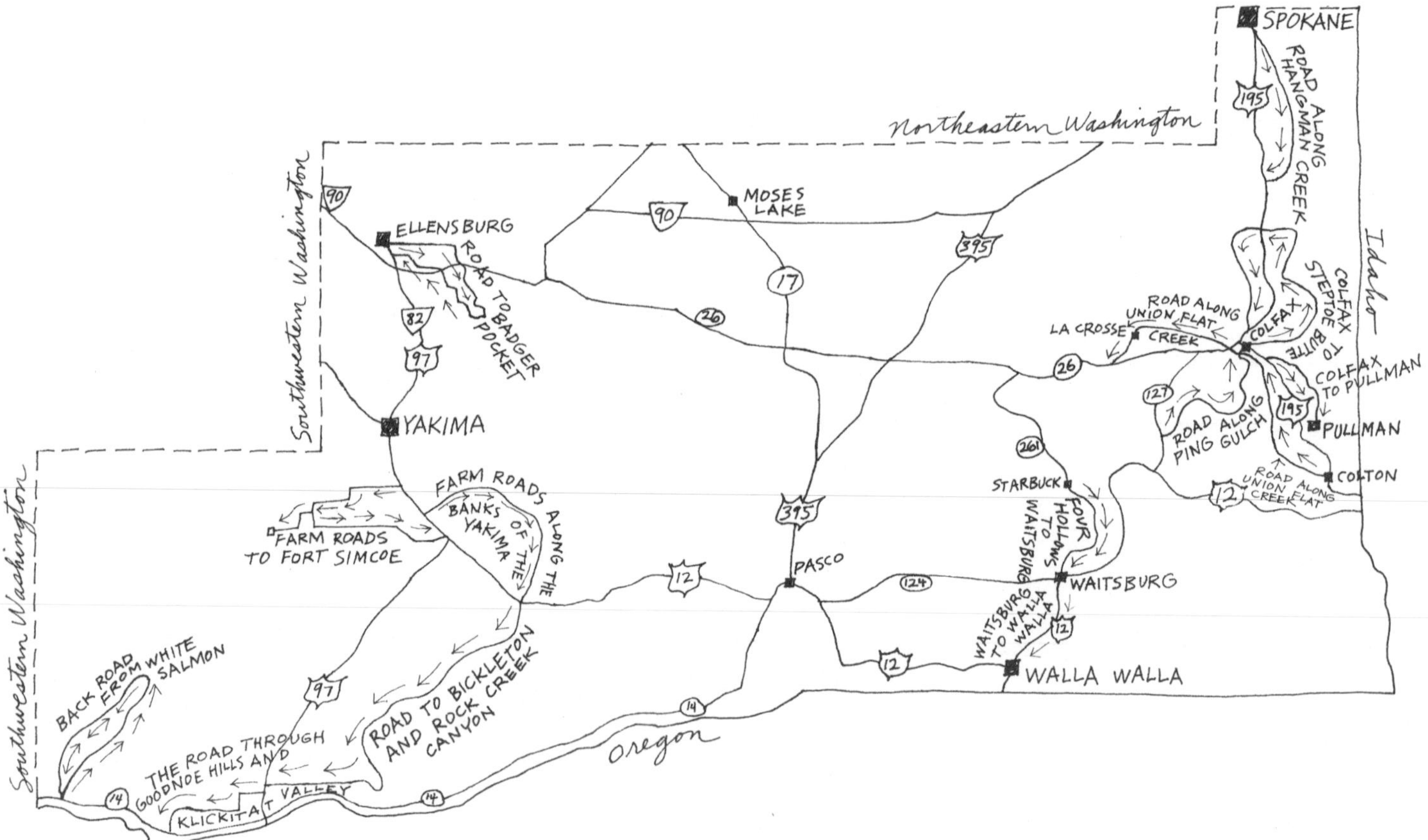

SPOKANE
ROAD ALONG HANGMAN CREEK
195
Northeastern Washington
Idaho
MOSES LAKE
90
ELLENSBURG
ROAD TO BADGER POCKET
Southwestern Washington
82
97
17
395
26
COLFAX TO STEPTOE BUTTE
ROAD ALONG UNION FLAT CREEK
LA CROSSE
COLFAX
COLFAX TO PULLMAN
PULLMAN
127
ROAD ALONG PING GULCH
COLTON
ROAD ALONG UNION FLAT CREEK
YAKIMA
FARM ROADS ALONG THE BANKS OF THE YAKIMA
FARM ROADS TO FORT SIMCOE
261
STARBUCK
FOUR HOLLOWS TO WAITSBURG
WAITSBURG
PASCO
124
12
WAITSBURG TO WALLA WALLA
WALLA WALLA
BACK ROAD FROM WHITE SALMON
ROAD TO BICKLETON AND ROCK CREEK CANYON
THE ROAD THROUGH GOODNOE HILLS AND KLICKITAT VALLEY
14
Oregon

# Southeastern Washington

I recall the fruit trees, grapevines, and the tall green of hops in Yakima Valley; the peas, asparagus, and sweet onion fields of Walla Walla; the dairy and grain country around Ellensburg, and the rolling wheatlands south of Spokane. And in late summer there is the drama of the harvest. By traveling the back roads, I witness the great agricultural achievement of the land.

Giant Blazing Star (bright yellow flowers), Klickitat County

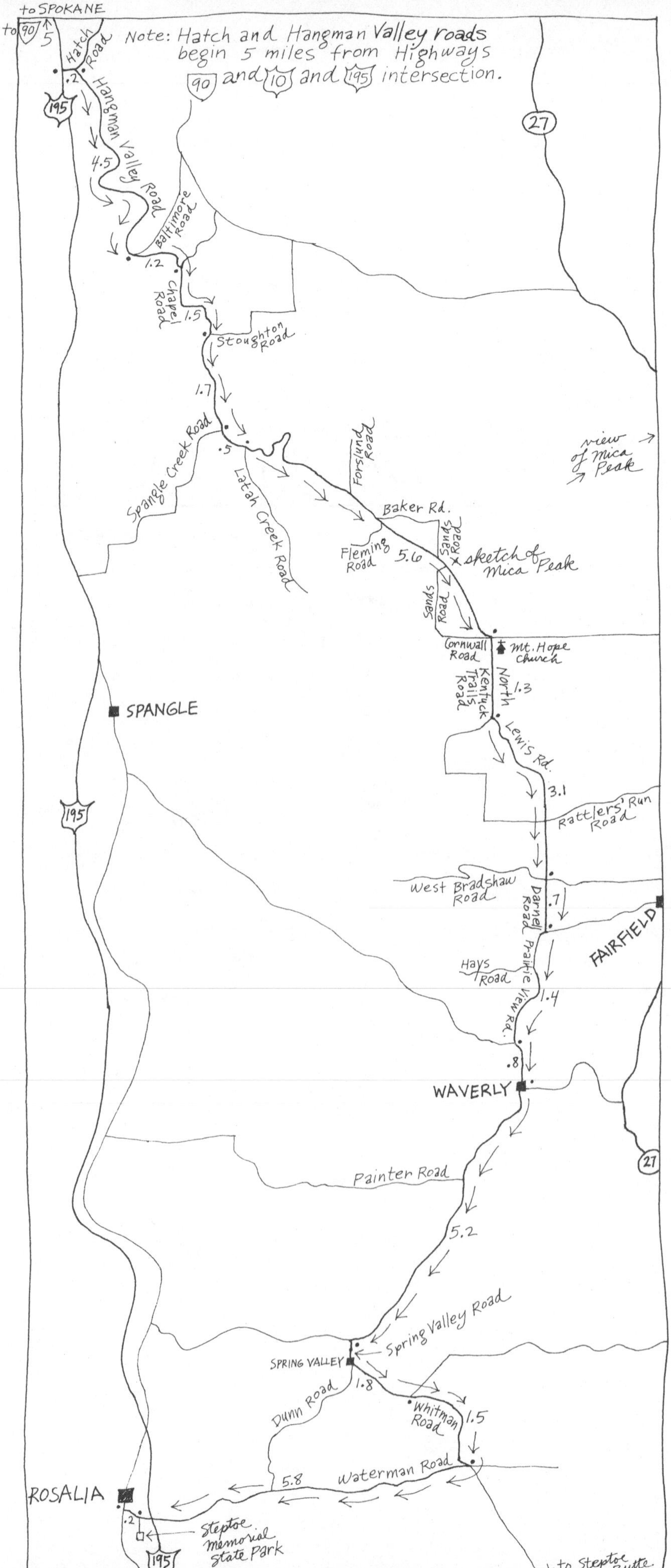

to SPOKANE
to 90
5
Note: Hatch and Hangman Valley roads begin 5 miles from Highways 90 and 10 and 195 intersection.
Hatch Road
.2
195
Hangman Valley Road
4.5
Baltimore Road
1.2
Chapel Road
1.5
Stoughton Road
27
1.7
Spangle Creek Road
.5
Latah Creek Road
Forslund Road
view of Mica Peak
Baker Rd.
Sands Road
Fleming Road
5.6
sketch of Mica Peak
Cornwall Road
Mt. Hope Church
Kentuck Trails Road
North
1.3
SPANGLE
Lewis Rd.
3.1
Rattlers' Run Road
195
West Bradshaw Road
Darnell Road
.7
FAIRFIELD
Hays Road
Prairie View Rd.
1.4
.8
WAVERLY
27
Painter Road
5.2
Spring Valley Road
SPRING VALLEY
1.8
Dunn Road
Whitman Road
1.5
Waterman Road
5.8
ROSALIA
.2
Steptoe Memorial State Park
195
to Steptoe Butte

## The road along Hangman Creek

Hangman Creek Road soon brings me to the rolling grain and grass seed fields south of Spokane. From one vista point I sketch Mica Peak and the extensive agricultural land surrounding it. Bluegrass fields are being burned in the distance, the smoke threatening the visibility of the mountain. The sound of harvesting machinery fills the air from beyond the nearby hills.

Harvester, Spokane County

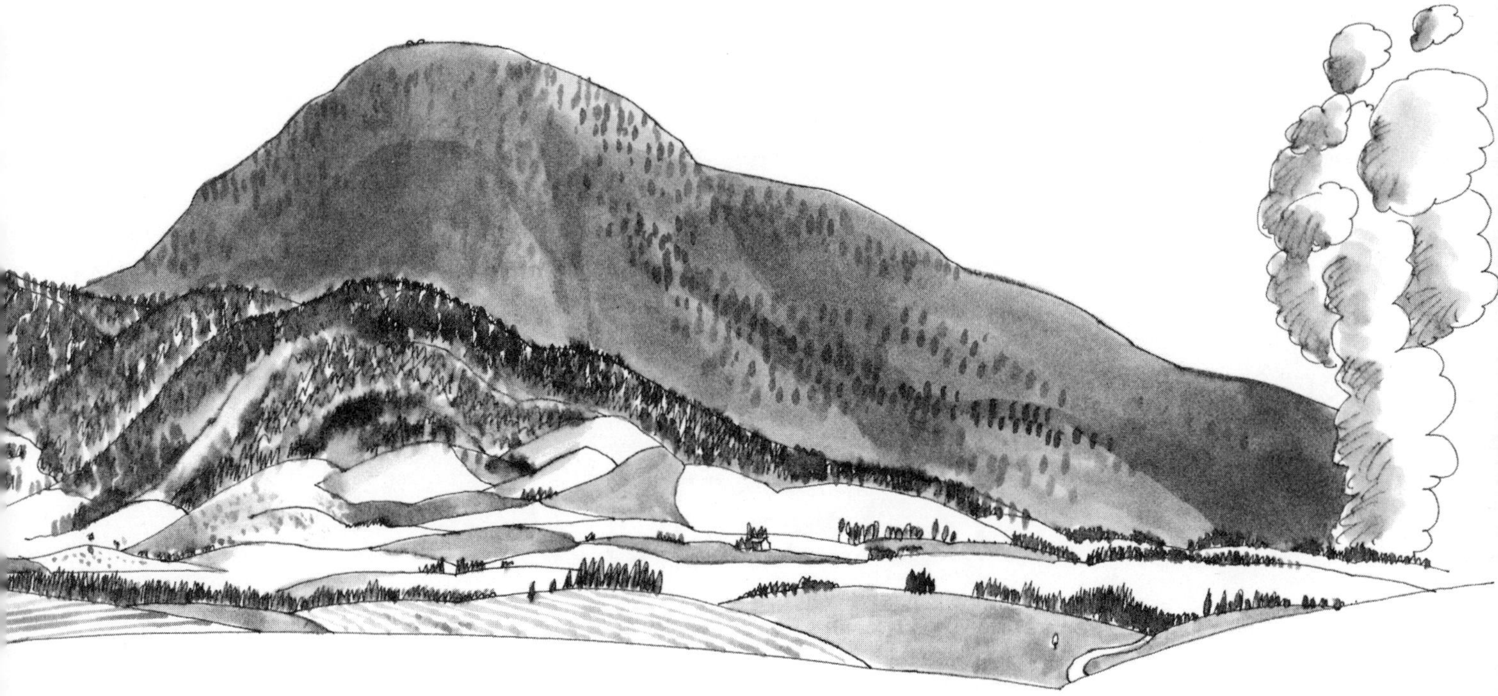

Mica Peak, Spokane County

## Road along Ping Gulch

From the campground along the Snake River at Central Ferry I see tugs pushing loaded barges. They carry oil, grain, fish, and wood—a variety of products from Idaho. An incredibly long freight train creaks over a trestle suspended high above the Snake. An image of Buster Keaton racing and leaping from car to car comes to mind. I am occupied counting cars for quite a while, for it turns out there are a hundred of them!

In Ping Gulch there are cows, rolling wheatlands, creekside willows, roadside sunflowers, neat farmhouses, and dogs running alongside my vehicle.

Ping Gulch ranch, Garfield County

At Lower Granite Lock and Dam on the Snake River I visit the Fish Viewing Room and the fish ladder. There are steelhead trout, channel catfish, carp, salmon, and many other fish to see.

The hills roll gracefully on either side of the road to Colfax. I feel that I am gaining more knowledge of the land and its farming people for taking this meandering series of back country roads.

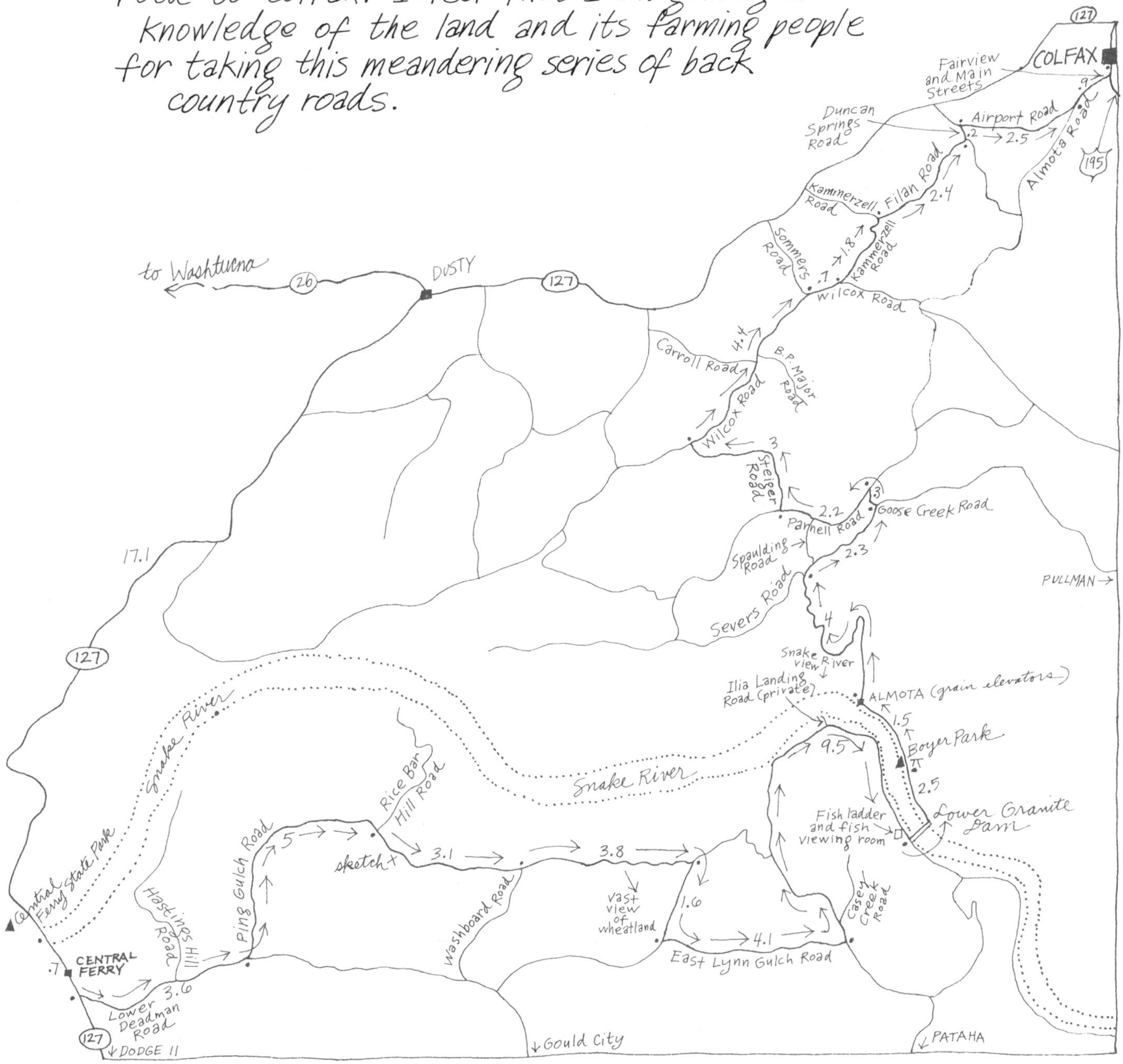

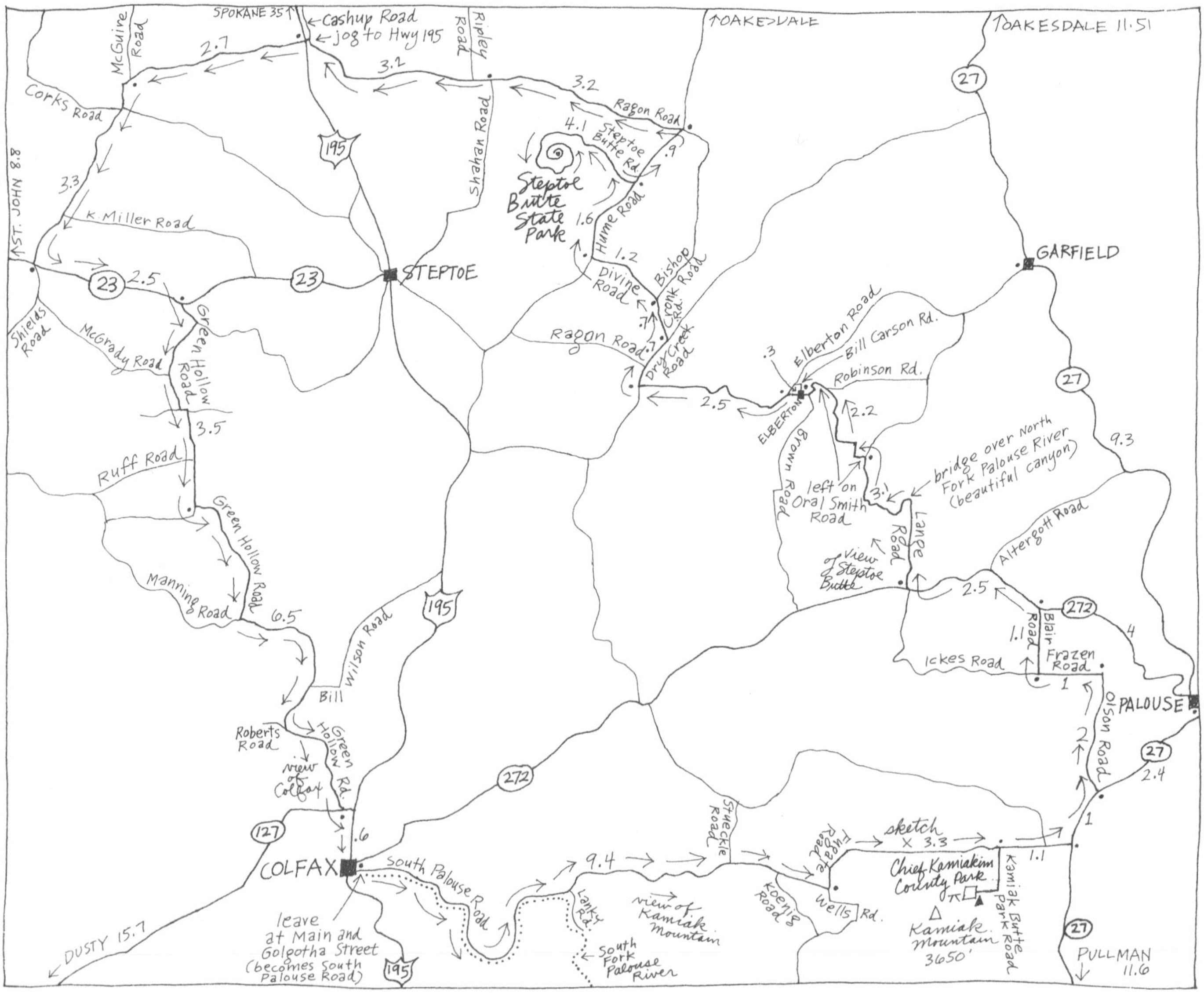


# Colfax to Steptoe Butte

I follow the Palouse River past well-kept farmhouses, their gardens adorned with flowers. Near Kamiak Butte I make a drawing of the rolling farmland. Kamiak was a famous Yakima Indian chieftain, and the butte named after him is now a county park. I cross the Palouse River, here flowing through a deep canyon, and proceed to the picturesque community of Elberton. Later, as I appreciate the view from atop Steptoe Butte, I reflect on the geology of this region. I am looking down from an ancient mountain that ten million years ago was

Surrounded by lava flows. Kamiak Butte is another old mountain that lava had surrounded but not covered. The rich covering of dirt and topsoil, layered over the old lava flows, today support the Palouse area's large-scale dry farming of peas, lentils, and wheat.

Landscape near Colfax,
Whitman County

# Country road from Colfax to Pullman

In Colfax, on Perkins Avenue near Last Street, you can see the 1884 Victorian house of the first permanent resident of the town, James A. Perkins. (If you wish to see the interior, write to the Whitman County Historical Society, Box 447, Pullman.)

The farmland in this area was once covered with bunchgrass. Early settlers called it palouse, from the French word for short, thick grass.

In a quiet valley I sketch the McIntosh Angus Ranch red barn and house. The black angus pictured here is particularly clean, for it has just been washed by a member of the McIntosh family. Other back roads beckon me to the delightful university town of Pullman, at the junction of the three forks of the Palouse River.

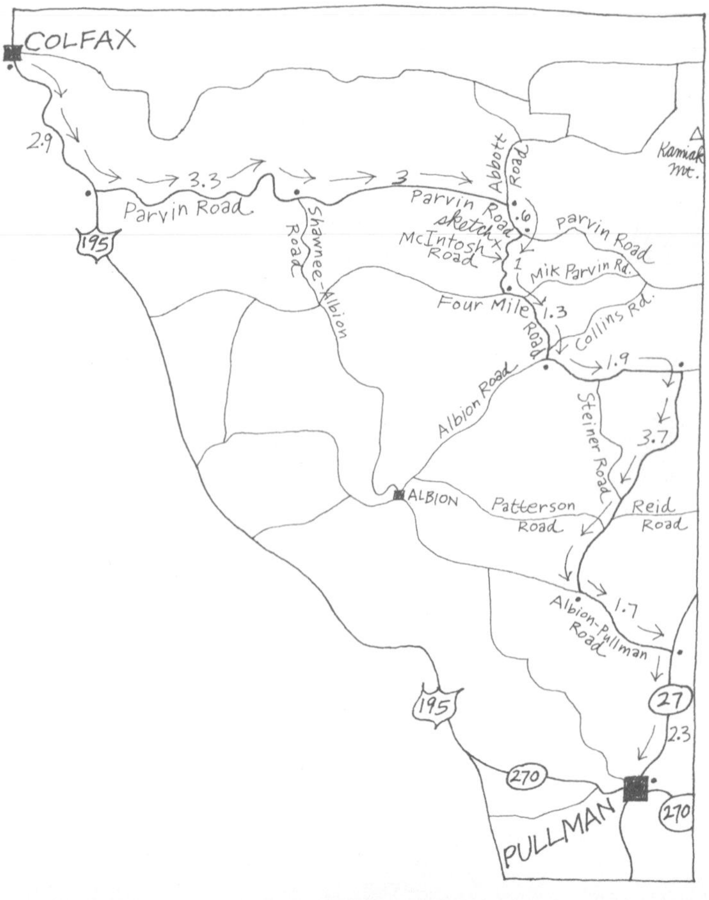

McIntosh Angus Ranch,
Whitman County

*Grain elevator, Union Flat Creek Road, Whitman County*

# The road along Union Flat Creek

I proceed through valley landscape past handsome farms and big barns. Willow trees grow along the creek. Klemgard County Park is situated on an attractive site for picnicking.

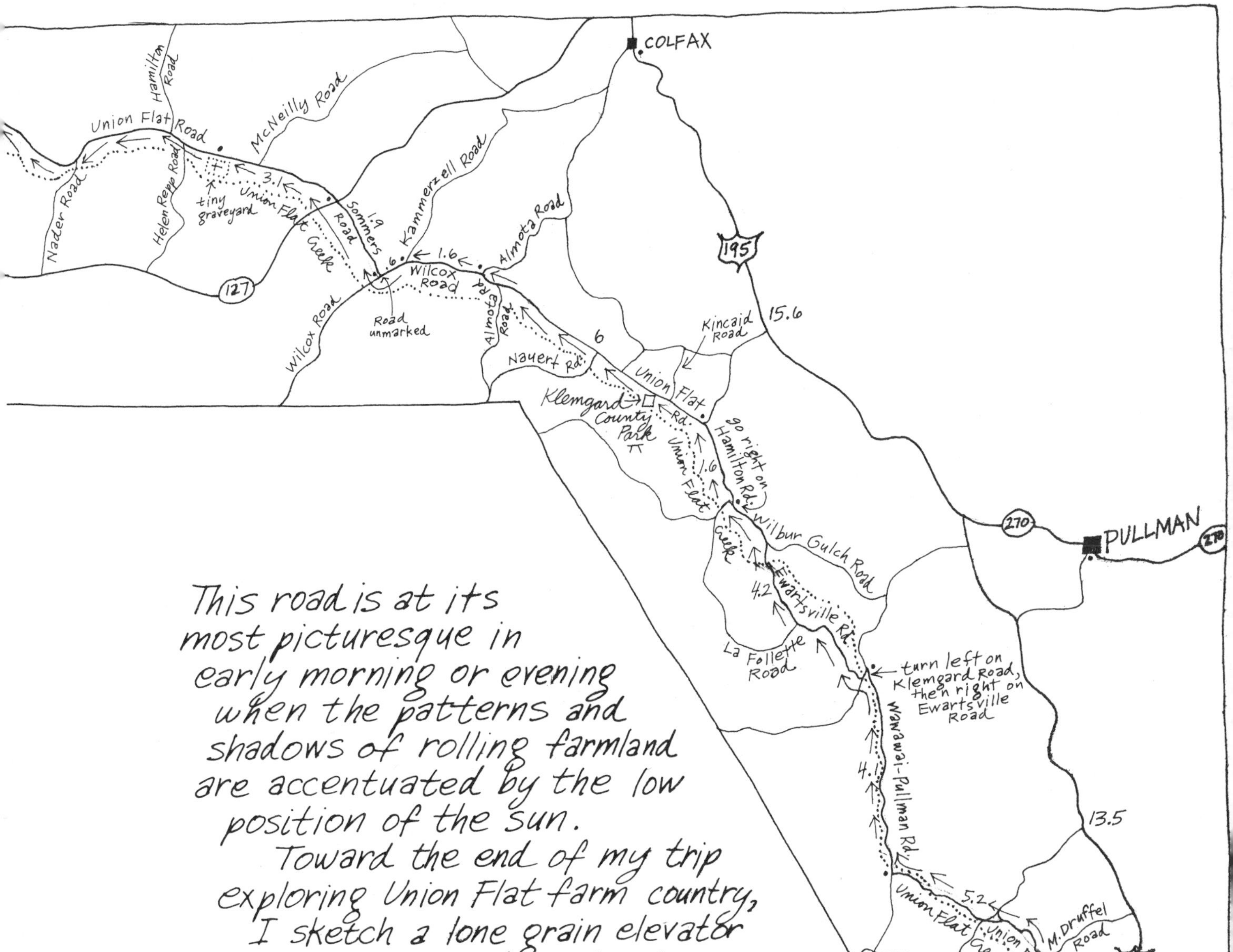


This road is at its most picturesque in early morning or evening when the patterns and shadows of rolling farmland are accentuated by the low position of the sun.

Toward the end of my trip exploring Union Flat farm country, I sketch a lone grain elevator poking upward to the sky.

1892 Drugstore, Waitsburg Walla Walla County

## Four Hollows to Waitsburg

South of Washtucna, Adams County, are two well-maintained state parks: Palouse Falls and Lyons Ferry. Crossing the Snake River at Lyons Ferry, I travel back roads with names like Smith Hollow, Whetstone Hollow, Thorn Hollow, Sorghum Hollow, and even Whoopemup Hollow.

Near Waitsburg, on Highway 12, is Lewis and Clark Trail State Park, where in May 1806, Lewis and Clark's party ate parsnips and dog meat, having nothing else to choose from. In historic Waitsburg I sketch two facades in the well-preserved old town. At the local newspaper, the *Times*, the editor informs me that the paper's 1888 building once had a decorative design at the top that has long since been removed. He suspects that the lawyer who used to have his office there had the peaked and turreted top taken off when the bricks and mortar began to show some wear. The lawyer, he conjectured, had been trying to avoid suit should a brick dislodge and fall on a passerby. However, the editor studied the prevailing wind direction, and it

The *Times*, Waitsburg, Walla Walla County

was his conclusion that should any part have deteriorated enough to fall, it would have fallen in the direction of the roof, not the street. The missing top accounted for the building's rather blunt roof line.

J. W. Morgan's 1892 drugstore has today been put to another use, but the well-proportioned, early Waitsburg design is still almost intact. Testimony to Waitsburg's interest in preserving its heritage of history is the Bruce Memorial Museum, at 4th and Main streets, which should also be seen while you are in town.

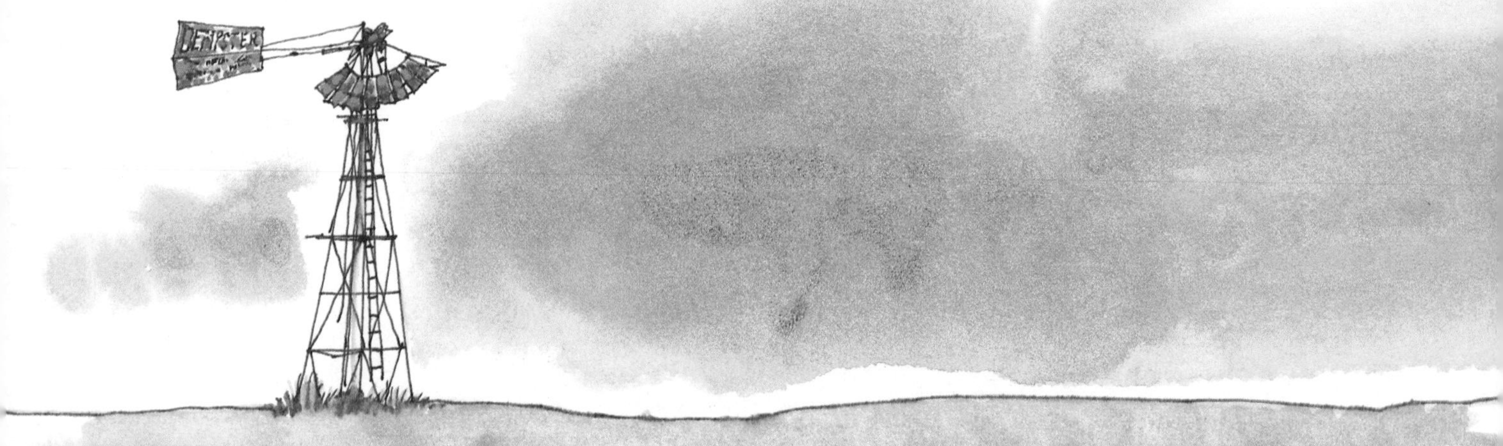


## Waitsburg to Walla Walla

This road takes me through the agricultural land north of Walla Walla, then east of the city to the "walk-in entrance" of Whitman Mission. It is a peaceful place of great beauty, but it is also the site of the massacre of the missionary Marcus Whitman family and other mission members by Cayuse Indians in 1847. The Cayuse had their reasons: one of them was that white settlers visiting the mission had transmitted a measles epidemic to the Indians that had wiped out half their tribe! When a cure could not be found by missionary-doctor Whitman, the Indians lost faith in the Whitman cause. There is more to the dramatic story; it awaits you at the Whitman Mission.

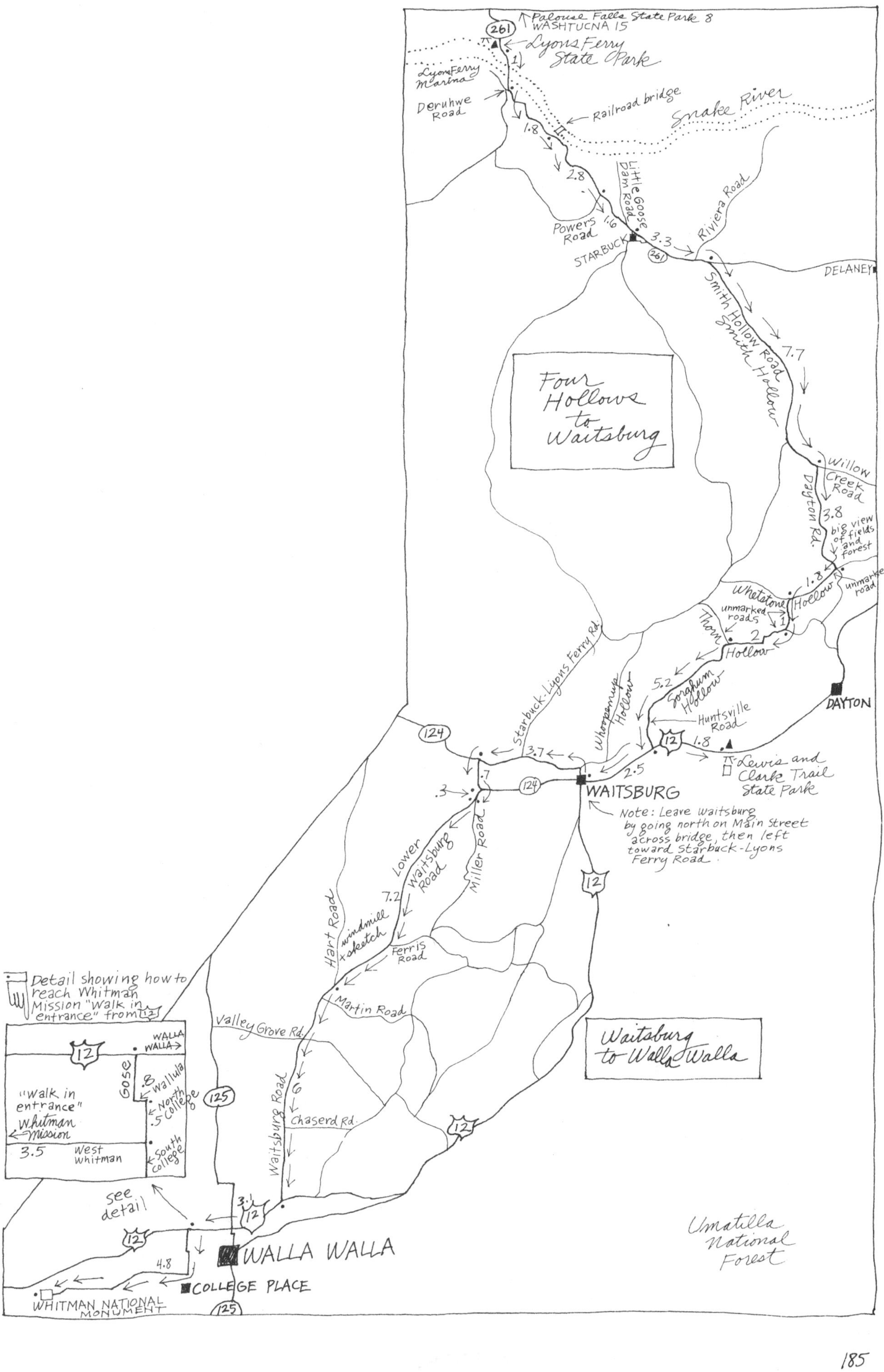

Palouse Falls State Park 8
WASHTUCNA 15
261
Lyons Ferry State Park
Lyons Ferry Marina
Deruhwe Road
Railroad bridge
Snake River
1.8
2.8
Little Goose Dam Road
Powers Road
1.6
STARBUCK
3.3
Riviera Road
DELANEY
Smith Hollow Road
Smith Hollow
7.7
Four Hollows to Waitsburg
Willow Creek Road
Dayton Rd.
3.8
big view of fields and forest
1.8
unmarked road
Whetstone Hollow
unmarked roads
Thorn Hollow
2
5.2
Sorghum Hollow
Whoopemup Hollow
Starbuck-Lyons Ferry Rd.
DAYTON
Huntsville Road
124
3.7
2.5
12
1.8
Lewis and Clark Trail State Park
WAITSBURG
Note: Leave Waitsburg by going north on Main Street across bridge, then left toward Starbuck-Lyons Ferry Road.
.7
.3
Lower Waitsburg Road
Miller Road
7.2
Hart Road
windmill sketch
Ferris Road
Martin Road
Detail showing how to reach Whitman Mission "walk in entrance" from 12
WALLA WALLA
Gose
.8
Wallula
North College
.5
"walk in entrance"
Whitman Mission
3.5
West Whitman
South College
Valley Grove Rd.
Waitsburg to Walla Walla
125
Waitsburg Road
6
Chaserd Rd.
see detail
3.1
WALLA WALLA
4.8
COLLEGE PLACE
WHITMAN NATIONAL MONUMENT
Umatilla National Forest

## The road to Badger Pocket

Frail ninety-year-old Clareta Olmstead shows me the old cottonwood log cabin built by the Olmstead family in 1875. Its historic furnishings include an 1870 Scottish spinning wheel. It is now part of a state park and is open to visitors most of the year. There are many other turn-of-the-century buildings in addition to the log cabin. As I sketch, peacocks strut about the grounds occasionally giving off plaintive, loud, babylike cries.

Olmstead Cabin, 1875,
Kittitas County

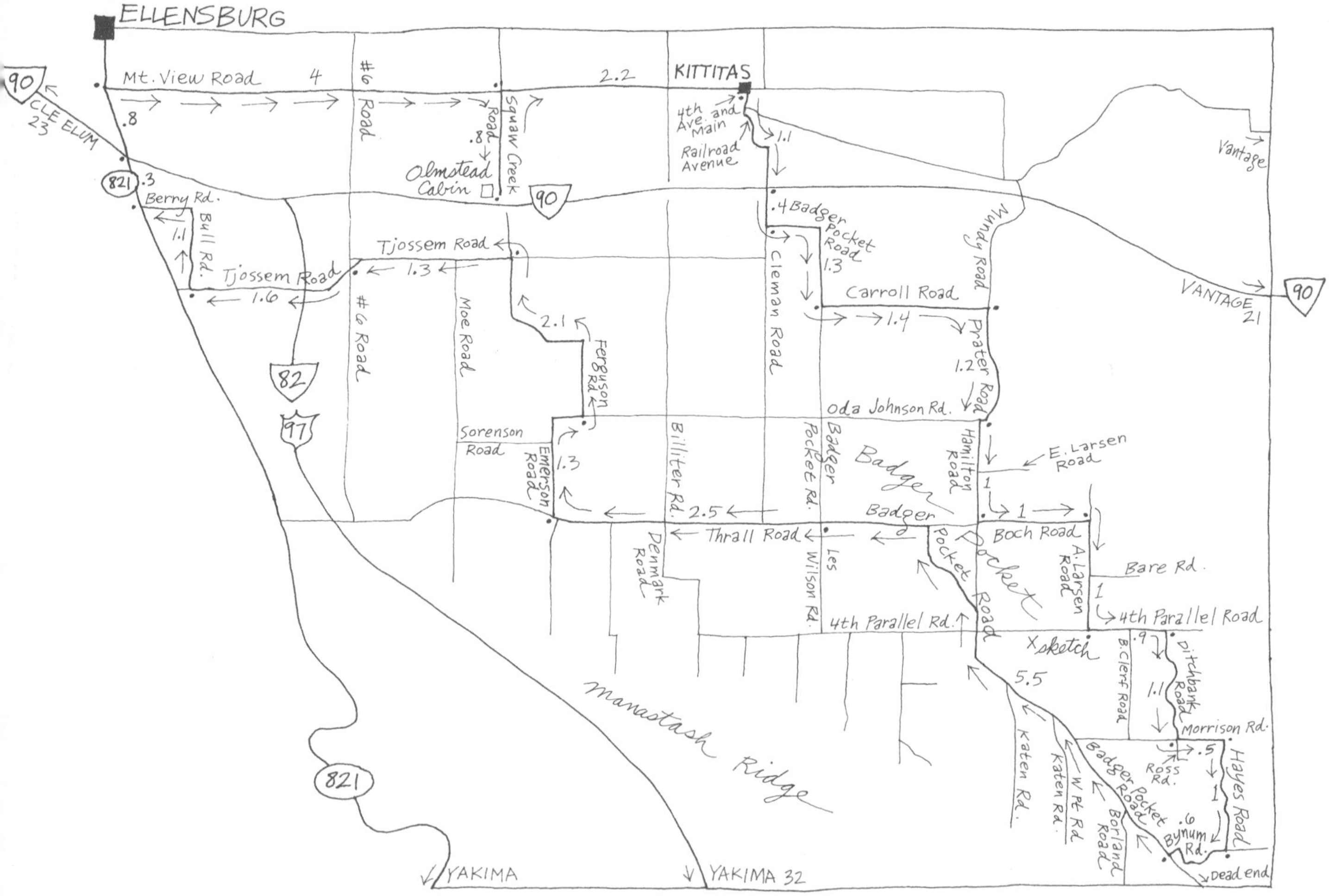

*Badger Pocket landscape,*
*near Ellensburg, Kittitas County*

Following this visit I explore Badger Pocket, where green farmland pushes up into the sagebrush-covered surrounding hills. This is rich dairyland, and green and golden hay crops and Hereford cattle are in plenitude.

Ellensburg, called Robber's Roost in 1870, contains many historic buildings. You should obtain a map showing them at the Chamber of Commerce.

## Farm roads to Fort Simcoe

Past apple and peach orchards, pastureland, fields of mint, corn, and hay, these roads finally lead to Fort Simcoe. Located on the Yakima Indian Reservation, the fort was originally built to oversee the Indians and to protect Yakima Treaty areas from land-hungry settlers. I liked Fort Simcoe for its spacious lawns and venerable oaks. The Yakimas called the location Mool Mool, a place of bubbling springs.

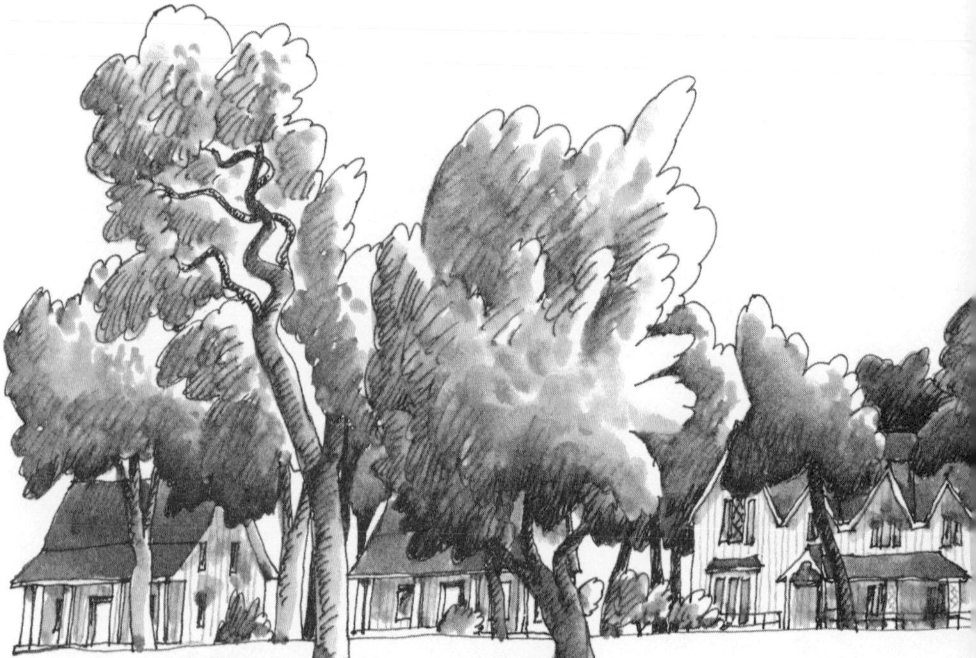

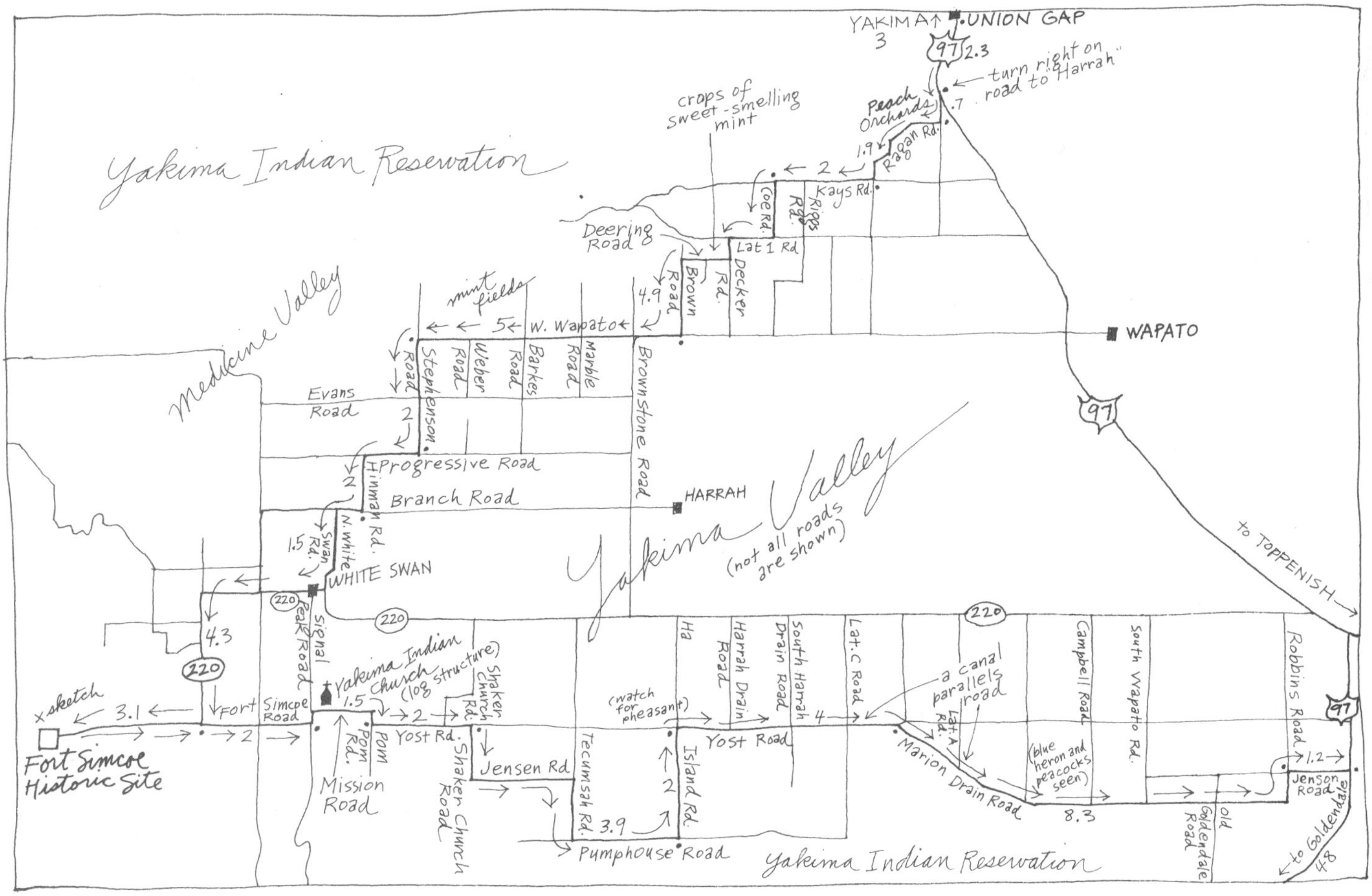

*Fort Simcoe Historical Site, Yakima County*

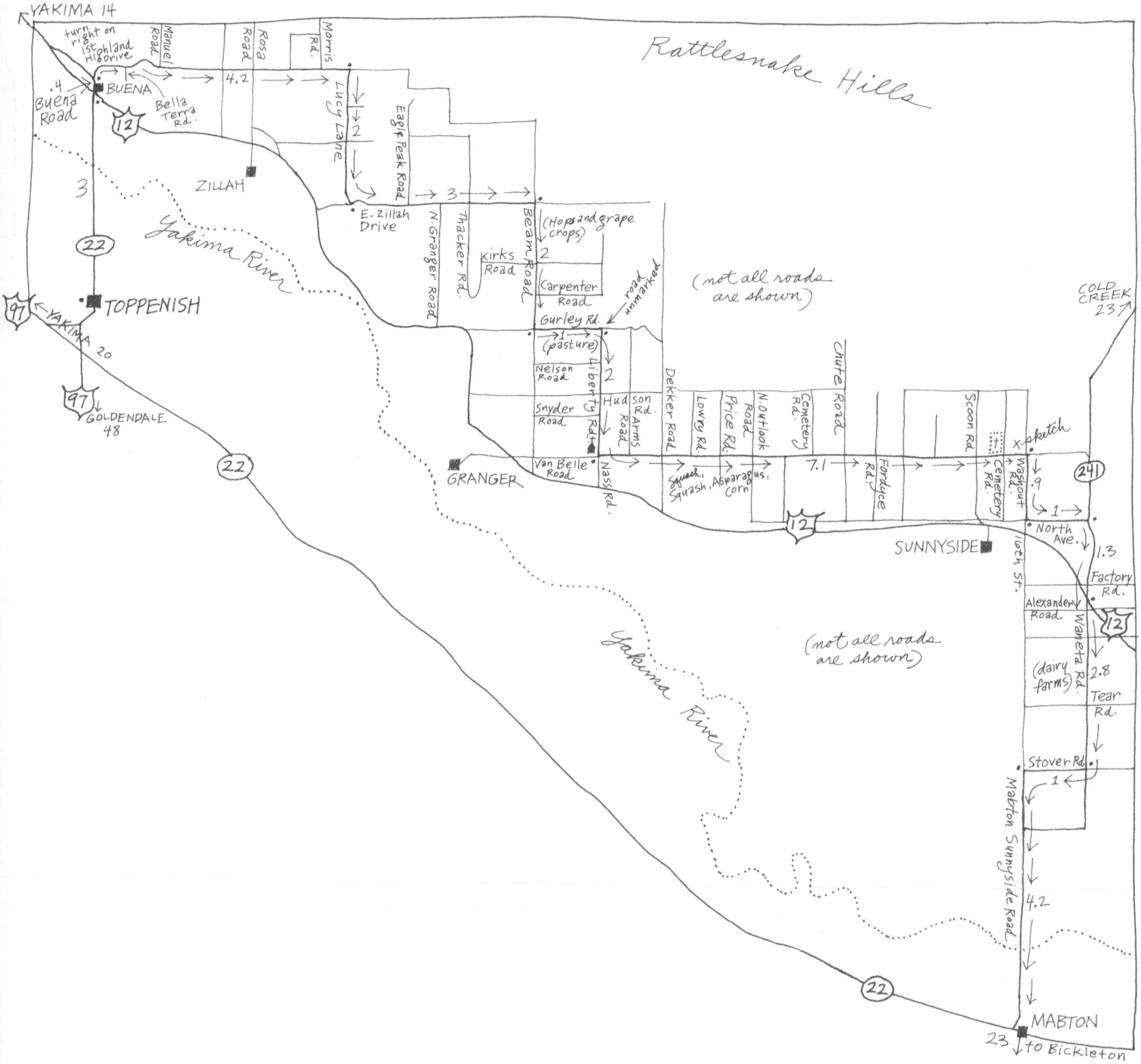
YAKIMA 14
turn right on 1st Highland Drive
Manuel Road
Rosa Road
Morris Rd.
Rattlesnake Hills
BUENA
.4
Buena Road
Bella Terra Rd.
12
4.2
Lucy Lane
Eagle Peak Road
ZILLAH
3
22
Yakima River
E. Zillah Drive
N. Granger Road
Thacker Rd.
Beam Road
Kirks Road
(Hops and grape crops)
Carpenter Road
Gurley Rd.
road unmarked
(not all roads are shown)
TOPPENISH
97
YAKIMA 20
GOLDENDALE 48
COLD CREEK 23
1 (pasture)
Nelson Road
Liberty Rd.
Snyder Road
Hudson Rd.
Arms Road
Dekker Road
Lowry Rd.
Price Rd.
N. Outlook Road
Cemetery Rd.
Chute Road
Scoon Rd.
sketch
241
GRANGER
Van Belle Road
Nass Rd.
Squash, Asparagus, Corn
7.1
Fordyce Rd.
Washout Rd.
.9
North Ave.
1.3
SUNNYSIDE
16th St.
Factory Rd.
Alexander Road
Wanetta Rd.
(dairy farms)
2.8
Tear Rd.
Stover Rd.
Mabton Sunnyside Road
MABTON
23
to Bickleton

## Farm roads along the banks of the Yakima

Apples, plums, asparagus, corn, hops, and grapes are some of the crops that grow along these roads. Hops are derived from a most decorative plant that has green garlands of leaves ten to twenty feet high. I sketch a house seemingly engulfed by grapevines. Premium-quality grapes are grown in Yakima Valley for Washington's fine wines.

Farm roads to Fort Simcoe and also this drive on the east bank of the Yakima River illustrate the agricultural abundance of the great Yakima Valley.

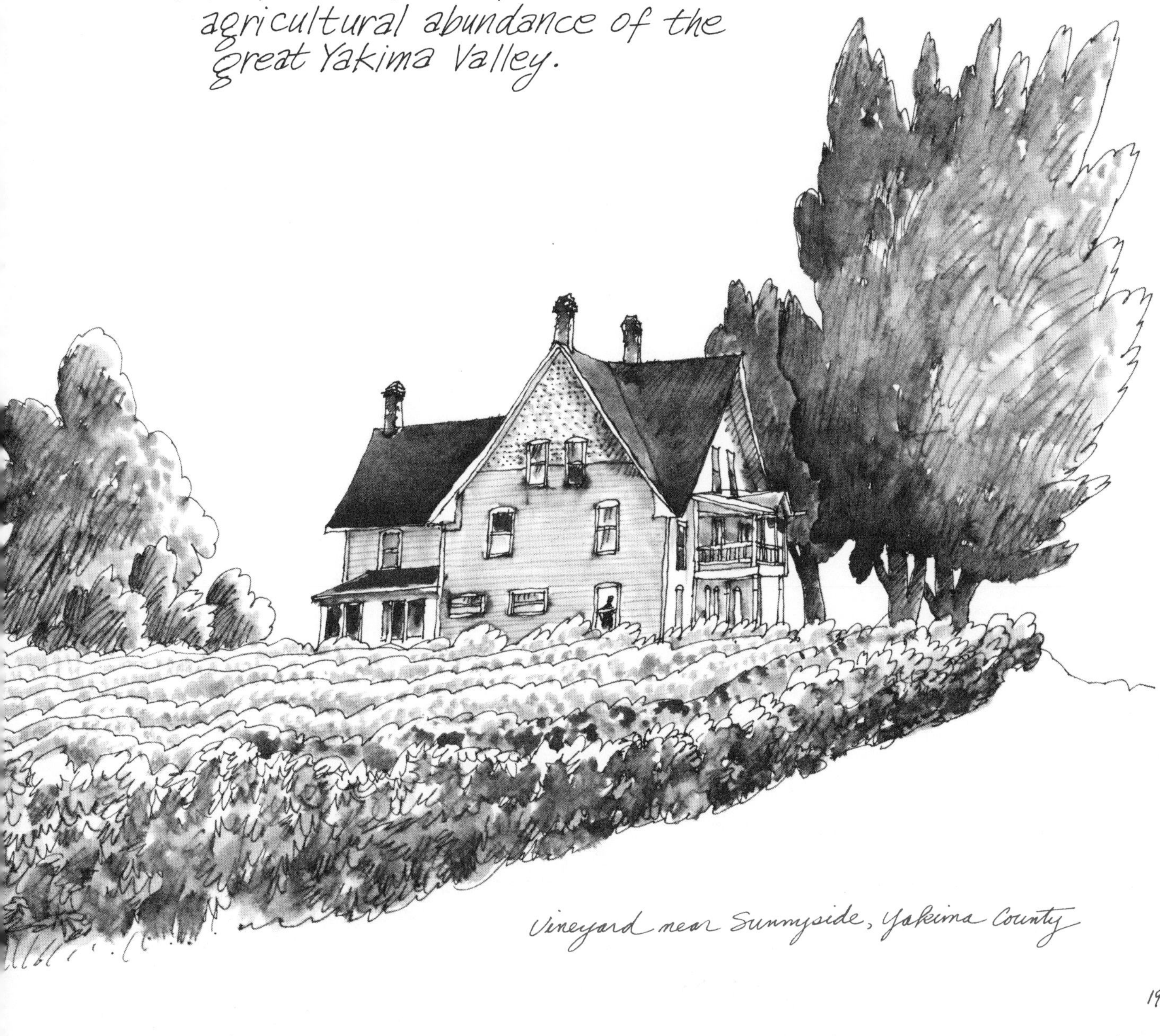

Vineyard near Sunnyside, Yakima County

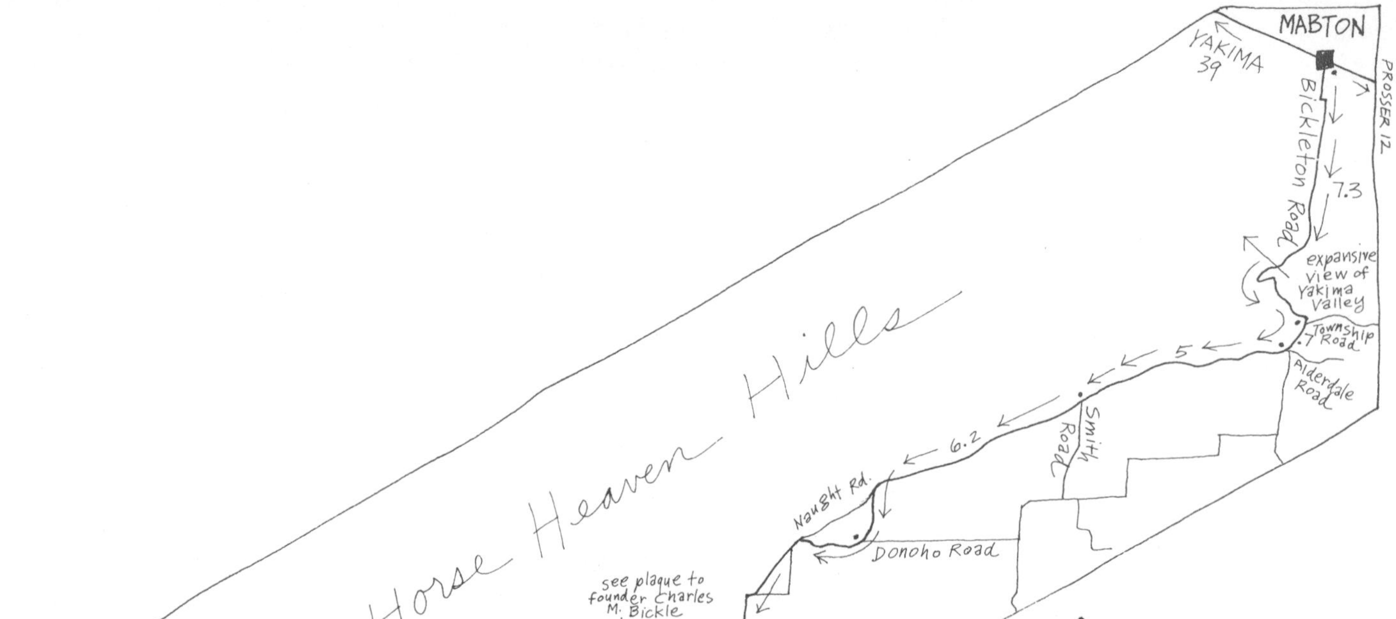


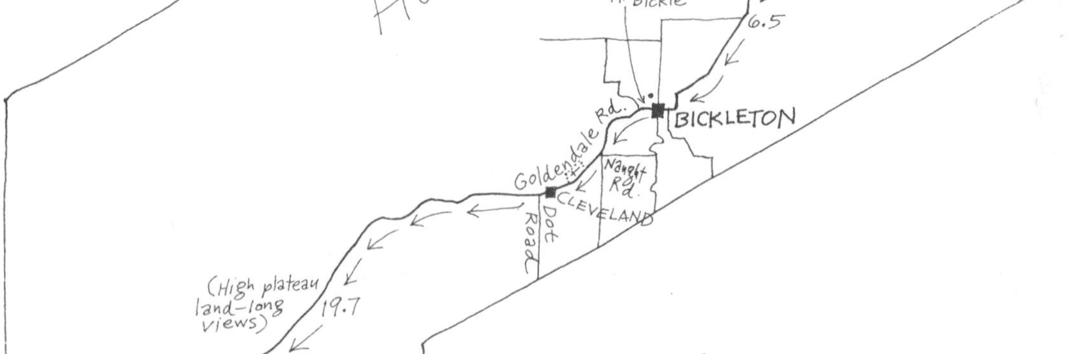

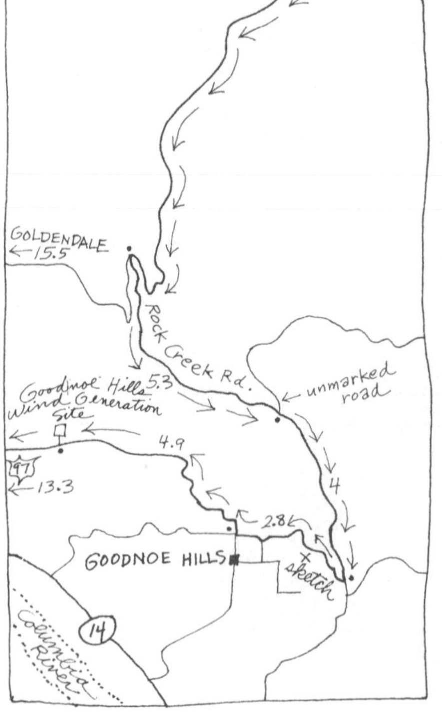


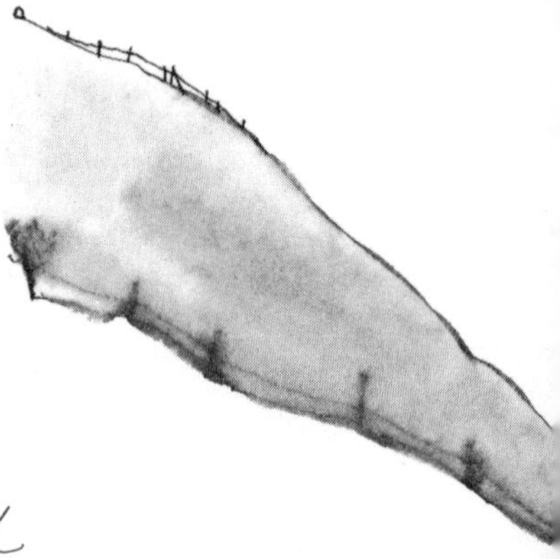

## The road to Bickleton and Rock Creek Canyon

The road winds through the sagebrush of Horse Heaven Hills, affording views of the Yakima Valley, which I am leaving behind.

Past the hamlets of Bickleton and Cleveland, marginal forest land begins. In Rock Creek Canyon the road hugs the creek bed with oaks, alders, and elderberry bushes growing in its narrow corridor. Leaving Rock Creek Canyon I sketch an abandoned, and slightly tilting, weathered brown house peaking over a barren hillside.

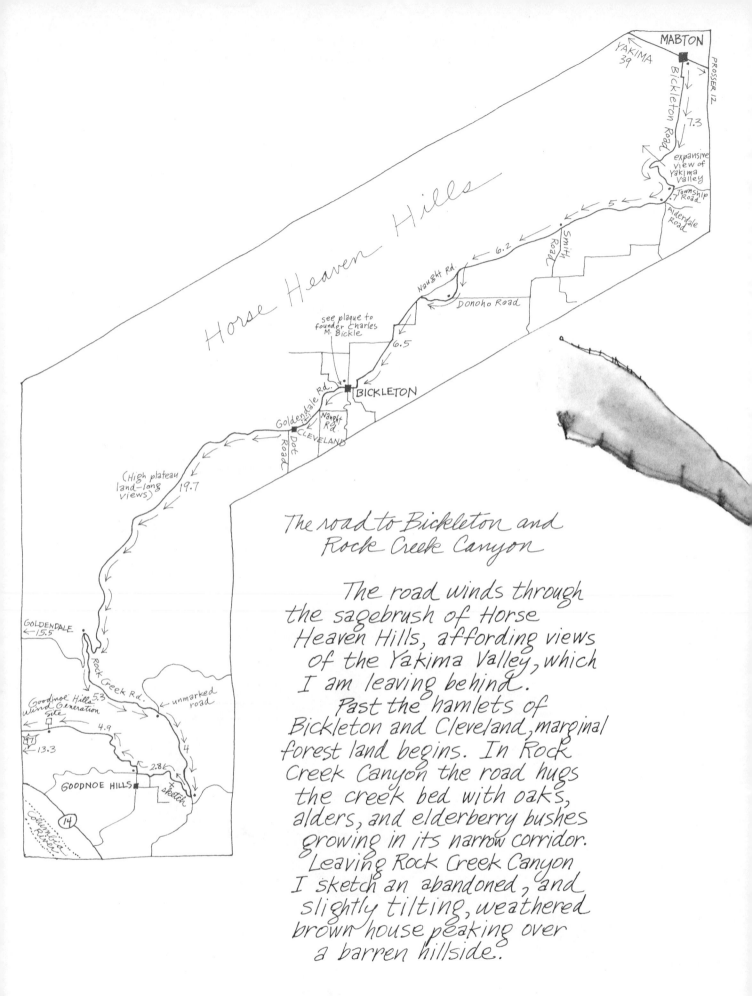

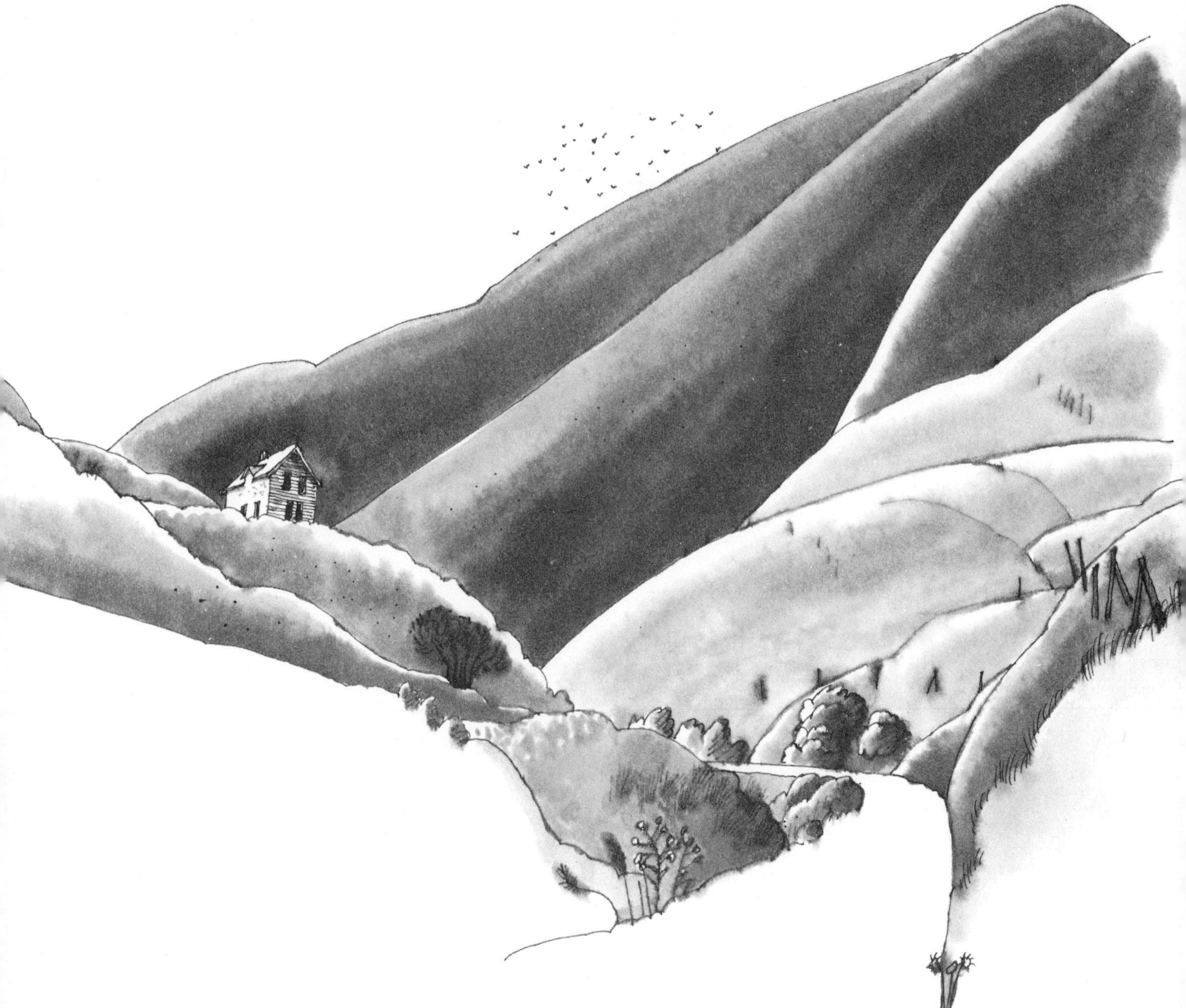

Ghostly house, near
Rock Creek Canyon, Klickitat County

# The road through Goodnoe Hills and Klickitat Valley

Good views of Columbia River country are along these roads, including the big mountains Hood and Adams. I pass the Goodnoe Hills Wind Generation Site with three of the world's largest and most advanced wind turbine generators, and proceed into the broad Klickitat Valley where I sketch a lonely farm.

The Dalles Mountain Road begins here, a slow, bumpy road over the Columbia hills. Once over the ridge I come upon a view that I will never forget. I imagine that I am looking south over the whole state of Oregon, its agricultural patterns continuing to infinity. The road is an exciting one both for its wonderful views and for the thrill of its precipitous mountain drive.

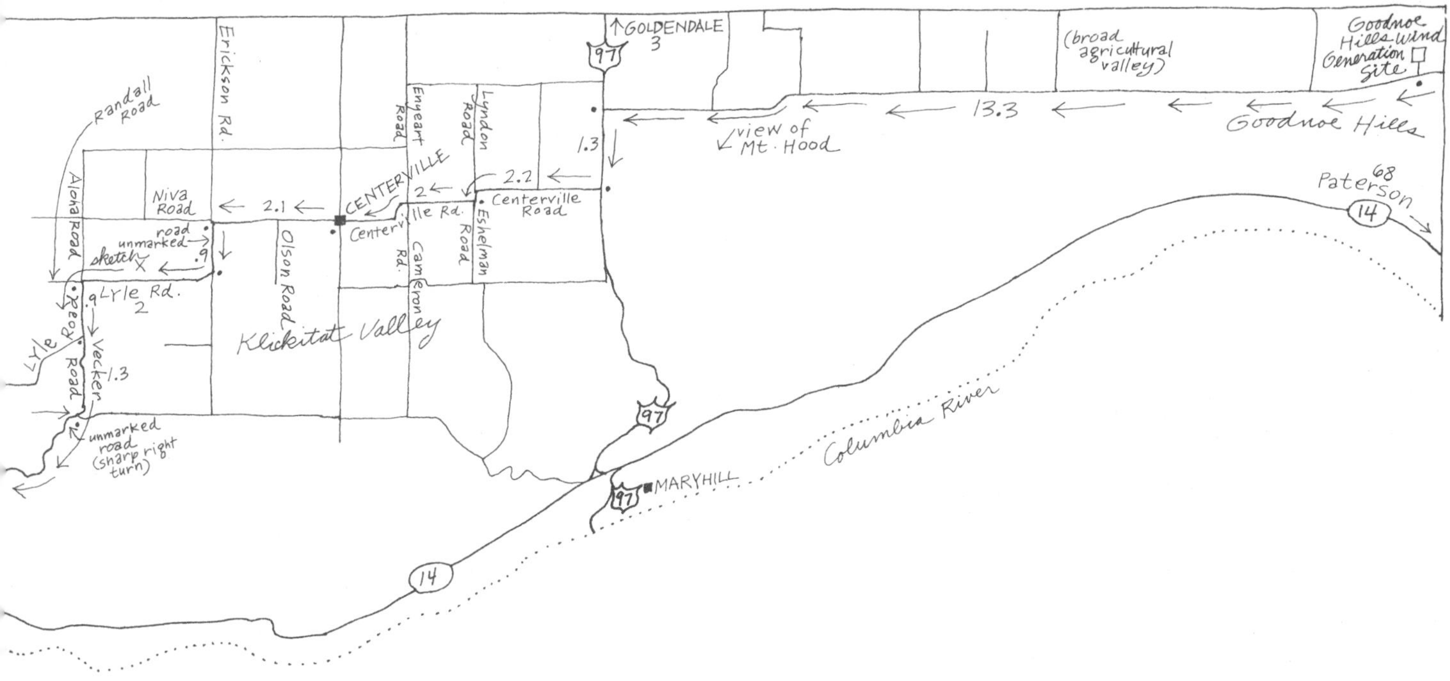


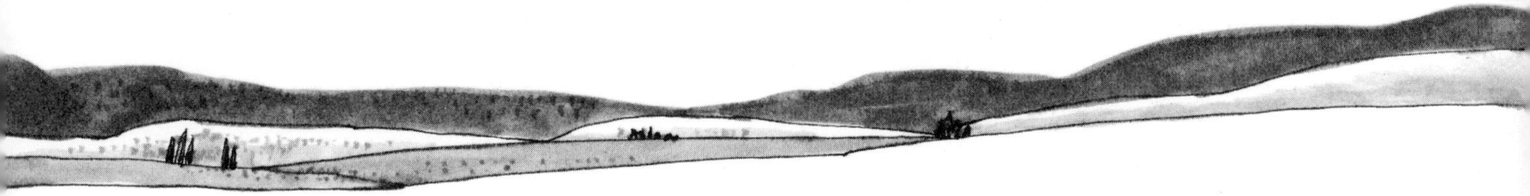

Klickitat Valley landscape, Klickitat County

View of Mount Adams,
near Glenwood,
Klickitat County

## Back road from White Salmon

Mountain and forest views, green meadows and old farmhouses describe the landscape along this back road. Near Conboy Lake I sketch Mount Adams, a ghostly old farmhouse in the foreground. Glenwood is a lively little town to visit; then I drive toward BZ Corners where I observe the pleasant dairy countryside with its cows, hay crops, and big old barns. It is a good road to end my memorable journey through the beautiful state of Washington.

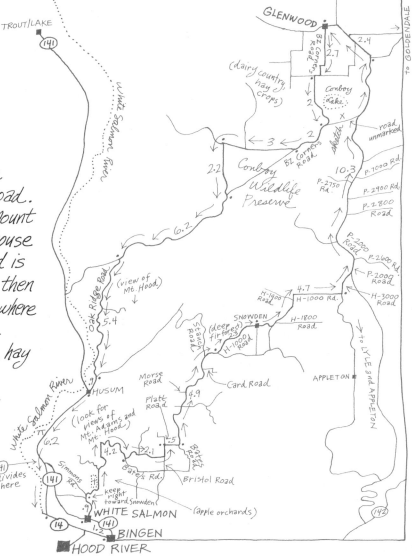

# Epilogue

Frog Rock, Bainbridge Island, Kitsap County

It is my wish that road builders will not straighten and widen our most picturesque back roads. And not even take out all the bumps. It encourages motorists to go ever faster, and to spend less time enjoying the trip. I agree that there must be fast highways and other fast roads, but there are also other roads that need not be.

As an artist, I am particularly concerned with impressions of nature, farmland and architecture. To make each day a series of remembered aesthetic experiences seems to me a happy goal. As my respect for my fellowman makes me proud to be human, so my respect for nature makes me proud to be part of it. I wish you many happy travels.

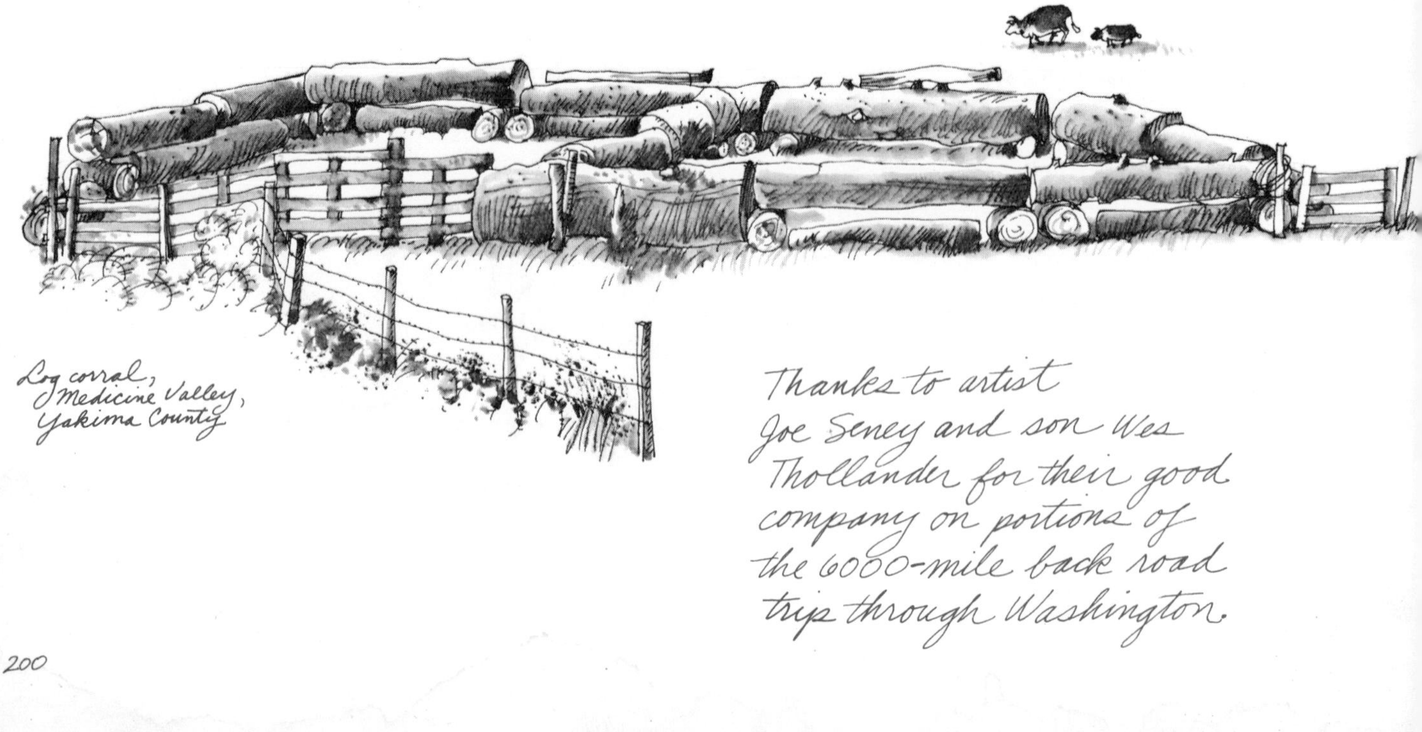

Log corral, Medicine Valley, Yakima County

Thanks to artist Joe Seney and son Wes Thollander for their good company on portions of the 6000-mile back road trips through Washington.